BOOKS BY WILLIAM M. BIRENBAUM

Overlive: Power, Poverty and the University

Something for Everybody Is Not Enough:
An Educator's Search for His Education

Something for
Everybody
Is Not Enough

Something for Everybody Is Not Enough

An Educator's Search for His Education

WILLIAM M. BIRENBAUM

Random House | **New York**

ISBN: 0-394-46037-5

Library of Congress Catalog Card Number: 74-117652

Manufactured in the United States of America
by The Book Press, Brattleboro, Vermont

2 3 4 5 6 7 8 9

First Edition

For
———

**Helen, Susan,
Lauren
and Charles**

Preface

First, the facts.

As I write this book I am the president of a college in New York City. It is one of the twenty free-tuition units of New York's giant public system called the City University. The annual operating budget of this university is approaching a half-billion dollars. Student enrollments are nearly two hundred thousand. There are more than eleven thousand full-time faculty members, organized into two trade unions and paid according to one of the highest salary schedules in the nation—a full professor for nine months' work may get more than $31,000. All of my employees—the secretaries, the security force, the janitors, the workers in the cafeterias—are unionized. Only the students and the presidents on the various campuses have not, as of this date, formed unions.

My piece of the action in this system is a community college in Staten Island. Staten Island is the balky borough of the city of New York. Its population now is a little over three hundred thousand. According to the 1970 census data, Staten Island is, in fact—as Robert Connor, the Republican-Conservative party borough president, proudly announces on placards at the entries to the island —the fastest-growing part of the city. A larger proportion of the population of this island was black at the time slavery was abolished here, in the 1820's, than at the time of the 1970 census.

Staten is an island which until a few years ago could only be reached by ferryboat or by other water or air conveyance. Now it is connected to the rest of the city by New York's most beautiful bridge, spanning the entry of the port. The Verrazano, one of man's most spectacular engineering feats, cost only a half-dozen human lives to build. But for Staten Island, the human cost is proving to be far greater. The bridge irrevocably joined the island to the city, linking its fate to the destiny of American mankind.

Once Staten Island commanded the port of New York. Its guns enforced the admission standards for the city. It was a beautiful island of gentle hills and rich forests, held in a girdle of magnificent beaches, some more beautiful and all more accessible than Long Island's. Now the forests that remain, a sixth or seventh growth of foliage, are being devastated. The hills have been gouged and scarred to accommodate the rows and rows of ugly development houses. And the beaches, of course, are all polluted. Still, Staten Island is greener than the rest of New York, and unlike the other parts, has a moment or two left in which to make some crucial decisions about its future.

Staten Island is the one borough of New York City in which the majority of voters thought Richard Nixon should be President of the United States. About 10 percent of its people preferred George Wallace. More than half of its people are Catholics of the Italian tradition. An unusual proportion of New York City's civil servants— its firemen, sanitation workers and policemen—have chosen to live here. My student body reflects this fact.

Like most of the blacks in the Bedford-Stuyvesant community, where I worked before coming here, most of the people in Staten Island still passionately believe in their own version of the American promise. They respect and honor the flag, and put decals and stickers on their automobiles proudly announcing that fact. I have grown very fond and respectful of the citizenry here. They believe in something, and on the whole they are brave, fearless and usually candid in the pursuit of their convictions, often at the expense of my peace of mind.

I arrived in Staten Island three years ago the hard way. That is, I've had a checkered and rather difficult professional career. Since leaving the University of Chicago in 1957, I've worked at Wayne State in Detroit, the New School for Social Research in Manhattan and Long Island University in Brooklyn. Then I became a part of Robert Kennedy's attempted revitalization operations in Bedford-Stuyvesant, and now I am at Staten Island. So far, four years is as long as I've remained in one professional position.

After World War II, the GI Bill paid for my own "higher" education at the University of Chicago, where my professional career began under Robert M. Hutchins during the Age of McCarthy (Joseph) and the Korean War. Since then, I have worked almost everywhere in the university—as teacher and administrator, board member and parent, in adult and graduate education, from the urban to the international field, in public and private institutions, large and small. Where I have worked there have always been too many students and not enough money, threats to academic freedom and assaults upon faculty democracy, excessive teaching loads and inadequate parking space.

I enjoy being a college president. Bernard Shaw once wrote Winston Churchill: "Dear Winnie, I have a new play opening in London next week. Enclosed are two

tickets to the first night. Please come, and bring a friend—
if you have one." Sir Winston replied: "Dear Bernie, I
can't make it to the opening night of your new play. But
I'll come the second night—*if there is one.*" As a college
president now, I have a pretty good idea who my friends
are—i.e., the non-friends have identified themselves. And
my current production has gotten through opening night,
though the duration of the run remains problematical.

So much for the facts. Now, a few opinions. A man in
my position is not supposed to write a book like this.
Unlike other teachers, college presidents are not expected
to share with others what they really know. Not while
they're still in office. Not if they want to stay there. At
least, hardly any have written a book like this.

This book is a special, personal act I had to commit
now.

I think I've had a rather rough time getting to where
I am. I don't mean getting to be a college president, I
mean getting to be me, while incidentally making a living.

If I had to make a choice between being me and making
a living, I hope I'd choose the former. Making a living has
imposed so many disciplines that confound and frustrate
being me. Making a living has compelled me too often to
do things I didn't want to do. Even worse, I have found I
sometimes enjoyed doing these things.

Sol Hurok, the New York City impresario, has said
about his own way of making a living, "If I was in this
business for business, I wouldn't be in this business." Of
course, Sol Hurok is in the business of being Sol Hurok,
and somehow he makes a living out of that. But about
what I do, he's right.

A few years ago, before I became a college president,
well-intentioned friends, meaning to show their high
expectations for me, would say, "Someday you'll be a college president." I didn't especially want to. Now, since

being a college president is not such a desirable thing to
be, well-intentioned friends, meaning to show their sympathy, say, "What are your future plans? What do you
want to be next?" Of course, I really don't know. I don't
think about that much. In fact, I've never been able to
think about me in terms of the job categories available.
Most jobs, including being a college president, leave something to be desired. Nevertheless, I rather enjoy being a
college president.

My work requires me to think very hard. It's very
difficult, but occasionally it comes off. I'm not sure
people in my position are supposed to think. Anyway,
when I think I usually get into trouble in my position.
There's another complication. When I think at the office
I find it very difficult to turn off the results, if any, when
I get home. And when I think at home (usually only after
being provoked to do so by my wife or three teen-age
children), I find it very hard to turn off the results of that
when I get to the office. The mass media and what people
tell me at cocktail and dinner parties or on the street often
excite me to think things while I'm at the office or at
home, and vice versa. Consequently, this trying-very-hard-
to-think bit tends to solidify my feelings about the importance of being me. I find that being me—while trying
very hard to think about Vietnam, Harlem, heroin, sex,
what's happening to my city, who's President of the United
States now—tends to turn aside and resist the hammer
blows struck in the name of the University, the Home, the
Flag, the President of the College, or the Overcharged
Patron of a Lousy Broadway Show.

Having been educated in the law and having been institutionalized for a long time (as a way of making a living),
I know that this continuity of things for me is a very serious compromise of both roles my position demands, i.e.,
my public and my private selves. Thus, when I'm compelled to think about dope on the campus, as I was when

one of my students killed himself in one of the johns with an overdose of heroin, what I end up thinking tends to influence my personal relationship with my own children regarding the use of narcotics. Or, what I've come to think as a citizen about the war in Vietnam tends to be what I think about Vietnam as a college president.

Unhappily, these habits deny me the protection of being two people: one who thinks about some things as a college president, but doesn't think at all (as a college president) about others. The so-called neutrality of the institution through which I make a living gets all mixed up with the positions I take, trying to be me. The lines between work and play, between the public and the private me's, get very thin. And soon I find myself caring about everything —almost too much. I have a hard time being detached, which they say I ought to be.

I must confess that because my public self has on an increasing number of occasions been declared a disaster area, I have been far more zealous in the purchase and protection of private pockets that are all my own, secret retreats, cozy refuges into which I can crawl all alone. Such are the little compromises some of us must make in order to make a living.

About the disaster areas: most of them result from my failure to accept gracefully the fiction of the academic corporation—the impersonal personality of the institution, its demand for a life of its own—brittle, abstract, sucked dry of human blood, but rigged so often to live off the blood of others. The fiction of the institution's impersonal personality is, of course, essential to the fiction that the institution acts objectively, that its conduct is neutral, that it really represents a collectivity of thought that gives its acts a (moral?) priority over the acts of any one person in it. The president of the institution, according to this position, should represent that collectivity. Today, at Berkeley or Columbia, at Harvard or Staten Island, if the president takes this position he may not represent much. But most college presidents do conscientiously try to represent a presumed collectivity. This is a part of the problem. Those holding real power in this country do not represent much at the moments of truth in the corporations and institutions they lead, and thus come to represent powerful forces subversive to my effort to be me.

I wonder if any of my young and untenured faculty members ever feel that way. Or any of our students? Or even any of those most senior professors, published and protected, who in these perilous times have come to question how *they* make a living? Whether it's worth it?

As violence and vulgarity have become more commonplace in my country, the search for consensus has become more frantic, the proclamations in behalf of social responsibility more strident, and the reassertion of the value of our traditional institutional forms more arbitrary, even though those forms seem less and less applicable to the solution of the new problems. The national climate makes the assertion of personal experience embarrassing, especially for those who hold responsible positions in our institutions. Perhaps this is because so much of the personal experience *is* vulgar, tolerant of violence, or even violent.

Perhaps more than ever before, the meaning of the public events intrudes into our personal lives and finds reflections in our most secret private acts. Conversely, more than ever before, the conduct of those who lead us— in government, industry, education, the arts and the professions—does embody and expose our innermost paradoxes, the fraudulence and sham of our personal lives. We *are* embarrassed, and our embarrassments take the form of retreat, disconnection, dropping out, alienation.

This intensified connection between the public and private, the social and individual, does not mean that our democracy is working better. Quite the opposite: it may only mean that to maintain some semblance of order we are further distorting the meaning of the public life, emphasizing the life of the institutions more than the quality of the life of the people they are supposed to serve. Instead of the institution more accurately representing the thrust and needs of individuals, individuals are expected, more and more, to represent the thrust and needs of the institution.

Because education is such a personal thing, this juxtaposition of emphases on the school versus its citizens is not only dangerous but potentially fatal: fatal to the proper balance and harmony between being ourselves and establishing a more perfect public life; fatal to a decent relationship between the younger and the older; fatal to the voluntary acceptance of the authority of reason and wisdom, to the only kind of relationship between the teacher and the student through which education can proceed.

In the preface to his *Education,* Henry Adams says: "Most educators of the nineteenth century have declined to show themselves before their scholars as objects more vile or contemptible than necessary, and even the humblest teacher hides, if possible, the faults with which nature has generously embellished us all . . . As an unfortunate result the twentieth century finds few recent guides to avoid, or to follow. American literature offers scarcely one working model for high education . . . Except in the abandoned sphere of the dead languages, no one has discussed what part of education has, in his personal experience, turned out to be useful, and what not."

"In his personal experience" is the deadly phrase, a usage now almost abandoned, for the personal experience —combining, as it always does, a man's thoughts with his actions—contains the authenticity of the man. And now, right now, with my students, with my own children, between my country and me, that authenticity is the issue.

Everyone mentioned in this book taught me something. I am deeply grateful to them all, but especially to Helen, my wife, and to my children, Susan, Lauren and Chuck. They are the most personal part of my experience, and in many ways have taught me what is most valuable.

W. M. B.

Contents

Something for
Everybody
Is Not Enough

Chapter One

Retreat at Waterloo

The Exploitation Principle

What we call school too often assumes that the difference between a teacher and a student is that one is a producer and the other is a consumer. According to this theory, an educated person is one who produces more than he consumes. The young, according to professional terms, are consumers until they are very old. One becomes a producer once he is old enough to exploit the young more than they exploit him.

As a student I often felt exploited. Such a feeling encourages one to master the art of exploiting others. Thus becoming professionalized, we earn tenure.

The Informer—Act One

I came to Chicago from Iowa via the United States Army Air Force. The Air Force was a strange place to be, especially during a war. It was hot in Washington and cold in Greenland. It was crowded in St. Petersburg and unbelievably lonely almost everywhere, but especially in Pawling.

The dormitories were great. Free food and lots of planned group activities. Cooperative living—we even cleaned each other's latrines. Friendly counselors with booming voices who were unafraid to relieve one of the burden of making his own decisions.

It was one of the most efficient schools in which I've ever been enrolled, concentrating almost exclusively upon what we needed to know in order to survive. It prepared me to fight Hitler without teaching me how to shoot a gun. It taught me things every red-blooded American ought to know in later life, like how to code and decode TOP SECRET messages on an electronic device (classified). I remember my excitement when I was given one of the first TOP SECRET messages to decode. It was during the build-up for the landings at Casablanca—on the brink, so to speak, of combat. I was at a strategic base in Greenland (classified), an essential link in the great northern air supply route. Calling upon my straight-B mathematical prowess in high school, plus what they had taught me in the cryptography training center at Pawling, New York, I laboriously converted something that read like this:

> BVDXT TYJNB XXMAR TPIQX CGLPQ EEPBV
> HSLKX YIPEW HIPPY GJOQW BAPHD
> LSXCN XCVEI BSLPQ WTERY BVJSF OYERI
> TWERP PXXXX

into the following war directive, which I assume has been declassified since Korea, Vietnam and all that, so I might share it with you:

> QUACKENBERRY LT COL PAREN UNCLE
> SAM MICKEY PAREN ESCORTING DIETRICH

COMMA MARLENE WITH UNCLE SAM
OBOE TROOP COMMA EASY TARE ABLE
ZERO NINE THREE SEVEN STOP FIVE PICK
UP JEEPS PAUSE POUR REGAL CHIVAS
XXXX

One of the ways we defeated Hitler was by always beginning and ending our TOP SECRET messages with uniquely
American words, like "Quackenberry" and "Chivas,"
which we thought would especially confuse the Nazi code
analysts monitoring our network from bases north of
Oslo.

I was tested and given security clearance for TOP SECRET
work in St. Petersburg. Given the German quality of my
name (it has a classical "e" in it), my final security interview with Air Force Intelligence Major Gunter Schultz
was a little tense. It was one of the few times I found it
useful to assert the family's ancestral origins somewhere
along the wandering borderline between Poland and Russia, and of course it didn't hurt to point out that this was
traditionally a Jewish enclave, for Jews were presumed
trustworthy in the war against Hitler.

Having been cleared for TOP SECRET endeavors, I was
amazed to be invited (I had been in uniform only three
weeks) to serve as an undercover agent for Air Force Intelligence Major Gunter Schultz. I have always thought
that it was my rather prominent ears that led the major to
point the finger at me. My assignment was to hang around
the local post exchange and enlisted men's beer hall, keeping my ears open for "suspicious remarks." If I overheard
anything pro-German or pro-Russian, or a GI under
orders mention his next destination (this was strictly
against the rules), I was (without arousing the offender's
suspicions) to find out his name, write it and the remark on
a plain sheet of paper, put it in an unmarked business-size

envelope and mail it to one Roberto Torres in care of the Pinellas Pineapple Company on a street in Tampa. I was given some petty cash in advance for postage stamps.

I was only eighteen, and this sensitive assignment was really the first constructive thing anyone had asked me to do about Hitler. I took it all very seriously, but it didn't work out too well. I loathed hanging around the PX watching other people buy things. I spent a lot of time in the beer hall and I certainly overheard some wonderfully interesting "suspicious remarks." But somehow, by the time I got back to the secrecy of the office on my barracks bunk to write it all down, things just didn't click. Finally, as I was about to be transferred out of St. Petersburg, I did send one plain white business-size envelope to Roberto Torres in care of the Pinellas Pineapple Company in Tampa. It contained the advance for the postage stamps, minus the cost of one.

Though I was a failure in my first attempt as an informer, the experience exposed me to another point of view, one which I am sure has influenced my subsequent outlook toward narcotics-squad, FBI and CIA plainclothesmen, who seem ever-present on the campuses where I've worked. I have yet to ask a member of the dean of students' staff to identify disruptive students so that a judge could issue an injunction. But trench coats are big on American campuses lately, and there are plenty of pineapple companies around.

Separatists

To be admitted to the converted prep school at Pawling for a cryptographic education, one had to achieve "high scores" on the United States Army Air Force College entrance board examinations. The placement tests at St. Petersburg separated the men from the boys and the black from the white. The tests confirmed earned high school averages and determined who qualified for what curriculum. Some low achievers were destined for horrible bases in Texas or Georgia and for advanced training in subjects like shooting guns, repairing airplane motors, assisting cooks and filing papers. My test scores put an abrupt end to my career on K.P. duty and precluded further physical-fitness training. Within weeks I was admitted to one of the better fraternities in the school, being issued staff-sergeant stripes and what amounted to a permanent weekend pass.

The only non-Caucasians I met during the war were the Eskimos in Greenland. They weren't integrated, being the main objects of the Danes' separatist policy. They were not too eager at first to be exploited further by invaders from places like Iowa. They traded ivory trinkets, painstakingly carved, for cigarettes. I tried at one point to explain to them what I was doing in Sondrestromfjord, but I don't think they understood. They thought I had come there to get something they had. They couldn't imagine one wanting to stay in a place like Iowa. They even had a hard time pronouncing it.

The Eskimos were avid but friendly separatists, quite ignorant about the ways of the school in which I was enrolled. Their huts stank, but they seemed to like living in them and they took great pride in their pile of tundra-covered rock squeezed in between the fjord and the icecap. The Eskimos could outwrestle, outrun and outshoot almost all of us who had so expensively been prepared to contend with Tojo, Hitler and Mussolini. But they were sitting ducks for our secret weapons, the unique products of the West—Danish beer, German measles and American syphilis. Compared to us, they appeared to be a happy, generous, impoverished people who, in their happiness, generosity and poverty, were quite unlike what I was accustomed to back in Waterloo, Iowa. Our sets of values were somewhat different. For example, they didn't even care who won the war! It took some time to adjust to the idea of that, but I finally understood they never would care.

After the novelty of the first few months, even Iowa began to seem like a reasonable place to go home to. That first winter, when the temperature first dropped below —40 degrees Fahrenheit, I was ready to leave the Eskimos to the peace of their Sondrestromfjord. But as things turned out, I was essential to the war effort for eighteen months in Greenland—long enough to study in depth the mating habits of the caribou. That, along with the Eskimos, they had neglected in my courses at Pawling.

The Soul Business

When I left Waterloo, Iowa, there were about a hundred and fifty Jewish families there who maintained the town's only synagogue. Their names were broadcast on the shoe, jewelry and clothing stores along the main street.

The synagogue was across the street from one of the town's largest Catholic schools, and by the time a Jewish boy was five or six, however bad his memory, he had ample reason to suspect that he personally had hung Christ on the Cross. He was reminded of this almost daily with taunts wrapped around stones that were hurled across West Fifth Street. Peace and windows were shattered regularly. The fights were bloody and usually lost, for the Defenders of the Truth outmanned and outgunned those of us who deeply resented being at the synagogue four days a week after public school, anyway.

Years later in Brooklyn, Robert (Sonny) Carson, a so-called militant black leader, cross-examined me in great detail about my *cheder* (Hebrew school) back in Waterloo —about what I had learned there, how it was financed, if the kids showed up regularly, and what made them come. Disenchanted with public education in New York City and

deeply committed in the downhill battle of Ocean Hill–
Brownsville to return control of the public schools to
the communities they are supposed to serve, Mr. Carson
thought maybe he ought to set up a *cheder* of his own in
an abandoned building in Bedford-Stuyvesant. Swahili for
Hebrew, Africa for Israel, karate for our guerrilla tactics
on West Fifth Street. He thought Five Great Books were a
modest production, and assumed his effort would be based
on something a bit more extensive than that.

To each his own traditions. It seemed to me that my
personal honkies back in Waterloo carried a grudge for
an awfully long time. I was in no position to argue history.
My identity crisis was a bit different. We thought we
knew who we were. The trouble was, so did everybody
else. We just didn't quite know what to do about it.

We often retaliated after Hebrew school by urinating
on the other side's doorstep across the street after they
had all gone home. This maneuver greatly agitated our
own teachers, who had ideas about fighting with
dignity and in conformity with the appropriate Geneva
Conventions. It was an exciting double-whammy—putting
the "enemy" in his place while also defying the rabbi and
his assistant, who kept us, against our better judgment,
from football practice and the other things red-blooded
American youth (Jewish) should have been doing after a
tedious day in Waterloo's public schools.

In Hebrew school we actually learned some Hebrew—
at least enough with which to chant the portions of the
Torah required as a part of coming of age at thirteen.
(Even in Waterloo we Jewish boys were magically transformed into men at the age of thirteen, which meant, so
it seemed to some of us, that our responsibilities increased
substantially without a commensurate growth of adult
privileges.) We learned about the ancient Hebrew heroes,
who, like us, were always outmanned and outgunned, but,
unlike us, lost with their dignity more or less intact. We

didn't hang Christ from the Cross in Hebrew school or anything like that, but we did sort of put Him in His place, a station or two below Moses, alongside Mohammed and Buddha, great men all, especially deserving our respect. *They* may have invented Christmas and all that, but we, after all, had started the ball rolling. We were the chosen people, all right. We just wished that the kids across the street would choose somebody else.

Being chosen in Waterloo, it often seemed to me, led uniquely to being saved.

One of the biggest neon signs in town sat on top of the fundamentalist Baptist church, announcing not only what the place was but also where the local people could go to be saved.

In the inexperience and immaturity of my youth, I did not think I especially needed saving. But my homeroom teacher in Waterloo West High School was a pillar of the church. She thought I needed saving (and that she knew the only way how). She wasn't anti-Semitic, i.e., she didn't discriminate. She thought *everybody* needed saving, and that I ought to be flattered by her special attention. She also tried to teach me geometry and algebra, and there were times when I thought it might not be a bad idea to be saved a little in order to get through her courses.

Mae Howell was one of the best math teachers I ever had, and a wonderful woman. But she had the strangest ideas about my Inner Situation. From somewhere in the New Testament, I know not exactly where, she produced conclusive evidence that Jesus was about to appear for a second time in the wake of the final and total holocaust which would erupt from Jewish misconduct in Palestine. (This was before Israel was reborn, a prospect which, according to her view, was probably part of the plot.) Anyway, she was hellbent to get me in shape, because wherever we were all going after the catastrophe, she wanted me to go along with her side. She was a genuine

Baptist missionary in the New Guinea or Black Congo style, and I was her private little native, emerging from my part of Waterloo's jungle five mornings a week to receive her inoculations and pieces of calico, along, of course, with the Word.

We transacted this soul business just before or right after homeroom period—but never, to my recollection, during classes. But my soul-saving sessions with Miss Howell *were* educational, even if a little illegitimate. She was very serious and dedicated about it all, and I came to feel a certain respectful duty, a special kind of responsibility toward the formidable challenge she presented. I tried to keep her hopes high, while struggling against her purposes as vigorously as possible, so that she could at least enjoy the anticipation of a truly worthwhile conversion, if she ever succeeded.

One of the fascinating aspects of this situation was how it enabled me to serve as an informal interlocutor between Miss Howell and the rabbi, who on four days a week between four and six, and on Saturday and Sunday mornings, was doing his best to save me at the synagogue, a few blocks down the street. Miss Howell would cite some outrageous chapter and verse, putting the five thousand years of the history of my people into some unexpected and spectacular new perspective (new to me, anyway). I would then trot down to the rabbi's mission to repeat the revelation, presenting it as something I had either read or thought up all on my own.

The rabbi was usually well prepared (or would be in short order), and in due course he would come back with some original chapters and verses of his own, plus commentaries, plus commentaries on the commentaries, plus some further original insights of his own. He armed me perfectly with just the right things to challenge Miss Howell. The more orthodox and scholarly my responses, the more spectacular her retaliations. Her supply of ammunition was endless. For all I know she may have had her own board of consultants back at the church with the neon sign on top.

It was something like I imagine missile warfare must be, where the superior technicians on each side push the buttons, never knowing or seeing the enemy. Only, I was the missile, flawed so that I was not about to explode, but aiming in each abortive flight toward one of the technicians or the other.

The Disruption Principle

The rabbi must have thought, even then, that I was indeed a very special "Jewish problem." (He certainly thinks so now.) And Miss Howell must have been reassured that there was a lot of me to be saved. However disagreeable their motives were to me then, they both taught me many things by their own examples. I didn't want to be bothered by them, but they bothered me. That is, they were disruptive. They upset my natural law and order, and violated my due processes. Outstanding teachers are always disruptive. They go out of their way to disrupt, and by bothering people who don't want to be bothered, they encourage them to learn something.

Miss Howell, somehow, seemed above and beyond the politics of her profession. The politics of promotion and tenure, and of planning curricula through elaborate treaties dividing up the credit-hour spoils by the numbers, suppress the disruptive function of teaching. Getting ahead in the academic corporation seems to depend more and more upon one's consensus-producing capacity. So much of the important business of the college gets transacted on the basis of gossip. Issues have become things to avoid. Issues-makers are seen as escalators and polarizers. There is a tendency to use knowledge mainly to confirm the validity of the given order. If we just knew more about it, presumably the status quo would work better and everything would be all right. Learn, and get a job. And if the learning is scholarly, get an academic job and master the art of perpetuating the consensus.

The decline of the disruptive function of teaching stimulates many students to be disruptive. Nature has a way of restoring balances, but we have learned how to upset nature's balances. A campus without disruption is polluted, like a river without fish or a defoliated forest along the Ho Chi Minh Trail.

Once a Jap, Always a Jew

The little contest for my soul back in Iowa happened in a climate which predetermined the outcome. A little later, right after Pearl Harbor, during my first undergraduate year at Iowa State Teachers College in Cedar Falls (and my last anywhere), I was suspended, temporarily, from the student newspaper. The ships had hardly sunk in Hawaii before the leader of the Iowa State Assembly, in a fit of patriotic fervor, proclaimed, "Once a Jap, Always a Jap," and promptly resolved to expel all students of Japanese descent from the public colleges and universities in the state. I wrote a column, suggesting that perhaps the State Assembly ought to be expelled, which appeared in the *College Eye*. Its brilliance blinded, momentarily, the good judgment of the poor president of my college.

Waterloo was the kind of town that proved Hitler was right when he said, "Once a Jew, Always a Jew." It was very difficult to assimilate in Waterloo. There was so little of it to assimilate into. In spite of Miss Howell (and the rabbi, too) it just never occurred to me that there was a viable option. If you were Jewish in Waterloo, you were Jewish, and that was that. As she presented it, Miss Howell's option seemed worse than the ailment it was meant to cure. She spent more time in her church than I did at my synagogue. Her complications were at least as bad as the rabbi's. I was embarrassed by the neon sign on her church. Even if I had been in a mood to be saved, I would have preferred to have it happen with a different style, and with a somewhat greater respect for my privacy, if not my integrity.

But the truth: it was a springtime in my life when the likes of me worried more about saving others than being saved. It was, of course, reassuring to have people I respected so concerned about me. But I daydreamed a lot, and there were moments—fleeting, I admit—when *I* thought of saving Miss Howell and the rabbi. They may not have saved my soul, or me—but they helped my ego.

I have sometimes felt on campuses I've been to lately that my black students are more interested in saving me than being saved. Once a Black, Always a Black. At places like Long Island University or Staten Island, into what are they supposed to integrate? They bring with them their complications. I have my neon sign. What are they daydreaming about? Perhaps the best I can do is to fortify their egos. But that's not possible until and unless they respect me first. They have put a price upon the grant of their respect.

Tokenism

Waterloo, as its Chamber of Commerce pointed out, was the state's fifth largest city, with over forty thousand people. It was about the size of Bologna when its great university shaped up in the twelfth century. The Rath Packing Company, the John Deere tractor and plow plant, and the Annual Dairy Cattle Congress summarized its prosperity. They were its monuments to the incredibly black and rich loam of the rolling farmlands that conceived them. Even then, hardly out of the backwash of the Great Depression, many farmers sent their offspring to Iowa City in shiny new cars. There were parking problems on the prairies.

We saw the world each day, according to our ranks and stations, through the columns of the Waterloo *Daily Courier* or the Des Moines *Register* or the Chicago *Tribune*. The *Courier* contained the local gossip. The *Register* kept one abreast of Statehouse politics and the daily grain-, cattle- and pork-market ups and downs. Each paper said something about the rest of the world, but Colonel McCormick's staff authoritatively developed the larger issues of the day. Iowa was to Republicanism what Mississippi has been to the Democrats. The quantity and the quality of corruption in each place were about the same. McCormick was a big man in the territory. He interpreted the corruption so that it became plausible.

As an officer of the debating society at the University of Chicago after the war, I visited Colonel McCormick once with an invitation to speak on campus. I was escorted into his impressive paneled office high in his Gothic tower on Michigan Avenue. He addressed me as one of "Mr. Hutchins' children" and kept me standing in front of his desk throughout our three-minute interview. He conceded at the outset that he knew many things that the students on my campus, unfortunately, neither knew nor even suspected. But he really didn't have the time or the inclination to travel south to the Midway to tell them what they ought to know. There was a better way. He handed me a nickel and suggested I buy a paper on the way out.

All of Waterloo's five or six hundred Jews were the town's House Jews. Indeed, almost all of the Jews in Iowa were the state's House Jews. We were separate and apart, but under the circumstances, tolerated decently. We were generally well regarded, and from my point of view, well treated. There were waterholes in the social swim which were off-limits. But most of our parents made comfortable, quiet livings, maintained houses in the nicer neighborhoods, and shared the limited supply of black domestics to keep the houses clean. Almost every year a Jewish boy among my own peers managed to be a local sports hero, a debate-team champion, or a recipient of some kind of civic prize or recognition.

The year I won the $50 second prize in the Elks Lodge essay contest "Why I Am Proud to Be an American," Allen Cutler, one of my best Jewish friends, won $75 for first. Our picture was in the *Courier* with a local dignitary, and the rabbi was very proud of us.

There was a time when I felt I was the rabbi's House Jew. He was young and eager then. Waterloo was among his earlier assignments. He put a lot into it. He did the best he could with what he found. He certainly put me through his hoops. He got me ready in time for my bar mitzvah, and even inscribed a book as a gift to me on that occasion, noting that I had recited the Hebrew passages from the Torah acceptably well. He often gave me books containing encouraging notes to mark the salient occasions in the development of my more valiant Jewish self. I still have a half shelf of them:

> For Shavuoth in the year of Our People 5698,
> *A Book of Jewish Thoughts,* by Joseph Herman Hertz, Chief Rabbi of the British Empire, presented to Bill Birenbaum as the Aleph Shein Scholarship Award of the Congregation of the Sons of Jacob, Waterloo, Iowa. . . .
>
> *Israel,* by Ludwig Lewisohn, to Bill Birenbaum with appreciation from the Rabbi, in the year of Our People 5701. . . .

The Jewish Contribution to Civilization, by Cecil Roth, to Bill Birenbaum as a token of appreciation for his whole-hearted cooperation. The Rabbi, March, 1941. . . .

The rabbi especially reminded me of the existence of Our People. I do not remember that he ever knocked Waterloo, but in an insidious way he put it in its place. I'm sure that he regarded Waterloo as a passing stage in his own career. He sometimes gave the impression that Waterloo itself was but a passing fancy. After all, it was a place dominated by the uninformed with but a very short history. Naturally, it was full of young people, my age, who would want to play football. What was one to expect? But we were different. We had the Books. And Traditions. We counted time in terms of thousands of years. If *they* should live so long, maybe they would know better. Meantime, he led us to believe that we were tolerating *them,* instead of the other way around.

There were no Jewish Studies in West High's curriculum, and it never occurred to me that there should have been. We saluted the flag each morning, and said a prayer, occasionally chosen from Our Book instead of *theirs.* And there were, of course, Mae Howell's little seminars privately conducted for my benefit.

Things that arose from time to time in the regular curriculum, putting my history in an improper light, simply created the presumption in my mind that I knew something *they* didn't—namely, the Truth. I'm sure this did not bother them; but it confirmed for me the fact that they were ill informed and I wasn't.

As I saw it then, all Gaul was divided into three parts. In the biggest province—the parts of the curriculum we had imported from an overseas civilization, such as Latin and the foreign languages, mathematics, English literature and European history—we were all exploratory immigrants, equal in our ignorance and claims to ill fame. In

the second, the American province, the great equalizer
was how one felt and performed. I felt as American as
anybody else and I was eager to perform as well as or better
than *they*. The third—the Christian part, the Christmas
carols and the bits and pieces of history and literature
which ennobled bloody Gentile causes or embodied the
majority's questionable prejudices—I may not have liked,
but I think I intuitively honored what it meant to be in
the majority. If one is in a minority, one of the things to
which he might naturally aspire is to be in the majority,
and one should not dishonor the object of his aspirations.
To each his own. And after all, I had my own literature,
my own private curriculum down at the synagogue, and
my own unfolding view of what it all meant, anyway.
One didn't have to be black to be Jewish in Waterloo.
One just had to have parents who forced him into the
rabbi's clutches.

Not too long after my bar mitzvah, the rabbi had me
teaching younger kids elementary Hebrew, and by the
time I was fifteen I was conducting a Sunday school class.
When she found out about all this, Mae Howell redoubled
her efforts. She really flipped when I reported that the
rabbi suggested that I too might like to be a rabbi one day.
This was a suggestion I did not casually reject for a while.

I think it is very important that the young have some
clearly defined heroes and villains in their lives. Things
should be somewhat clearer when we are young, and woe
to the young who grow up in doubt about whom they
should admire and hate. Franklin Delano Roosevelt was a
hero, and the Chicago Cubs. Albert Einstein was born
Jewish, and what a mind! The rabbi, Tarzan and Judy
Garland were all very special. Hitler was wonderfully hate-
ful, and the New York Yankees. The Catholic kids across
the street from the synagogue really served a useful pur-

pose. I grew to dislike the idea of Colonel McCormick, and the reality of the family dentist.

I took my knocks trying to make the football team at West High—sprained ankles and pulled tendons. But the only real physical pain I recall was produced by the family dentist, Dr. Hoxie. Dr. Hoxie was a big and beefy man with an arm equal to the hammer-and-tongs operations he performed inside my mouth. He talked a gentle line, and he must have been a good dentist, for I still have a couple of silver slugs he carefully inserted into my teeth. But I still associate Dr. Hoxie with a profession I would never want to practice.

Dr. Hoxie had a son, Gordon, who preceded me by five or six years in West High. I never knew him in Waterloo. The honor of our acquaintance was reserved for later years in New York. He turned up as the chancellor of Long Island University, a man for whom I worked when I was appointed provost of that institution's Brooklyn campus. He came to have some serious doubts about my capacities as an educator—so much so that he finally told me to shape up or ship out of Brooklyn. As things happened, I was shipped out.

Hoxies and pain go together for me. But in retrospect I must admit that the son, like the father before him, performed some operations inside my head that have permanently changed the biting edges of my mind.

The Stone Farm

As we grow older our heroes, if we still have any, are different from the ones we had when we were younger. My Aunt Sarah really liked the rabbi, and I really liked Aunt Sarah. Besides my mother (her sister), Aunt Sarah was about the only adult I knew who had mastered the knack of talking horizontal. (No matter what, my mother never talked down, never talked below people's heads, and she still doesn't. She talks horizontal. Whether the object of her words is six or sixty, she instantaneously shifts her mental gears and her idioms, and broadcasts loud and clear, no static. She communicates, but especially with the young, so that her age is not the problem—what she *says* is sometimes a problem, but even the young disagree with each other. People like that sometimes sound a little nutty, unless you are the one talking with them. But their conversations are always fascinating. Things I have heard my mother exchange with my own children are often unbelievable, except they seem to believe each other.) Aunt Sarah struck me as being a little nutty, but always fascinating and believable. Nothing pleased me more than spending a few weeks of summer vacation at her house. We'd sit on her front-porch swing for hours talking about animals, people, and other interesting things, like "being Jewish."

For years Uncle Max struggled with an old-fashioned corner grocery store (with barrels of things sitting on sawdusted wooden floors) in Chariton, Iowa, saving his pennies to realize his primeval dream—to own a piece of that famous fertile Iowa soil. According to one of our family legends, this urge to own land was a common denominator on both the maternal and paternal sides. My ancestors came to the United States in the latter part of the nineteenth century from the East European Pale. Many of them had spent their lives managing other peoples' lands. Arriving in New York, they asked where in America they could get their own land. Even today when "farming," "hayseed" and "land" are brought up, smart-alecky New Yorkers think of Iowa. Naturally, their sophisticated advisers on the Lower East Side told my grandparents to go to Iowa. So they went, and their lives are histories of

backbreaking peddling and shopkeeping in generally un-
successful efforts to amass capital for land.

Uncle Max finally begged, borrowed and earned enough
to acquire a mortgage on one hundred and sixty acres in
the southwest corner of the state. When the glaciers de-
posited their rich lode on Iowa, they meticulously stopped
at the fences along the edges of Uncle Max's farm. He
owned about the only spur of the Rocky Mountains east
of the Missouri River. Uncle Max was an unlikely
farmer. He had the physique of a corner grocery-store
owner and the temperament of a confirmed indoorsman.
Insofar as one could tell, he knew absolutely nothing about
growing eatable things. His traditions and style were to
hire tenants, and through them he tried to grow corn,
which, of course, collapsed into the clay. He tried alfalfa,
which always emerged stunted and exhausted through the
crust of stones. He tried cows, and even—perish the
thought—pigs. The animals had enough space to walk
around in, but supplying them with food was a problem.

After years of disaster, Uncle Max tenaciously hanging
on, it dawned on him that all he would ever grow on his
place was stones. The translation of dreams into realities
is always a nitty-gritty business. The big light that went
on in Uncle Max's head was the idea of a stone farm. To
make a long story shorter, he finally crushed his stones, and
sold the stuff at the very time that Iowa began the conversion of her millions of miles of mud ruts into super-
highways. Eventually Uncle Max became a gravel man of
some substance.

Uncle Max and Aunt Sarah were my Super Jews. Even
in Chariton, before they moved to the big city—Des
Moines—they, alone among our tribe, kept kosher. This
was no simple practice in Chariton, to which all of the
specially slaughtered meats and many other essentials had
to be imported via Des Moines, St. Louis or Omaha from

Chicago or points east. Uncle Max proudly maintained intense and sustained personal relationships with his Maker, the Lord of Hosts. Once he moved to Des Moines, he conferred with Him at length every morning in the synagogue on Polk Boulevard, where he virtually lived on the weekends. His home, the synagogue, the gravel pits and his children were Uncle Max's life.

Uncle Max and Aunt Sarah were not only Super Jews in Des Moines—they became pillars of the People throughout the state. Des Moines was the Jerusalem of Iowa, and the dozen or so rabbis in the state often had business in Des Moines. From time to time rabbis from the East would travel to this hinterland to give the people the Latest Word about our collective plight in this new as well as in the older world. Aunt Sarah came to do with rabbis what President Roosevelt did with stamps: she developed a passion for collecting them. Nothing gave her greater joy than to wine and dine any rabbi who hove into sight. She really thought (at least at the beginning) that all rabbis, by the fact of ordination, were scholarly, decent, honest men who did her house great honor simply by gracing her table, however much she may have slaved to prepare the board. Her kitchen was a factory producing an endless supply of kosher gelfilte fish balls, stuffed roasted chickens, sponge cakes and salty pot roasts. Her Russian teapot overflowed-eth, and she became the Pearl Mesta, a Hostess of Lords, for our part of the world, with a reputation that spilled over into Missouri and Illinois, and at times reached out to Cleveland, Cincinnati and even New York. I imagine that finally her house came to be posted on the bulletin boards of the Jewish seminaries back East with a triple-A rating—one of the "in" places to visit when one went to Des Moines on business.

Aunt Sarah, like Mae Howell, was in the saving business; and like Miss Howell, she did not discriminate. Anything that was young, male and Jewish she was happily determined to convert into a rabbi. If she had had her way we would all have spent our time teaching one another, I suppose, guiding one another ceremoniously through a life transformed into one unending gala Passover fete, a joyous Sabbath ceremony, a party floating on a flooding river of tea and cakes of lemon sponges. Sarah was disappointed in my mother and father, who took a more relaxed view of my future. But she put a lot of faith in the rabbi, who for a while was one of the favorite pieces in her collection. Together, for a time, I saw them as a powerful conspiracy in behalf of my rabbinical future. I didn't trust them when they got together.

One of the rabbi's greatest virtues (especially in the view of one who would regard him as a hero) was that he was always clear about where he was. He still is. His likes and dislikes, his positions pro and con could be ledgered, put in discreet columns like credits and debits, added and subtracted and totaled into a Grand Final Solution. Naturally, Germans were not to his liking. When Stalin signed up with Hitler, that only confirmed what he already knew about the Russians specifically, and the Slavs in general. The British, with their Balfour Declarations and all that, were devious, double-dealing and untrustworthy. Japs were the American enemy, and he *was* American. Arabs were unspeakable. Catholics of all shapes and sizes were suspect. (Negroes, Indians, and Chinese didn't figure much in Waterloo, though the former came to be ledgered later.) The remainder grew smaller and smaller, until the real chosen people (and the reasons why) began to emerge more and more clearly: all five or six hundred of us in Waterloo. Poor Mae Howell—she and hers never had a chance. Like so many of us, she was on a list without even knowing it.

What Hitler was doing to Our People at this time—the horrible stories that increasingly filled the columns of the Chicago *Tribune*—made us in Waterloo feel both guilty and in a strange way proud. Being chosen meant, beyond a shadow of a doubt, that we had every reason to be chosen, right there in Waterloo. If we had not been chosen because we were better, or smarter, then clearly we were chosen because we were, as a matter of principle, more oppressed than anybody else. Naturally, the Catholic kids threw stones at us. It was their way of confirming God's choice. Not only were we different, but our differences were something to be worn like badges of courage. By osmosis, what we were suffering specially armed us with special insights into the meaning of Waterloo, West High School, Iowa, America, and everything else. Consequently, we knew something *they* didn't. And knowing was superior to not knowing. The ultimate good feeling to come from being hurt from a distance is the feeling that you would not do the horrible things to others that others were doing to you, remotely. Try that sometime, if you want to feel you've got it all under control.

Much as I thought I hated going to Hebrew school, I never doubted that I had to go. I cannot remember a single discussion in my family about whether I should go to college and to *cheder*. Going to college was just one of those things you did, like going to kindergarten. The only questions were: Where, and for what? So it was with most of my friends. You went to the bathroom; you went to Hebrew school; and you went to college. You knew why you went to the bathroom. But one of the interesting things about the other places was worrying about why and for what.

The whole attitude about expectations, I think, was rather remarkable. There are black parents who confront me now, suspicious about why we are keeping their offspring from work and from making money. And there are others, who see me with increasing frequency lately, demanding to know why we're keeping their children out of college. We all react to the expectations others have for us. In this respect we are all programmed toward ends about which we do very little thinking.

The rabbi was one of the first great leaders of an American separatist movement I ever knew. I am sure that a big part of his effort to get us "in" was so that once we got in—into Waterloo—we could show *them* who we were, not only in terms of their "in" game, but also in terms of our immutable, ancient, persistent and glorious dissents. I don't think he meant to be disruptive, but the end of his road was the most dangerous kind of disruption. He converted our weaknesses into strengths by making it respectable for us to assert our weaknesses more effectively than our detractors did. This made an imaginative young man like me dream impossible dreams. And when others, like blacks in New York, played this same game with me, I knew the rules and was prepared to play.

To my astonishment, the rabbi showed up in Greenland once—a United States Army chaplain—to conduct Passover services for us Jewish GI's. His very presence there reminded me of his assumption that I was still under some obligation. He returned to Waterloo and told my parents that I was handling the Hitler thing okay. (He didn't know about the Eskimos and all the other things really going on, on the tundra.) He showed up in Sondrestromfjord shortly after Marlene Dietrich had been there under USO auspices to entertain the troops (without regard to race, color or creed). Miss Dietrich and the rabbi were both, by their respective and overlapping constituencies, much appreciated during the desolate wasteland of that war. But somehow, during the short two years between Waterloo and Sondrestromfjord, I had moved quite a bit from the rabbi's right arm toward Marlene's left leg. Like Miss Howell, the rabbi had had it.

When I arrived in New York years later to be dean of the New School (America's first university for adults), the rabbi was there to greet me. He had become one of the top functionaries of the New York Board of Rabbis. He took me out to lunch at a dairy restaurant on the West Side of Manhattan to celebrate my arrival in the really big city. He met me with an old confidence of knowing me well, but as he was to find out later, he really didn't. It was during the battle of Ocean Hill–Brownsville—the black community in Brooklyn which came to symbolize the struggle for the decentralization of New York's public schools. Against a backdrop of press releases from the Board of Rabbis warning the people about the evils of "Black Nazism," and the alleged storm-trooper tactics of the militant young blacks, we sat together during the summer of 1968 in one of the inner circles of a Jewish "power bloc" —troubled men deeply worried about how to defend themselves.

There was a group of blacks headed by Mrs. Kenneth Clark who had decided to buy a full page of the *Times* on which to state the case for the demonstration school district in Brooklyn. The sponsoring committee had lined up thirty or so prominent black names from the arts, education and politics to sign the page. They were looking for a few white and, hopefully, a few Jewish names to join them. They were having a hard time with the Jewish part. I agreed to participate in the venture, and when the ad appeared there was my name, alphabetically listed right after James Baldwin and somewhat before LeRoi Jones.

When our little bloc next met, the rabbi was furious. How could I sign the same piece of paper that LeRoi Jones had signed? He told me then for the first time that "Once a Jew, Always a Jew" was not necessarily so. There were different kinds of Jews. There were "Black Jews"—and then there were JEWS, presumably non-black (i.e., white?). It was then that, sadly, I reminded the rabbi that he had been my bar mitzvah teacher. He had led me through the rites of entering manhood. If he had neglected to teach me certain things, he should forgive me for not having learned them.

We teachers should, I think, be a little modest. If we succeed, naturally we run the risk of being repudiated. We can only do so much; those we teach must do the rest. We should be content when our students repudiate us. If our students—even one or two—come to teach us something somehow someday, we should rejoice. We should rejoice if our students think they are teaching us something even when they aren't. The attempt to teach is to be encouraged.

The rabbi and I probably disagree now about what it means to be Jewish in America. But in his own way, he is still to be respected. He taught me something lately—sadly.

Wrestling

Ruth Updegraf first showed me where most of the black people lived in Waterloo. She took me there personally, across the Illinois Central railroad tracks where they lived in ramshackle blocks. I saw some from time to time, brawny ones in blood-splattered undershirts walking home from work at the packing plant where they slit the throats of the animals. Many of their wives worked during the day for people like my mother. The size of the black population of Waterloo must have been about the same as the Jewish. Being an All-American–type town, it even accumulated its minorities with some sense of proportion.

The UAW was in the forefront of the battle for social justice for the workers at the John Deere tractor plant, but it was a time before the union had seriously thought of blacks as workers. The only time I can remember seeing a group of more than four blacks together at once in Waterloo was on a picket line at the Rath Packing Com-

pany fence during a strike. For most of us in Waterloo, a
strike was a most irregular event—a curiosity. A picket
line was something you went to see, like the Annual Dairy
Cattle Congress. Retrospectively, it was rather amazing.
The Great Depression, the Great War, the Great Peace—
through all of this greatness it was possible for a large part
of America, probably the larger part, to live and die without seeing more than four blacks in a group. And then, a
curiosity.

Ruth Updegraf must have been six feet tall. She carried
herself like a drill sergeant or a United States admiral. I
had not seen or heard of her for more than fifteen years
when she read about my adventures at Long Island University in the *New York Times,* and wrote me a note
reminding me to be brave. She wrote that she was something over ninety and living in a home for the aged back
in Iowa. But I see her even now quite clearly. She was one
of the great disruptions in my life.

Miss Updegraf was supposed to teach what was called
civics to junior high school kids in Waterloo. She had this
crazy idea—somewhat at variance with the position held
by a certain Greek—that kids barely out of puberty could
know and understand that there were some politics in their
future. She didn't teach government. She made you govern
something. She led you to believe that you might even
govern yourself. Forcing you to read about political figures
was not enough for her. She did everything in her power to
make you one. She reminded us of Aristotle's dictum that
if you want to learn to do something, you'd better try
doing it. Telling fourteen- and fifteen-year-old kids in
Waterloo about Aristotle was itself a considerable educational innovation.

Miss Updegraf would have been a great athletic coach.
She was a severe taskmaster whose classes were tightly
disciplined drills. But somehow, out of her stern tutelage

and rigid expectations, a unique kind of freedom emerged. It was like hard training for wrestling or gymnastics. You practiced the moves over and over again, but when you finally got on the mat or the bars in real competition— especially if you were any good—it was the greatest freedom of all. To the spectator the movements of an accomplished athlete always appear effortless, but behind such a performance there is always a Ruth Updegraf.

She ran us all over Waterloo looking for corruption. She made us read newspapers other than the Chicago *Tribune,* and then encouraged us to resolve all of the earthshaking problems we read about. She was a practical woman. She saw a command of written and spoken English as an essential weaponry system. She taught us rhetoric with the detached coolness of an engineer explaining the mechanics of a nuclear device. From her point of view there were no such things as Republican-English or Democrat-English, socialist-rhetoric or fascist-rhetoric. Atoms for Peace or Atoms for War were not her options. She was interested in Atoms.

Naturally, while they were subject to her authority, most of my classmates hated Miss Updegraf's guts. It was only after she was done with you, and you with her, that you began to understand her reality. And her morality. For the moral dimension of her self-view, of her professional practice, ran through everything that she did. She was not neutral at all about her overall intent. She was so deeply convinced that we ought to be experienced in the practice and art of being free that she was fully prepared to be the ultimate tyrant to see that we were. When you made mistakes in the operation of the freedom machinery, she was there, a skilled mechanic, to help you fix it up. But she charged a high price for her services. And you also learned, as you worked the levers, that not only was Miss Updegraf watching you, but so was the machine. You learned that you had an opportunity, however modest, to control the damned thing. You learned that you could be in charge if you were willing to pay the price, to take the risks.

Mythology

More than fifteen years after I graduated from Waterloo West High, I was asked back to address the annual homecoming pep assembly. The homecoming football game was clearly the big event in the school's year, an extravaganza with much color and emotion. I remember sitting as a student in the auditorium with fifteen hundred others, listening to some old man, a grad who had gone out into the world and become famous, return to tell us how great the Old Rose and Black was during his days at the school. And we would all wave our pompons, hoarsely chant ridiculous cheers, and generally go berserk in anticipation of a football game. And here I was, the old man returned, returned from the world (Chicago) and fame (I had become a dean of students at the university), full of reminiscences of the greatness of the Old Rose and Black during the good old days.

Football was played rough and well when I was a student at West High, and the school almost always turned out to be among the Powerhouses in the state. I was not a natural athlete, and football was not my favorite sport. But for several complicated reasons (not the least of which was that you had to do something athletic in that school to be in with the girls), I tried assiduously for four years to make the team. Coach Strowbridge favored the unbalanced-line approach, with a running right or left guard who was compelled in most plays to pull out and do leaping blocks to clear the way for the ball carrier. It was, as I saw it, a low-visibility, high-risk position. He tried very hard to make a decent right guard out of me. I was probably the best-conditioned athlete ever to grace his bench for four years. You had to put in a certain number of actual game-playing hours to earn your award letter for the season. Wearing your sweater with the letter was one of the top status acts one could commit in the school. It was embarrassing: to earn my letter required another ten minutes of game play as we entered the very last game of the last season I was in the school. Fortunately, by the last half we were winning that game big, and the coach, with great compassion and some feeling that effort, however fumbling, should be worth something, took the risk of putting me in. With but a few seconds to spare I earned my letter, and concluded that illustrious part of my educational career.

I guess there was a time when, as a part of their education, it was felt necessary to inspire the young with myths, to depart a bit from the truth for inspirational purposes, especially when the truth itself did not quite suffice. Coach Strowbridge was supposed to introduce me at the homecoming rally, but he introduced instead, with consummate grace, someone else I had yet to meet. The kids were to know that a conquering hero had returned: I was fearless and had been full of team spirit; I was aggressive and agile—one of the greatest right guards ever to pull out of the Old Rose and Black line; I was tenacious and hardworking; I played the game for its own sake, and for the glory of the school. He went on and on, and I felt older and older. He was great, and led me to the greatest heights I had ever climbed, in that five-minute introduction. What does one do with the truth in the face of a mob of screaming and inspired kids? If your myth gives them a glimpse of how it might be, do you tell them how it really was? Tell them how their tuition money is really being spent? Tell them of the deals upon which their alignments of credit hours really depend? Tell them you really played the game? Of the compromises? Of the way you cheated? Of the things you did which in retrospect seem so stupid? Tell them the truth about how the letters get "earned"? I told them the truth that time—something perhaps they would have preferred not to hear.

The Truth Gap

Once, shortly after arriving at Long Island University, I opened the confidential files in my office to the executive committee of the Student Government so that they could see for themselves the truth which had always been withheld from them, especially about the Center's budget. The more they understood what they read, the less they believed that the truth was the truth. For a while they saw the files as a plot contrived to mislead them.

Mythmakers have the power to condition their audiences to distrust the truth. Given the time and some effort, we can create great confusion by making people think they are not confused.

The lawless act of the students who broke into Dean Ford's files at Harvard was indefensible. It was almost as indefensible as what they found in the files they unlawfully seized.

Americus, Cedar Rapids and Oshkosh

When I returned to Waterloo for the homecoming, several of my old high school friends and classmates entertained me. They had all gone to college, gotten their degrees, and most of them had returned to Waterloo to live. There they were doing essentially what their fathers before them had done. The houses were a bit grander; the problems, perhaps, a bit bigger. But in the eternal way of somebody's

God, it all was reproducing itself. And most seemed content that it be that way.

I felt like the black sheep—the one who had strayed. Clearly, I was a case of Local Boy Makes Bad. It was one thing to read about Chicago in the *Tribune,* but it was another thing—an insane and inexplicable thing—to live there.

Now, when I leave New York City, as I frequently do, to visit campuses in Ohio or South Dakota, in Colorado or in Kansas, in Georgia or in Texas, I wonder whether I am leaving America or going to her. Is St. Paul the way it is, or El Paso, or Iowa City, or Omaha? America! Where are you?

In spite of *Life* magazine once a week and CBS from coast to coast every night, I still think it makes a difference where we grow up, and how. Or is it all reduced to the same size and consistency of an orange as seen from the window of an Apollo capsule a hundred thousand miles out?

I am still astonished when I meet someone in New York City who was born there. I am convinced that New York City is run by people who were born and raised in Americus, Cedar Rapids and Oshkosh. But I am equally astonished to meet young people, born and raised in Flatbush, who've never been west of the Hudson River.

When I was at the New School, the basic constituencies came from the middle- and upper-middle-class Jewish enclaves on the sides of Central Park, in the Village and from the nearby bedroom suburbs. At Long Island University the four hundred thousand Jews in Flatbush were an essential base. In Bedford-Stuyvesant it was, of course, the four hundred thousand blacks living there. And at Staten Island it's four hundred thousand living in that borough and the adjacent parts of Brooklyn, the majority of whom are Catholic of Italian descent. Will the real

America please stand up? In New York City, everybody should stand up?

For Mr. Nixon, Waterloo stood up. It may be increasingly difficult to tell the difference between a new Ford and a new Chevrolet, between the Zenith Super Chromatic Model and the Philco Stereocolored deluxe. But between Waterloo and Harlem, between the rabbi and me, between Mr. Nixon and being young—there are differences.

Being saved or saving others is no longer the issue. Perhaps it never was a proper issue, for Miss Howell, for me or for Christ himself! Finally, each of us must save himself. John Kennedy should have saved himself. And Mr. Evers. And Malcolm. And John's brother. And the last Panther to get a hole in his head. And Waterloo. The whole damned country must save itself—or so my younger friends tell me.

I enlisted in the United States Army Air Force at the age of eighteen and I left Waterloo shortly thereafter. America, where are you? Are you still there, along the Blackhawk Creek and the Cedar River, nestled among the tender green cornfields so recently incorporated into a giant new subsidized industry, lodged in the imagination of Ruth Updegraf's aging hopes, waiting for some new Mae Howell to save you? Come out, come out, wherever you are!

Chapter Two

Father Dearborn

The "Know Better" Principle

The moral dimension of growing up in Waterloo was educational. The educational part of being in Chicago was moral. Too often we dishonor what we think by the way we act. Too often we subvert our most cherished beliefs by the way we refuse to think about them. One way to gauge the condition of your education is to measure the distances between your conduct and what your best thinking argues ought to be done; between your values and what your highest order of thought indicates ought to be cherished most. The greater these distances are, the more room there is for the plain meaning of the words we use to orbit toward the exact opposite of what is intended. These are the Orwellian inner spaces in which, in the name of peace, we wage war—in the course of showing our love, we hurt people; in the cause of freedom, we impose tyranny.

Our children have an intuitive capacity for measuring

these distances with a harsh and deadly accuracy. They always understand at an early age what we don't know far better than they ever understand what we know. They understand our pretension far better than our reality, our hypocrisy far better than our truth. Naturally, our children tend to think we are more or less uneducated and, by and large, immoral. Naturally, we resent and resist this tendency among them. This situation accounts for a very serious problem encountered in all educational efforts and systems. *We* are supposed to be educating *them*, even while we are having a hard time keeping our own credibility patched up.

Ultimately, if too hard pressed about our ignorance, we will defend ourselves with our superior power. Ultimately, we will prescribe and enforce their education because, on the basis of our ignorance, we "know better." Most of our schools are monuments, first and foremost, to the fact that we know better.

Choosing

Neither the University of Chicago nor the city of Chicago made any pretensions whatsoever about being either democratic or loving. The university organized and conducted itself as if it were the city of Chicago, which it was not. The city was organized and acted as if it were a real center of learning, which it sort of was. Between the two of them, over the next decade, my mind blew.

Chicago is what He did before He rested on the seventh day. My marriage, three children, deeply ingrained habits of thought, attitudes, outlooks, two broken front teeth and the formal credentials on which I have transacted most of my professional business—all were products of Chicago. Naturally, Waterloo was essential to the production. Every Chicago should have its Waterloo, and almost always does.

Chicago stank and shouted, and at first left me so much alone I could have cried. From the beginning it was a wonderful and overpowering place, with its pockets of Sullivan and Van der Rohe, its thriving Second City theater, and cells of Algren and Lonigan aficionados, its heroic lake views, loop spires and Southside slums, its marvelously corrupting smells from the stockyards and the mayor's office.

Whatever I went looking for there I got, plus some other wholly unanticipated things. At the outset, that first spring and summer, I made choices madly. Worst and most wonderful of all, the choices I made seemed to have consequences. Nothing had quite prepared me for that. Very soon I met many people who were not choosing the same things as I. The chancellor of my university, Robert Maynard Hutchins, used to say that controversy was imperative to learning. I learned very quickly that about this, if about nothing else, he was right. Choosing automatically got you into trouble. Of course, whether it all meant anything, whether the choices had any significance, whether the conflicts were worthwhile—these were the questions that made life interesting. It was not enough just to *live* in Chicago. Chicago raised a very fundamental question about what *living* was. Chicago tried to organize me to learn—which is what any great city does to its citizens. But learn what, with what purpose, and why?

The Tale of Two Ghettos

There were parts of Chicago which were not citified, and I encountered them early in the game: one, the Southside black ghetto, because I practically lived in it; the other, the University of Chicago, because for practical purposes I was enrolled in it. Believe me, living and being enrolled are two different things, or at least they are meant to be.

Both were places in which the formal programing did everything in its power to preclude the need to make choices. In both, almost everything was prescribed by the classes. In the ghetto there was one master survey course in which all subject matter was thoroughly oriented and integrated. One did not have to worry about passing this course; if you survived it you automatically got a gentlemanly D. If you missed this mark you were likely to end up in one of the city's jails, or dead.

Things were different at the university. There you had one fundamental choice to make: to pass or not to pass. If you conformed to the university's style of street life, given the emphasis placed upon getting in, presumably you could make the grade. If you didn't conform, you didn't exactly go to jail—you transferred to Northwestern or some way-out place like that.

The outcome of World War II was pumped right out of Chicago's heart, there beneath the football stadium which Amos Alonzo Stagg had made so famous, the place where Mr. Hutchins substituted one game for another. For it was under the stadium bleachers that the laboratories were built in which the first chain reaction was achieved.

The chain reaction had a certain self-sustaining quality, a beauty all its own, which held great promise. I saw the plaque on the stadium wall, and soon heard some of the Manhattan Project legends,* like the one about the janitor who dumped a bucket of heavy water down a locker-room drain, compelling the excavation of a good part of Fifty-seventh Street in order to reclaim a part of America's future down there in the sewers.

For a while Chicago had one of the most exciting foot-

* Chicago—the city—has always been a little self-conscious about being second, and its great university invariably looked East for the glow against which to measure its own shadow. It was altogether fitting that the university's great contribution to fighting World War II—the production of the atomic bomb—should have been called "Manhattan."

ball fields in the world, but the chain reactions when I arrived were going on elsewhere in the ghetto. Fermi, Borghese, Urey and Szilard (the science giants in the project) were in the classrooms, and they were beginning to publish their guilt through their lectures and what they were writing. Hutchins was fighting the Joe McCarthys with one hand while trying to federalize the world with the other. The split atom was clearly a split-off. In spite of the Hutchins College (in its third or fourth revised form), and St. Thomas, we were all clearly there for one main purpose —to learn how to survive, comfortably, cleanly, from nine to five each day. The thesis of the atom had been written, microfilmed, catalogued and published. The decent war had been fought and apparently won. The educational problem of the time was to get the operation of the important things, like the world and the Illinois Central commuter trains, more or less back to normal. It was a place where the Great Books represented normalcy, and those books, of course, were really great, especially for those who could and did read. But the university had added a few volumes to the shelf as a part of its special contribution to winning the war. There were the isotopes, and the new Institute of Metallurgy with its dazzling giant cyclotron anchored in Chicago's most colossal hunk of cement. That project represented a formidable challenge to any fund-raising university chief executive. Sustaining its researchers required an endless supply of dollars above and beyond the university's regular budget.

Sitting In

Among the things which the chain reaction did in the University of Chicago ghetto was to create a new administration building. Deans, presidents, chancellors and directors, who had been scattered all over the campus, were brought together at last under one Neo-Gothic roof in a building which miraculously, though no higher than the four-story Gothic one next to it, contained *six* floors of ready, willing and able computerized space. Presumably now more decisions would be made more efficiently with greater impact on more people. Every ghetto should have its own central administration building, a point New York's Governor Rockefeller is trying to make in Harlem just as Senator Robert Kennedy tried to make in Bedford-Stuyvesant.

Before the new administration building was completed, we students didn't exactly know where to "sit in." On the few occasions when we were moved to demonstrate publicly against our own Establishment, we just marched around the quadrangles rather aimlessly. There was the time we struck to recover the football Mr. Hutchins had stolen—to obtain the funds for two intramural teams, which, subsequently, were ordained the Platonists and the Aristotelians. And there were the sporadic outcries against the subversive attempts to tamper with our beloved core curriculum in the College—the SAVE OUR SOC THREE and DON'T MESS AROUND WITH HUMANITIES ONE banners. These parades by torchlight usually ended up at the chancellor's residence, for want of a better place to go; and it never occurred to us to compromise the inner privacy of the place where he lived. We were even careful about messing up his grass.

But the completion of the new administration building brought the situation into focus. Now we would know where to sit in, what to take over. The university was preparing itself for its future. And so was Chicago.

God Is on the Sixth Floor

Mr. Hutchins, at the time, was not the kind of academic leader his students could hate. Some members of his faculty and large numbers of the general public hated his guts. But we were inclined to worship him. Mr. Hutchins, accommodatingly, was abundantly worshipable. He was strikingly handsome and sufficiently remote from us to be mysterious. His public utterances were cool and dazzling, precisely cut, many-faceted diamonds. He fearlessly fought the political pygmies and industrial dwarfs around the state who kept calling us students "whiz-kid queers" and Commies. He even gave the appearance of standing, against great odds, for educational change. (It was not until sometime later that I understood that against the backdrop of the monotonous homogeneity and mediocrity of American higher education, Mr. Hutchins gave the appearance of pointing toward the future by his singular but very articulate exposition of the past.) Mr. Hutchins, at an early age, possessed the stuff of which legends are made. And to us, he was legendary.

When he was finally shaken off his throne, after twenty years of reigning, it was rumored that he was a failure as a fund raiser. I don't see how that could be. There was the story about one of his sorties among the rich ladies on the North Shore in quest of unrestricted funds. He appeared at their luncheon, handsome as a movie star, the breathtaking aquiline profile, the abundant and gently waving coiffure, the physical grace of an aristocrat, and with a reputation for brains to boot. It was a production sufficient to fluster any bosomy middle-aged dowager. And when the chairlady rose to introduce him, disarmed and stammering, her biographic notes trembling in her hands, she said, "Ladies, he is the chancellor of the University of Chicago. What more can one say about a man whose *Who's Who* is eight inches long!" In the estimate of his students, Mr. Hutchins' *Who's Who* was longer than eight inches.

Nevertheless, few students at that time ever met Mr. Hutchins face to face, man to man. We were occasionally in his audiences and we read about him in the newspapers.

But seldom if ever did we penetrate the sixth floor of the administration building, where academic men proposed but God disposed of our affairs, allegedly.

The University of Chicago during those days had more deans per square student than any other academic institution in the world. There was a dean of almost everything, including a dean of deans. Efforts were made to enforce channels, and this meant that if one wished to see a vice-president (of which there was also an abundance) or a president (appointed to relieve Mr. Hutchins of the daily routine of running the place), let alone the chancellor, one appealed first to the director of student activities, then to the assistant dean for student affairs, through him to the dean of students, who then checked it all out with some vice-president. Months later one might find out, if one of the memoranda had not been lost, that your target was really too busy, and the problem, if you could remember what it was, should properly be solved by the director of student activities. The university was organized to teach us self-reliance.

During my second year in the Law School, two profoundly difficult problems overtook me at once, filling me with a despair I felt only God himself might dispel. I was desperate. You had to be, even to think of calling Heaven direct. But call I did, on the telephone, without advance notice of any kind whatsoever to any dean, assistant dean, or subordinate administrator. And Lo and Behold! Thanks to that simple strategy, eight days later I was actually ushered into His Presence. Later, even my most cynical student colleagues saw this as a bold, stunning maneuver.

His secretary was statuesque and beautiful; his office was book-lined, carpeted and spacious; and there He was, alone in the room with me, looking just like Chancellor Hutchins ought to look.

My first and most serious problem was really his fault.

The university had restored my youth and was, so it seemed to me after the first year there, threatening to subvert, to stultify my education. But I did not tell him on this occasion how I came to be there in the first place. Like most American collegians, I had chosen my university scientifically after the most careful consideration—of the sort one uses when he buys a tube of toothpaste.

I was there because sometime during the last year of my fight against Hitler, *Life* magazine ran a story about the University of Chicago. It was wonderful. There, in *Life*-size pictures, were the ersatz Oxonian stage sets, the Nobel laureates and assorted nuclear physicists, and the strong young leader presiding over it all, front and center. Wedged among the photos was the text, containing a line or two about the tests. According to the story, no matter what your age or the disrepair of your previous formal education, if you took the tests and passed them you would get in. In fact, there were lots of tests, and the more you took of them and passed, the deeper in you might get.

This, potentially, was my panacea. There I was, aged twenty-three, and virtually uneducated, i.e., without credentials. The only piece of paper looming in my future at that point was the anticipated United States Army Air Force degree, the honorable discharge, which, except in a negative way, has turned out to be the most useless credential in my limited arsenal. I had no bachelor's degree and no master's degree (and still don't), and I thought that someday it would be nice to be a lawyer. I saw myself stooped and gnarled, bald or white-thatched, bearded and trembling with the infirmities of the senile before I hatched from my formal educational shell to scratch the real earth. Meantime, the young and the brave were inheriting the earth. I was developing quite a grievance against Mr. Hitler. But thanks to *Life,* Chicago's tests were a glimmer of hope, a chance, however slim, to grow young again. It was all a part of the Hutchins' Plan.

So I went, paid the fees, and during a week or so of un-mitigated hell, took the tests. Now, it may be that Chicago was hard up for students. The war had depleted the ranks, and I was among the first to get out, having been among the first to go in. Anyway, they let me in. Not only that, they let me in *sans* B.A. and admitted me, after another battery of tests, directly into the Law School, where I thought I wanted to be. In less than three weeks I prac-tically dropped three years! Eureka! The Hutchins' Plan was sensational. I was young again!

The trouble developed after a year of Contracts, Torts and Property. It became increasingly clear that the action was not exactly where I thought it would be. The action was in the College, the College from which the tests had excused me, the College where Reisman and Schwab, young Miekeljohn, Champion Ward, Bell and a dozen or more other young Turks were holding forth. In the Law School they were really obsessed by the Law. But over in the College, at least in the view of those who believed in Reason, they were really getting down to brass tacks, like redesigning the Spaceship Earth. Among the student body, the College seemed to engage the most interesting types. They were almost the exact opposite of the bores in Medi-cine or the School of Business, whom a substantial num-ber of the students in the Law School resembled, according to their peers over in Medicine and Business.

But there was trouble. It wasn't cricket to attend the Law School and the College simultaneously. There were rules and fees and all sorts of complications. I explained all this to the chancellor, thanked him profusely for my rejuvenation, and assured him of my capacity to handle the law school classes, the library assignments, and selected courses in the College simultaneously. Without comment, he wrote a sentence on a piece of his letterhead addressed "To whom It May Concern," a paper I treasure still, excusing the fees and cutting through the red tape, permitting me to audit freely throughout the College at my own peril. And so, over the following two and a half years, I did. I didn't get to everything, and of course, I didn't get the undergraduate degree. What I got remains one of the most interesting and important, if not the most disciplined and truthful parts, of higher learning.

My second problem was more mundane, but at the time equally pressing. The United Nations organization was being born, and for a while the birth of the UN was to us returning World War II vets what the death of Vietnam is to today's potential vets. It occurred to some of us that what turned out to be the first intercollegiate United Nations Assembly should be convened on the Midway. Between this thought and its realization, as we saw it, stood $8,000. I asked the chancellor for $8,000. He had a few questions about that, but after they had been asked and answered, he picked up his phone, called Dean Strozier and told him to set up an $8,000 account. This turned out to be a profoundly important decision, for not only did the Assembly begin an enduring student activity on American campuses but it also introduced me to a new hero, Adlai Stevenson.

My visit to heaven was probably less than twenty minutes long—but what a revelation I had had at the gates. It was the beginning of a friendship with Bob Hutchins. It was the first revealing demonstration to me personally of his extraordinary capacity to make decisions, of his unusual use of the single word or of the simple sentence to cut through complicated tangles and knots. And sometime after I left the sixth floor it occurred to me that it is better to go to the top. Even if you didn't get what you went for, you could find out promptly where you stood. Not only that, it turned out that God was easier to see than many of the priests He ordained to carry out His various commandments.

Walls

Coming out of Waterloo, you didn't need *Life* magazine to tell you about Chicago. You were ready for that discovery.

Cities are cultural discoveries of the first magnitude, like the use of fire or the wheel. Like all things cultural they were born of necessity—to help us defend ourselves more efficiently from ourselves, and to transact the business of day-to-day survival. Naturally, the early cities arose at places convenient for the collection and exchange of food and the materials for clothing and shelter. Naturally, like Fort Dearborn, they had walls built around them. The walls had gates, and the gates, like Chicago's, had keepers. City politics almost always center on the contest for control of the gates.

The success of the ancient city depended upon the impregnability of its walls. They not only kept the enemy out but also established the authority of those in charge within. The keepers of the gates kept our civilization. When we began to build our cities of learning in the image of the cities of man, from medieval Oxford to contemporary Columbia, Berkeley, Harvard or Chicago, we perpetuated a deeply felt defensive obsession with walls. The politics of city-states concern who shall be kept out, i.e., who shall be admitted to citizenship on what terms. For more than eight hundred years now the politics of educational systems have been the same. Our admissions thresholds separate the boys from the almost-men, and even define, arbitrarily, which is which—the child from the adult, the ignorant from the smart, the lower from the higher. Like slavery and aristocracy, doctoral degrees and high school diplomas both depend upon stout walls. The books upon which we relied in the Social Science I sequence in Chicago's College were entitled *The People*

Shall Judge. And so they shall, at least some, depending upon who keeps the gates.

Becoming civilized changed the function of the walls of ancient cities. There was a subtle shift over time from *keeping* things out to *sending* things out—from a protective tariff policy to one of freer trade. Instead of an obsession with invaders from distant places, the people in the cities became obsessed by the far-reaching consequences of their own creations. The defensive success of the walls released incredible new internal offensive forces. The city was transformed, not entirely but substantially, from a defensive fortress to an aggressive staging ground.

Of course, like civilizations and people, cities decline and die. (Universities seldom die. They just fade away, merge or raise tuition.) Every war involves finally the defense of somebody's cities, Dubček's, Robert Hutchins' or Grayson Kirk's. But in modern times the ability to wage war springs uniquely from the urban capacity. The prime targets of the bombs are the primary producers of the bombs. In the history of warfare, the walls have been far more successful in keeping things out than containing what is generated inside. This is not to say that civilization is its own worst enemy—quite the opposite. Becoming civilized enriches tremendously the store of treasures in our museums, where halls full of the relics remind us of how wonderful we have become, how far we have risen above the pyramids, the sacrificial altars and the need for ancient walls. The trouble is that the creative explosive force knocking down the walls from the inside also destroys the defensive power of the walls.

It is the *success* of the academic elite which now undermines its elitism. It will be written in the history of the academics not that they were slaughtered by the unlettered, illiterate mob storming the walls, but that they committed a bizarre kind of hara-kiri, by the ranks, with tenure, at a union meeting or an annual convention in a

Chicago ballroom. Class warfare often ends that way for the aristocracy.

The Law of Reason

The Law School at Chicago, at least in the estimate of most of those enrolled there, was *the* aristocratic part of the university. This was not a consequence of some spontaneously generated élan. It was the result of a careful indoctrination which, over a period of time, did lead to a certain morale.

The university had its walls. But the Law School was its inner city, an enclave within an enclave, the ultimate defense of the whole, the final fort. In due course, it segregated its students into separate dorms. The College was less than a fourth of the whole. With its early-admissions policy, and its recruitment of the allegedly superbright and hyperprecocious, it had developed a certain mystique which the graduate divisions and the professional schools, with some discomfort, tolerated. But, clearly, the main locus of power and prestige within the university was with the graduate and professional schools.

Among these there was an informal pecking order—at least in the view of those naturally recondite students (like me and my crowd) who thought about it. The Medical School was like a cancer—its buildings and budgets forever wildly multiplying, an ever-ending threat to the life of everything else, though somehow remote and quite beyond understanding. It was virtually impossible to talk with medical students. Most of them responded to everything as if they were already presidents of the AMA. In our view they were generally dull in conversation and hardly worth the trouble in the lexicon of things that counted. Whether you wanted to fight the Communists or Joseph McCarthy, you didn't count on medical student allies. If you wanted to talk about the theater, justice, or even women, you just didn't talk with medical students. They lived in another century, and it might just as well have been another world. To most of us, *their* faculty was invisible. As a part of certain secret rites and initiations we conducted, we occasionally had some business with the cadavers in the formaldehyde tanks with which they worked. But as a general rule, that was as close as we ever got to them. True, some others viewed the law students as we viewed those in Medicine. Even so, I think as a group, awful as we were, we were nonetheless a little looser.

Our peers in the School of Business were simply square. In general they were what we were all specifically against. But even they looked down their noses at what was going on in the School of Education. There were a few students who occasionally got off the head of the pin on which Theology was based, but it was a time when they were still looking for God in the third part of a syllogism.

There were, of course, a few exceptions. There was Carl Rogers and his squad issuing their non-directives from a wartime prefab; and a psychiatrist or two over in Medicine who stirred things up once in a while; and Havighurst and Redfield in Education; and if you wanted to know something about accounting (but not economics), for some strange reason you had to go into the School of Business. But the real power and prestige were in the graduate divisions in science, the social sciences and the humanities, in a few interdivisional committees like Human Development (which had nothing to do with Physical Education) and in the Law School. Mr. Hutchins had come to Chicago from the deanship of Yale's Law School, and he still even taught an occasional seminar—for credit.

The Age of Reason was nothing like Reason's Age on the campus at this time. There was a pervasive feeling everywhere in the university—even in Education—that there was virtually nothing the human mind could not achieve. We *thought* about everything, everything that humans could do. We thought about everything that humans couldn't possibly do. Everything! And then we thought about that. Everything about the place encouraged us to *think*. The intent of the official programing was to keep us so busy thinking that we never had to worry about doing anything. In fact, if we followed the official prescription, we would never do anything. Doing something, anything, was bound to get you into trouble. To do something was low camp, a distraction, a contamination of thinking. The official postwar position, pursuant to that climactic burst of Western civilization's conduct represented by the Nazis, was *to think*.

But on a campus where reasoning was supreme, legal reasoning was most supreme. On those rare occasions when faculty members talked to each other in public at the university, the ones from Law were always the most formidable. They often were the most successful in the invasion of, and sustaining an authoritative position in, others' territories of expertise, realms about which, in fact, they often knew very little. They came armed with a way of thinking, expressed in a jargon all their own, which others, naturally, could not possibly understand. Everything had a special meaning. And the meanings, the concepts, were all supported by the precedent of "experience," the trial of practice, other people's practice, naturally. It was a way of thought in which, if you accepted A or B squared, everything else followed right down to Z, period. Of course, their colleagues from Political Science or Sociology, anticipating the traps, always struggled mightily against taking the bait on A's hook. But it was always at this point that the legal scholars would simply assert that *they* knew how things really were, or that the stupid sociologist, who knew nothing about how it was in court, would find out the hard way what lawyers already knew if they ever got there.

The climax of their position was that life consisted mainly of keeping out of court, or getting out in one piece if you ever got in. Life, in other words, was thinking the way they thought. They modestly gave the impression that humanity existed primarily to get into trouble which lawyers, harassed, overworked, distracted and constantly fighting others' ignorance, would get it out of, if it would but listen, and learn, i.e., retain a good lawyer.

In my later wisdom I have come to regard the law as just another social science, about as imprecise, muddle-headed and confused as economics (before the computers), sociology and psychology (after the computers), and history. But there is a difference, a very important difference. The law, unlike the others, brilliantly *organizes* its imprecision, muddleheadedness and confusion. The organization is its wonderful discipline, and words are the vehicles by which its organization moves. For this reason, societies based upon sophisticated and mature legal systems are bound to be verbal. In the United States a superior command of the English language, spoken and written, is the ultimate weaponry system for the transaction of business, government, science and almost everything else. In the United States the best way to keep the blacks and the Spanish-speaking down is *not* to teach them English. To keep them powerless, subject them ruthlessly to the law, but never teach it to them. In fact, this is a pretty good way to keep white middle-class youth powerless while they are in college. At least it's worked reasonably well so far. Preach law and order to them, but keep them guessing about what you mean. If they ever find out what you mean, you're likely to be in very deep trouble, which means: *You* will need a lawyer.

One of the first essential and extremely difficult steps toward the mastery of legal reasoning is to sweep away the cobwebs in your head connecting the law in a tenuous and complex way to anything resembling justice. Of course, the law does have something to do with justice, but not exactly what the neophyte law student or the layman may naturally think. The law is a marvelous mechanism for the regulation of power relationships among the citizens, and between them and the various public authorities to whom they are responsible. Occasionally the outcome of this regulation is just. If you are a plaintiff or a defendant who wins his case, the law is just. If you are a plaintiff or a defendant who loses his case, the law is not just. And if you are a third party, observing the final score in the contest, whether the result is just or unjust depends upon your point of view and a lot of other things, like how you currently regard your own vested interests in the future.

Combat is implicit in the administration of Anglo-American law. Advocacy is its highest art form. These are basic points too often lost on academic administrators who act as if the community life of a university and its relations with the rest of the world should and in fact will proceed on the basis of some magically conjured consensus. One of the big surprises contained in the campus disruptions is the revelation that students, any students, would advocate anything. Deans and university presidents, and local urban politicians too, have been outraged and personally offended by the advocacy forms and practices adopted by some of the students, the blacks and the poor. But the high art of advocacy is also a subject practically omitted in the education of the young. There is another way that the art of advocacy can be mastered; that's through the practical experience of defending power, which presumes, of course, that you have some power to defend. Our students are learning the hard way, and so are the blacks. As things have turned out, except in the defense of their own positions, most of the people in charge in America have not proved to be especially accomplished advocates themselves. What do they expect from the powerless, who not only are inexperienced but have little reason to want the experience in the traditional way? We may predict with certainty that more deans, college presidents and urban politicians will be outraged and personally offended in the near future.

Most of the Law School curriculum was organized along the line of a simulated game, like Let's Pretend. The reality of advocacy was simulated. Courtrooms were simulated. Fellow students were simulated legal colleagues. Faculty members were simulated judges. Trial practice was simulated. Even simulated justice was occasionally covered in a simulated discussion. It was the case method mainly, based more or less upon Anglo-Saxon mankind's One Hundred Great Cases. In the final comprehensive examinations, a great case was one whose outcome pursuant to reasoning was very different from the correct one pursuant to legal reasoning. The right answers on those tests were notoriously unjust, as were the grades I earned on some of them.

We all knew, of course, that in Chicago and the world—in fact, down the street a few blocks from the Law School—law was being practiced, justice administered, and tests given that were not simulated. And the conduct of our own faculty was often a marked departure from what it officially preached. Our faculty, at least its stronger members, continuously translated what it thought into action. Several had practiced law or held important positions in government. Many actively consulted, in Chicago, New York or Washington. Their publications sometimes took the form of real briefs really pled before real courts, including the Supreme one. They won or lost real cases, sometimes making real legal history. The best of them were thoughtful men of action even while they promised us that we might someday be like that too if we would but *think* now in the expectation of *acting* later. We were the novice monks in the charge of the fathers superior who traveled to Rome regularly to keep an eye on the Pope. We were excused from society while we *thought* uninterruptedly for three years or more. We were the consumers, and they, the producers. We were being educated, but they stood for the morality. They produced us.

The Informer—Act Two

The one time I was asked to *do* something *as a law student,* as distinguished from being induced to act as a plain student or just as a human being, I rather wished I had deferred acting until I got out of the monastery three years later.

I was approached by a representative of the Lawyers' Guild or the Legal Defense Department of the NAACP—I forget which—to perform voluntarily some legal service over at the Airport Homes. The Airport Homes was a relatively new public-housing development on the southwest side of the city near Midway Airport in an almost exclusively Polish Catholic neighborhood. The first Negro family had been moved into the project, and for over a week crowds, a few hundred to several thousand people, had besieged their front door, shouting obscenities, threatening and committing acts of violence. A police cordon had been thrown, shoulder to shoulder, around the block. Food and other supplies had been brought in by white officials and friends to the frightened family, who had not dared venture out during the siege. There had been rocks and broken windows, and an abortive fire bomb or two. During the day, crowds of babushka'd women and young children kept the watch. After work in the evening their ranks were swollen by the hundreds of returning breadwinners and the older children. The vigil went on by torchlight throughout the night, small squads taking shifts in the early predawn hours.

The assignment for which I had volunteered required that I mingle in the crowd, gathering the kind of facts that could subsequently be used in a court. I would identify under oath ringleaders and committers of acts of violence.

Following instructions, I prepared myself for unobtrusive mingling. Dungarees and an old sweat shirt. I even dirtied my uncalloused hands a bit. I was driven late one afternoon to within a mile or so of the neighborhood and then took a bus nearer to where the action was, riding through streets of neat little houses with neat little front yards, and gardens, all, I suppose, neatly mortgaged too. There was a crowd of several hundred people, mostly female, but the men were beginning to arrive. I moved through it toward the police line, and for thirty minutes or so listened to and watched the ugly beast. Suddenly it turned on me.

He was about my age and size, and he asked, "Where do you live?" I said, "Down the street a couple of blocks." "Let me see your wallet, your identification." "Let me see yours," I replied. And then he struck out at me, shouting to his friends all around, "Another Commie-kike! Over here, a Jew-bastard!"

The police watched the fight calmly, and I did the best I could. The attack from the rear was what got me. The girls—the Polish, amazon girls. Strong as the peasants in the fields, they got me on the ground and kicked. The boys made a pretense of fighting like men, but the girls, they are really the stronger sex. Finally the police reached over, picked me up and pulled me behind their lines. For a while they debated whether to arrest me on charges of disorderly conduct, while I held a handkerchief to my bleeding nose. Then they put me in a squad car, drove me far away from the beast, and told me never to return.

In the summer of 1967, years later, a good young friend in Bedford-Stuyvesant said to me, "Where's the freedom, man? It's in the streets. The streets are free! The streets are free!" And so they are, depending upon when and where, and for whom and how. Later I discovered that two pieces of my upper front teeth had inadvertently been left on the streets of southwest Chicago, meager offerings on the altar of the God of the Informers. Would His wrath ever be satisfied? Would I ever make a decent spy? It seemed doubtful.

The Order of Combat

The best teachers in the Law School were sometimes the most brutal. In spite of all that we don't know about group dynamics and sensitivity training, and our natural, human sentiments in behalf of the cooperative learning environment, I am convinced that certain aspects of the education of grown-up people (and young ones too) necessarily must involve a little cruelty. Learning is not all love, and education is not all fun. In part I suppose this is a genetic matter. We have a tendency to defend the private territories of our ignorance aggressively, and after all, there is an authoritarian dimension in the educational relationship which, bearing as it does upon our most personal and precious possessions—our minds and our spirits—we naturally resent.

In the Law School the best teachers prepared us for the harsh realities of the combat in advocacy practice. Among the brutally best of these was Ed Levi, who became dean of the school while I was there, and since has become president of the university. Levi, I think, wrote the original legislation making ignorance a crime. To enter his classes unprepared was unthinkable, unless you were ready to die. To think you had prepared adequately was a perilous act of overconfidence. Levi was a specialist in What You Didn't Know. He was merciless in his cross-

examinations, which always exposed, for the world to see,
What You Didn't Know. His sense of humor was sly and
underplayed. By the time you found out you were a
jackass, he already had the saddle on you. He delicately
sliced up your mind, and then pasted the strips of it on
the blackboard. Your fellow students laughed at your im-
becility, knowing full well that a few moments later you
might laugh at theirs. We seldom found occasion to laugh
at Ed Levi, and at times this seemed cruel. If you accepted
the official premises of the Law School, Levi was among its
best exponents.

Bill Crosskey was a rumpled renegade, a real credit to
the Law School because it tolerated him, kept him
equipped and let him do his thing. I don't know if Crosskey ever pleaded before the Supreme Court, but if he ever
did, it would have been a day the Court would never
forget. Crosskey was not a man for small legal problems—
like going bankrupt, paying income taxes, making a will,
suing an insurance company, selling the Empire State
Building or negotiating a contract to buy the Brooklyn
Bridge. He was interested in slightly bigger ones, like
what in the hell did they write the Constitution for in
the first place? But if you, ever had a problem like that,
he was clearly the counsel to engage.

He was supposed to be teaching legal history, but like
some black students now, he had a certain view about what
the historians had been doing to American history. He
thought the history was fine, but he felt that most of the
historians, wrapping their cloaks of academic freedom
around their allegedly objective scholarship, were self-in-
dicted libelists. He made us lug the five weighty volumes
of Madison's notes of the Constitutional Convention
around for a year. His views of the Convention and of the
early Supreme Courts, and of the principal actors in those
dramas—Hamilton, Jefferson, Madison, Jay, John Mar-
shall and the others—were slightly at variance with what

they taught over in the history department, and if ever adopted, would have put most of the scholars in the Law School out of business. But he was no simple debunker. His exposés of Madison's forgeries, of Jefferson's duplicities, of the cracker-barrel politics in which the Founding Fathers indulged, were consummately illustrated with impeccable scholarly research. He subjected the watermarks in pieces of their paper to chemical analysis and applied isotope techniques in the determination of the ages of their tomes. By the time he was through, the Library of Congress was probably sorry that it had kept the records.

Crosskey lurked, shaggy and unkempt, in a disorderly office, papers and books piled haphazardly everywhere, notes oozing off the shelves and heaped on the floor, an incredible maze only he could master in the course of writing his own Great Book—a course that seemed to extend on and on and on.

In many ways Crosskey was the opposite of Levi. Between them ranged the rest—the declining, aged great authorities, the prestigious new ones robbed mainly from Yale, and the crisp, acid-tongued, razor-sharp young men the dean was acquiring who so often seemed like replicas of himself. They were a motley crew, and I dwell upon them only because they, along with Dick McKeon over in the graduate philosophy department, provided me with the only formal higher education I have ever had. Being the way they were, they deserved credit for the fact that by the beginning of my fourth year in what was loosely regarded as a doctoral program, they had without realizing it persuaded me that I did not want to practice the law. As guidance counselors, they were pretty good, albeit expensive.

Nevertheless, almost a decade later, with the special permission of the state's supreme court, I finally passed the bar in Illinois. I was about to leave the jurisdiction, and at a lunch with Ed Levi he bet me I couldn't pass it, so I tried, and I did. My certificate hangs in my study, its gold seal a glittering testimony to how great the Law School really was. The one thing they didn't convey at all in the Law School was the legal knowledge necessary to pass a bar exam. Passing that examination on my first try proved to me the staying power, the durable and deep value of my Law School education. What they had taught me was how to acquire and then use the knowledge required to pass the bar. It was a style of thought, a way of venturing with one's mind which transcended the law itself, and at times has even been helpful to a college president—given the world in which college presidents live these days. But it's a style of thought, I've learned, which, if carried too far, leads deep into marshlands far removed from where the people live, and from the solution of their problems. Our views of law and order, and due process, should embody great restraint, and some sense of balance.

Finally, about the inner city—the higher it built its walls to keep me in, the more it excited the likes of me to get out. Its insistence upon its elitism, its fascination with its own perfection, its conviction that it really was the inner city of our minds, forced me to look elsewhere for significant parts of my education. Of course, if you tried to get out, the law, its school, and what they represented, abused you. But even the abuse was helpful. It toughened your hide, and eventually showed you *their* limitations as well as something new about your own.

Chapter Three

Who Shall Judge?

Fads

Each time produces its own fads, and the adoption of each time's fads is a part of that era's survival prescription. For example, if you want to survive long as a college or university "leader" these days you should pledge allegiance to student participation and faculty democracy, personal humility, quality education and maintaining standards, personal humility, the injunction and a winning football team, personal humility, patriotic peace in Vietnam and higher salaries for the faculty, and personal humility. And if you want to succeed in marriage these days, you should be for children's participation and family democracy, equality of the sexes and color TV, a house in the suburbs and at least three expensive vacations each year, and personal humility.

Now, these things are so self-evident that one wonders why so many college and university presidents are having such a rough time, why the divorce rate is so outrageously high, and so many of our children alienated.

Constituencies

Obviously it is not what we *say* that counts, but what we *mean*. All I gather Mr. Nixon is trying to do by memorializing that deeply un-American phenomenon—the Silent Majority—is to Americanize it, i.e., to provoke it to end its silence and speak up—in his behalf, naturally. If college and university "leaders" (and husbands and wives) ever said what they really meant or lived the way they really want to, they'd all probably be in much deeper trouble than they're already in. Rich as we are, we still can't afford to do business on the basis of what we think—only on the basis of what our constituents think. And if you can't beat them, join them, especially if you don't want them taking over the place illegally, without a bill of sale, and dirtying up your office.

Unfortunately, we are all somebody's constituents. That's democracy.

All Management Is Mismanagement

Proclamation:

> ACADEMIC FREEDOM IS A UNIVERSITY'S
> GREAT BULWARK AGAINST THE SUBVER-
> SION OF THE PURSUIT OF TRUTH!

Faculty democracy is the machinery through which academic freedom works. Due process on the campus is a function of these verities, adjusted, of course, by clauses in the contracts with the labor unions (faculty and other),

by the outlook and deportment of the institution's governing board, the political climate of the jurisdiction (is it
California, New York or Mississippi?), and the cultural
tone of the community in which it is located (is it Harlem,
Haverford or Hoboken?).

Footnote:

> Freedom, academic or some other kind, finally is a
> legal concept, politically charged and power-laden.
> Nobody has a freedom problem until he tries to *do*
> something.

A psychologist like Bruno Bettelheim, a critic like Paul
Goodman, or a board chairman like William Zeckendorf,
may discuss freedom academically. But once a working
authoritative relationship is established with other people,
once we accept that kind of responsibility, and once we
lead the other people to believe that they are to enjoy
some kind of freedom practically, then we are politicians,
whatever else we are, possessing and disposing of power.
Then we can hurt people, however much we may intend
to help them.

There is a banker in Staten Island, of whom I am quite
fond, who likes to argue that I don't have the guts to
manage my own campus. If I had, he claims, I would
simply issue a memo putting a stop to the "obscenity" that
crops up from time to time in our student newspapers. My
banker friend makes no claim about being an educator,
but he has every reason to assert his expertise as the man-
ager of an important bank. I think I know how he would
handle his employees, though I wonder what he does
with some of *his* more demanding customers. But putting
aside fine distinctions between faculty members and "employees," between students and "customers," *universities*

simply are not managed. Universities are governed, or should be.

True, our academic institutions are issued corporate charters, own land and often operate through pipe lines like Standard Oil. But in an important, intrinsic way, either a university is a *community* or it isn't much of a university. It is a community in the ways that a sociologist, a political scientist, an engineer, a policeman or an economist would think and act about a community. A university has to be governed, even if it is a community of scholars, which, once in a while with luck, it turns out to be.

Overdue Processes

The decay of the university as a community, like the experience of the black people in America, has a long history. The academic responses to the great events of our time have not exploded suddenly like an atomic bomb. They have been carefully cultivated, like rare orchids. In one of his essays Harlow Shapely says that it took Harvard's faculty more than a century to put its official stamp of approval on the authoritative evidence that the sun, not the earth, is the center of our planetary system. Academically, caution is not only the better part of the valorous truth; it *is* the academic truth.

Two years before its uprising, Columbia University announced a far-reaching reorganization which was hailed nationally as a model for institutional reform. In the last book he wrote before his great disruption, the former president of Cornell said: "The student is a student. He is at the university to learn, not to manage; to reflect, not to decide; to observe, not to coerce." A few years later, in the midst of his disruption, he told a student rally, "No community can be considered legitimate in which we or those of us who ask for the right to participate in its decisions have that right denied." Naturally, at the proper times, the *New York Times* certified editorially the propriety of both of these propositions.

Now we are compelled to learn quickly, though what there is to learn has been around for a long time. Indeed, the seven members of the corporation at Harvard have been a self-perpetuating body since 1644. Perhaps no dynasty except the ones headed by the Pope and the Queen of England can lay such an ancient claim to the right to rule. A distinguished professor of Harvard's divinity faculty told me that very few members of the university's faculty and practically none of its students knew the names of those sitting on the corporation when the trouble hit. Naturally, a university with one of the most distinguished conglomerations of faculty talent in the arts and crafts of government would also, itself, have a government which, utterly paralyzed at the moment of its own truth, was incapable of governing.

The invasion of the cities by our people has been rapid, but it has not happened all at once. Harlem has been visible from university windows for a long time. On campuses where the students sat in because of faculty dismissals, hiring and firing practices have remained more or less unchanged for a long time. Guns are not new on our campuses (ROTC units and campus police officers have possessed them for a long time), but only the perverse outlook of some students about who should possess the guns and for what purposes. When the former president of Harvard told his student leaders not too long ago that the Corporation invests its great wealth in places that "selfishly are good for Harvard," and that the university does "not use its money for social purposes," he was not proclaiming a new policy, but simply restating a tradition.

It is embarrassing to be reminded now by some of our

students that the order we defend derives in large part from medieval bodies of law. Because some notion of freedom is, always has been, and must be the ultimate defense of our academic claims, it is embarrassing to find out in the way we have that our students know so little about the practice of freedom. What sad desperation must have moved that white student at City College during its disruption to proclaim that occupation of a building was the only base of power left open to him and his peers—the only basis remaining for a dialogue between them and those in charge. Such desperation is the source of our peril. The activities of some of our best and brightest students may now combine with the conduct of some of our most decent and enlightened academic leaders to prove the most dangerous and obnoxious of the propositions for which the Ronald Reagans and the Weathermen stand. Is it possible that what we are defending is so powerful and so corrupt that it cannot possibly be changed through processes which respect the professed American values?

The disruptions prove either that our students, the young adults in our free society, are sadly inexperienced in the possession and use of freedom power or that the system we defend, the privileges and interests we represent require us to keep them in ignorance about the power of being free. Either we have failed and are failing the students in their education or our high educational purposes require us to keep them in ignorance. In either event, the deficiencies so many of them embody in the use of the English language and standard-numbers systems are like nothing compared to their inexperience and ignorance concerning the operation of the principles of parliamentary government, the discipline of self-regulation, and the implications of freedom. We have apparently assumed that American babies—black and white, Spanish and English-speaking, rich and poor, from Waterloo and from New York, even in Chicago—are born free. They aren't.

How to Run a Ghetto

A compulsory ghetto fails as a community because its inhabitants lack the power to develop common goals and to pursue them effectively together. It fails too because of a fatal disconnection between the possession and use of power and the cognition that knowledge, as a form of power, carries with it political responsibility. In these respects the campus is now like the compulsory ghetto.

Those who deplore a view of the university in terms of its powerful political role in American society must account for the institution's use of political power in its own terms, for its own purposes. I have come to feel lately—partly, I guess, because of the legal reasoning styles to which I have been exposed—that those playing around with the structure of their universities these days are playing with tinker toys. New committees, new senates and new student-participation formulae do not necessarily mean that anything has changed. Indeed, if Berkeley, Columbia, Harvard and Chicago are valid examples, restructuring turns out to be one of the brilliant new inventions for sustaining the status quo. The vested interests and essential privileges involved in current efforts to restructure the university have yet completely to surface. A substantial part of our melting iceberg is still below the waterline.

That part of the student critique of the university which most deserves our attention bears upon what we teach, how we teach it, and the terms on which it is taught. One of the interesting things their critique points out is that our building programs, corporate investments, relationships to the immediate community and to the society, and our views of citizenship inside the university, all turn out to be projections and applications of what *we* call or have called education. Their critique suggests the perfectly absurd conclusion that there is a relationship between their long hair and our long war, between being a nurse and being a Negro, between the freshman political-science course and the pollution of fresh air, between education for freedom and being free. Obviously, the contemporary American student activist is crazy.

We have probably made a mistake by revealing to our students that there really is too much to know, and only one way to learn it—our way. They have come to accept this as gospel, and it has encouraged them to view curriculum development as essentially a sophisticated art of selection, interpretation and emphasis in which *they* have a vested interest. Understanding this, naturally they have begun to ask the key political questions bearing upon *our* vested interests and privileges: What experience and talent should be empowered to select? Who should be empowered to employ those who will interpret, and to deploy the wealth required to support the enterprise?

Obviously the control over who will be kept out and over punishment-and-reward systems inside is extremely important. While our students still generally concede that the older adults who teach them may know something they don't, they are also asserting the uniqueness of their own experience, claiming that they may know something which those now in charge don't. They have returned to the kindergarten level to rediscover a principle long revered in American education—that the student plays a positive and active role, that he has something definite and essential to contribute to his own education.

The young—suspended precariously in a society obsessed by Vietnam violence, race violence, crime violence and culture violence—are restating the eternal questions about education: What is important to learn, and how may people best learn together? Regarding these enduring questions, they are also asking the eternal question of a society which officially encourages its young to grow up free (even while keeping them in bondage), namely: Who shall judge? Regarding the problems these questions suggest, academic tradition responds through an uptight delineation of jurisdictions and powers within the university.

Whatever erosions of faculty power may have occurred, the curriculum, the expenditure of the credit-hour currency, and the hiring, firing, promotion and tenuring of one another, remain at the heart of faculty power. It is not an absolute power, but it is a power to initiate and to create, not merely to veto and to react. The academic freedom tradition is at the foundation of this power, and faculty democracy is its superstructure. Where there is no faculty democracy, academic freedom is a slogan rather than a way of life.

The new demands for student democracy arise in academic communities where there is in fact very little faculty democracy. On the campuses where the faculty does vote on anything important, the franchise is usually limited to those who possess tenure. Getting tenure is mainly a function of the passage of time. The usual residency requirement is three to five years—i.e., 300 to 500 percent longer than the usual residency requirement for the franchise to elect a President of the United States.

Tenure is generally associated with the two upper ranks. As student populations have grown, more and more persons have been recruited to teach full time who either have just earned a Ph.D. or are still working on it. Throughout the country, something substantially less than half of those who teach full time possess tenure. Most of the associate and full professors, department chairmen, deans and possessors of the distinguished professorial chairs are over forty, and the majority are over fifty. By and large, faculty power, as well as administrative power on our campuses, is in the hands of the grown-up children of the Great Depression, the New Deal, the struggle of the trade union movement, and the war against Hitler. Prestige values pursuant to the publish-or-perish dogma mean that those most successful in research and publication usually remain aloof from faculty and campus politics, except in the moments of crisis. The result is that among the minority empowered to decide, even a smaller clique generally rises into day-to-day control. *Faculty power is oligarchical,* and the success of its exercise is really the work of a relatively few. It is these few who give academic freedom its real operational content.

Faculty power has been exercised mainly to expand the curriculum without really reforming it. After the sciences, the technologies got in. The expansion of graduate education has naturally meant the admission of new professional curricula. Now that we have stumbled upon the black part of American society, there will be new courses and new electives, black. But all that is "new" is jammed in a disorderly way into the old packages—the old credit-hour and course systems, the old methods for selecting what is important and relevant, the old dogma about how action pursuits contaminate scholarly endeavor, the old standards for judging talent and performance, the old walls around the campus meant to protect the neutrality that was never neutral. Within these old boundaries the faculties have contributed mightily to the store of the new knowledge— which is not quite the same thing as contributing mightily to the advanced education of more students, to the possession and use of what is known.

At an immediately practical level, faculty leadership has achieved, especially since World War II, a marked improvement in the working conditions, salaries and fringe benefits attending faculty status. Salaries have risen at annual rates of between 7 and 15 percent. Teaching loads are steadily dropping to a common standard of twelve or nine hours per week actually spent in the classroom in the two-year colleges, nine-hour loads in the four-year colleges, and (not uncommonly) six hours in the graduate and professional schools. We are talking here about nine- or ten-month contract years, about full professors, for example, who are required to teach nine hours a week or less for nine months at salaries often above $20,000 per year, and in City University now, on a scale that goes as high as $31,000 for that kind of service. These are, of course, only base-income figures. To these numbers a skillful moon-lighter may add substantial sums from consulting and lecture fees, book royalties and from teaching an additional course or two during a short summer term or at night beyond the assigned schedule. Not bad, all things considered.

These work loads are often arranged within maximum three-day weeks, allowing increased free time for the consultations, the outside lecturing and publication. In the great cities, where expressways are congested at the beginning and end of the workday, there is a tendency to schedule the three-day weeks between the hours of 10 and 2 or 3, especially for the senior faculty members who have an influence upon arranging the schedules.

What does all this mean? It means the rising cost of an inefficient deployment of physical facilities at a time when educational wealth is moving toward short supply. It means enlarged class sizes at the same time that students are not only more numerous but more varied in their needs for individual attention and more anxious for informal learning opportunities. It means perpetuating the powerlessness of the younger full-time teachers who are often psychologically as well as chronologically closest to the new student outlook, discouraging their impulses for change.

But the most serious consequence of this situation is its subversion of remaining opportunities to develop a sense of community among those who teach and those who are taught. The system puts all personnel in fast motion, at greater and greater distances from one another. Within the framework of complex and harried schedules and larger and larger classes, the people on the contemporary campus pass one another like ships on a foggy sea—tentatively, remotely, suspiciously, and with horns blowing louder and louder. The course-credit way of packaging the knowledge emerges as the one sure, computerized beacon breaking through the fog. It tells everyone exactly where to go. And all, like the lemmings responding to some deep inner primeval need, relentlessly go.

With the advent of collective bargaining, especially in the public sector of higher education, we may expect to see more and more of the critical issues affecting class sizes, the deployment of university wealth, the criteria for evaluating professional performance, and even the character of student life resolved in closed forums by labor-management experts who are neither the students, the teachers, nor the campus-level administrators whose day-to-day lives are reordered by the terms of the "negotiated" contracts.

In the growing regulation of the American university through collective bargaining, the representation of the public interest is distorted. In the combatant context of negotiation, the governing board no longer governs. It is compelled to advance the interests of management which often are not coincident with those of the consumers—the students, their parents or the taxpayers. Collective bargaining threatens to formalize and congeal the pursuit of professional self-interest in education, and speed the transformation of the learning community into just another American corporate enterprise. In this process of negotiating our academic affairs, the higher purposes and commitments of the nation—blacks, equal opportunity, peace, cities—may be submerged in the combative pursuit of narrower goals. Trade unionism, inspired by democratic values, may, in academe, distort those values.

Officially Designated Ignorance Areas

During the 1969 disruptions at the University of Chicago, a leading member of its faculty proclaimed that democracy in a university is the enemy of academic freedom. He felt that students, being the ones who need to learn, represent ignorance, and that ignorance is no proper basis on which to make decisions in a university.

In a department of economics, everyone outside that department represents ignorance when it comes to the decisions affecting research, teaching and the educational programs in that department. And within such a department, a select few represent knowledge and wisdom when it comes to the selection of leadership, hiring and firing, promotion and tenure, budgeting, the assignment of credit hours, and the ultimate decisions about what should be taught. But even at the University of Chicago there are some tenured members of professorial rank in the department of economics who expect to be taken seriously when they advise the president of their university about handling disruptive antiwar students, or the President of the United States about controlling inflation. The officially designated ignorance areas in the contemporary American university finally extend to all the neighborhoods except those in which the currently empowered oligarchs reside.

Community control is properly a priority issue in a nation whose people have lost a sense of control of their lives, and where the conduct of public life is reduced to an incomprehensible and remote managerial process, a collective-bargaining negotiation. Flash, one of our students at Staten Island, says, "Your guys don't make the proper distinction between special people and people who know special things. I put my pants on one leg at a time, just like the professors around here when they get up in the morning."

When it bravely faced Joseph McCarthy's assault, when it finally, timidly, ventured beyond its Gothic walls into the slums huddled in its own shadows, and when it converted its football stadium into the laboratory that produced a chain reaction, my great university in Chicago put its pants on one leg at a time. Learning in places like the Law School sometimes seemed like learning for a one-legged man, a crippled man. But assuming that we are forever destined to be lame, it was a magnificent, a heroic crutch.

Now is a time when we are invited to reconsider our assumptions. Large numbers of Americans are suddenly showing up, eager to learn to walk on two legs.

Chapter Four

Loyalty Oaths

A Grecian Urn

While I was a student at the University of Chicago I was sure that I had thoughts no one else in all creation had ever had before. There were times when I understood so very, very clearly how my parents, and their parents, and their parents before them, had screwed it all up. There was a time when I was the earth's most accomplished artist, when designs and forms, symmetrical, graceful and delicate as an ancient Grecian vase were lovingly shaped by the hands of my mind. Making such brilliant discoveries and creating such rare objects of art, I knew that it was only a matter of time before this battered planet would return to its proper orbit, and the flowers would somehow magically bloom again under the elevated on Sixty-third Street.

But since then, walking along a crowded street or looking at the pictures in a newspaper, I have more than once come across a man, a total stranger, who, I see with a sudden shock, is my twin. How astonishing to chance unexpectedly upon another who in his countenance, his physique, the set of his eyes, the way he walks, is a replica of yourself! But there you are, among the billions, suddenly no longer absolutely unique, perhaps not mass-produced like the latest Ford, but in what you read or what you see, what you think, or through some extraordinary genetic fluke, not quite an utterly original production, but created in the images of other times, other places and even other people! It is like walking into a room for the first time and knowing that you've been there before. Or seeing your personal soap opera replayed like an old film on TV.

I find it hard to believe even now that I could have given a speech to some students in Pennsylvania in 1955 entitled "The Decline of the Student Life." But even before that, *Time* magazine had discovered the new American collegians and ordained them "the Silent Generation." Of course it was not *my* generation which *Time* had discovered, but worse than that, the immediate offspring of my breed, the very ones to whom I had personally handed my exquisitely turned Grecian urn. They were the ones we meant especially to inspire. We had handed the torch to them, and according to *Time,* they had dropped it.

In Pennsylvania, though it was but a few moments after the Great Events, I spoke nostalgically, like an eighty-year-old man on the front stoop of his retirement-village villa baking in the Florida sun. Surely it is a sign of aging, at any age, when we look back, even a little way, and see the moment of our greatest hopes—unique, irreplaceable and utterly beyond the reach of those who follow. I said,

"Eager to re-enter civilian life, impatient to make up for lost time, headstrong about the future, the World War II veteran took the ivory tower by storm. . . . He was no mere kid. He'd been around. He had lived with the Russians and the Indians. . . . In the carnival-mirror of war he had lived life in its exaggerated and distorted forms. He had smelled death. He had voted for a President at least once. Many were married—had children. He was not there just to fill out those difficult and often empty years between seventeen and legal majority. He was there with a purpose, born of war, because of Hitler, not merely to reaffirm the meaning of Europe or of the American Dream or of Asian and African aspirations, but to rescue the meaning of the civilization for which he had fought and, somehow, survived. . . .

"He brought fresh versions of two ideas to the campus. He believed that students like himself had rights, and that the old forms of academic life had to be democratized. And he stood for an international brotherhood of students, for the use of knowledge to reunite old friends and old foes, Germans and Poles, Shintoists and Christians, capitalists and Communists, white, brown, yellow and black brothers. . . . He upset mightily his deans, the bursars, and his teachers. What an extraordinary promise the vitality of his movement contained! But by 1950 the awful scope of his disaster was apparent. His promise was never realized. . . ."

Retrospectively, this was a restrained description of the disaster. For we had yet to bask in the deeper warmth of Eisenhower's Indian Summer, that strange interlude before the stormy season, bound to come.

One other point: it is possible I was a little romantic in the recollection of the significance of my peers—of what I meant myself then. Perhaps I saw us as I thought we should be, not as we actually were.

Births

During the war the University of Chicago must have been a place for the very young and the very old, and of course, for the girls. At least it seemed that way when we arrived on the Midway. The girls were glad to see us back—that was our impression. For the very young and the very old, our arrival must have been a very mixed bag, indeed.

But old Mother Midway, waiting patiently in her squat, graying manner for a new love affair late in life, merrily took us in, whatever her ulterior motives. Soon the seminal juices of our new altruism impregnated the campus and led to the birth of a whole new family of organizations, causes and movements. For those who were trying to keep the campus cool, our new offspring must have seemed like a noisy bunch of bastards. And by the time Congressman William Jenner and United States Senator Joseph McCarthy were attracted by the uproar, there was plenty around to look into.

The American Veterans Committee was born, and the Labor Youth League, the Lawyers Guild and CORE, the National Students Association, the *Bulletin of the Atomic Scientists,* the United World Federalists, the Henry Wallace student movement, and more. Competing literary journals, ribald and obscene, reactionary and leftish, rose and fell with regularity. The *Maroon,* rejuvenated and rambunctious, got its editors suspended and reinstalled, and did its very best to keep the deans, the faculty and our enemies in the world at large, upset. Elaine May, Mike Nichols, and others, were putting together the stage for their kind of new theater. Philip Roth was in and out, preparing his complaints.

All of these happenings announced more than new births. They were really rebirths. Each embodied not only hopes for something new in the future but also intense critiques of something old from the past. It was not just that the American Legion and the Veterans of Foreign Wars were old; they stood for things that the American Veterans Committee was aggressively, specifically against. We knew even before the San Francisco Conference was over that the United Nations was a cause stillborn, so that it could not even be lost. When Adlai Stevenson sat in one of the dormitory lounges and patiently explained to us that "The United Nations will never make the peace, but only keep the peace that the national governments decide to make," he only confirmed our deep conviction that we had to federalize the world in the morning.

Twenty of us cooked up the National Students Association. Student government then, like now, was strictly Mickey Mouse. We were grown-up men with global matters to set in order. No time to quibble about jukeboxes in the cafeteria or whether the fraternities should be allowed to serve beer. Counterparts abroad, sometimes friends we had met in foreign armies, had gone home to leadership in national student unions, European, Asian and African, whose proclamations commanded the ears of cabinet ministers and whose manifestoes shook entire governments. But here in the States, with so many things to say, we had yet to find a voice. And then there was the peace to make, the peace *we* would make, our peace, whole cities to rebuild, entire nations to restore, and newly freed people who reached out their hands, we thought, to us—or to the Russians. There were the Russians, our gallant allies, already becoming former, whose wartime braveries and massive postwar armies and diplomatic coups inspired and captured the imaginations of some of my best friends. There was the deepening understanding of Hiroshima's meaning even as we occasionally kicked the soccer ball around the field where its explosion first echoed.

The campus was instantaneously politicized, and master political parties, cutting across several organizations, formed. Even the Greeks broke into right, left and center. And when hundreds of the American Veterans Committee's members assembled every two weeks for their meetings in the lecture hall of the chemistry building, the left caucus automatically pre-empted the left side of the hall, the right, the right, and the centerists, the middle.

The corner tavern on Fifty-fifth Street became the headquarters for staging the new world order. When the
libraries closed at eleven, a significant part of the campus
came to life and things began to get done—or so we
thought.

Red Power/White Power and Black

The Maoists of that time were more numerous than now,
though like young socialists at any time or place, they
broke into as many factions among themselves as the Slavs
in the Balkans or practicing psychologists in New York.
But for many, Stalin's wartime leadership was the inspira-
tion, and the heroic performance of the Russian people
at Stalingrad was freely confused with the merit of postwar Stalinist prescriptions for the liberated people everywhere.

The Labor Youth League flourished, and its influence,
or versions of it, was felt everywhere—in AVC, NSA, student government, and of course, in the support of Henry
Wallace as an alternative to Messrs. Truman or Dewey in
1948. Young Communists presented a formidable and
unique challenge to the rest of us. Though always a minority wherever we confronted them, they had a powerful
capacity to paralyze our own machinery. And yet, to ex-
clude them presented a painful American issue. Senator
McCarthy confused the issue, for he had a loud and clear
solution to the problem—a solution none of us could
accept then, because it was based on the separation of one
kind of American from another. It was a time when there
were heated debates about whether a member of the Communist party should be allowed to teach at the university.
And when the investigating committees entered the picture, the Fifth Amendment was the respectable assertion

for almost everyone—Communists and anti-Communists, students and teachers alike.

Our Communist foes compelled most of us for the first time seriously to study their ideologies. It was the only way to contend with them in free and open debate. The best way to beat an enemy is to know his strategies and tactics at least as well as he. This is as true for the pages of Roberts' *Rules of Order* as it is for the wrestling mat. We organized informal seminars, and for the first time many of us read Marx; we even began to study (not for credit) the structure of Soviet government and law. And, strangely, the deeper we got into all that, the deeper went our probes into the meaning of our own beliefs and values, the structure of our own system and traditions. These were not abstract drills. Sometimes they were like cram courses, studies urgently pursued to get us ready for the test of the next night's meeting, debate and resolution.

One of the most promising invitations I've received lately came from a group of blacks in Brooklyn who wanted me to teach a course on White Power in a street "college" they were organizing. This was to be a part of a three-course sequence they planned—Black Power, White Power and Power.

People like me, who are in charge of things that activist white and militant black students sometimes find themselves opposing, know only too well that *they* are usually their own worst enemies. Too often they let their bitterness get in the way and confuse the intensity of their feelings of opposition with the cool logic of knowing well what they oppose. So long as their ignorance can be exploited, they've had it. But for people in my position, for those in charge of every part of American society, this reality frames very tough educational and political problems. Too often those who stupidly oppose what we represent are right. First, we must inspire them with the desire to learn—to know, not just to feel, that we are wrong; and then we must teach them how to cope with what they know —how to beat us at our own game. This is to ask a great deal from those who are in charge. There are very few historical examples in which those in command voluntarily relinquish their power, in which the enemy takes the initiative to reveal his own weaknesses. The prerequisite for Thinking Black is probably an introductory course on How to Think White. And until we get over this color thing, we probably ought to organize our undergraduate curriculum to include this sequence. This would be a modest first step in a voluntary transfer, in the revelation of what must be revealed.

We did everything in our power at the University of Chicago to resist our opponents' invitations to force them underground. Our forms of participatory democracy allowed for *their* participation, and we fought it out on those terms. The price of this strategy was often dear, but probably not as expensive as the alternatives they sometimes dangled before us so temptingly. Not only that, playing it this way compelled us to work out our own internal differences before we entered the larger arenas. It was often the only hope for winning.

I am sure that once our current crop of black students resolve some of their deep internal, factional and ideological differences, they will not only participate more effectively in the larger arenas, but they will also be far less insistent upon their separate privacy. In struggles of this kind, the most precious strength, next to knowledge, is common purpose and a sense of unity. Where the opponent attaches very great significance to very small differences of opinion within his own ranks, there are his Achilles' heels, the points to attack to destroy his unity of purpose. Those who maintain ghettos in order to exploit them know this very well.

The Constitution

In 1947 at the University of Wisconsin's campus in Madison, American students for the first time drew up a constitution for themselves. It was a remarkable achievement, at least as remarkable as Woodstock, which the students did not make for themselves, or the Moratorium March on Washington, which has yet to reveal an enduring political meaning beyond the fact that it happened.

The Constitutional Convention of the United States National Students Association (USNSA) brought together the representatives of more than 350 colleges and universities, 1,500 or 1,600 students. They came from everywhere—from the Southern state universities and from parochial colleges, from the great private urban universities and the large Middle-western public ones, from the West coast and the East; Catholics and Communists, right wings and left, racists and civil righters, isolationists recoiling from the war, and One Worlders pursuing in their own way its consequences. They had about ten days together, and in spite of their very substantial differences, they made a constitution, wrote it down and for many years thereafter more or less lived by it. And even now the students left in NSA have that constitution, nearly a quarter of a century old.

NSA's constitution regulated its affairs through its lean years (none have been fat), through the assaults from the left in the late forties and from the right during McCarthy, through the Silence of the Eisenhower years, and the tumult of the Year of Dallas and all that has followed, including the monstrous CIA connection. But whether it will survive what it is in now remains to be seen, for in the backwash of the Disruption Era, America's students, speaking with many voices, seem to have no need for a voice, much less for a constitution. In the pursuit of their various and sundry purposes they no longer seem willing, or perhaps they are unable, to organize and persist in behalf of common purposes. It may be that they have disrupted themselves more than anything else, which, if true, would not be all bad, but even self-disruption deserves to be organized in order to make its meaning clearer.

At Madison I presided over the constitution-making committee. After that, no faculty meeting has really upset my balance. My chairmanship catapulted me into a race for the first presidency of USNSA. But when the ballots were finally counted, a bright young history major from Berea College in Kentucky—Bill Welsh—was elected. He has gone on to an interesting political career, which has taken him in and out of Washington at the most exciting times. In fact, when I first visited Washington after John Kennedy took over, I was impressed by the number of young men and women there who had been delegates at the Madison Convention, who had joined JFK's team in the crucial second-, third- and fourth-level positions, where the programs really get shaped up, the speeches actually written, the research done, and the patronage transacted. Those who were a part of NSA's creation and its struggles during those first years never seemed to quite get over it.

NSA began its life with a student constituency on the campuses of more than a million. Two overriding purposes compelled the leaders of this constituency to make themselves a constitution and find themselves a voice at Madison, and then, to speak.

The first was to confirm the legitimacy of the constituency itself, to remark upon its existence—something almost everyone else had done except the students themselves—and to assert, because of its existence, its possession of a right to pursue its own interests, the interests of students in the United States. Campus-level self-government was a primary goal. And the first American Bill of Student

Rights was issued. That bill spoke of the student as a citizen, not only with rights, but with responsibilities to pursue his causes on campus and off, into the national and then the international arenas, wherever his versions of his future might take him.

The second purpose was to demonstrate to student friends and foes abroad that America's students had grown up during the war, at least an inch. When they spoke to us now, no deans of students, learned societies or Washington bureaucrats need now respond for us. We would reply for ourselves, and in due course, hopefully, we would enter upon our obligations on the larger scene where young men and women, our age or only a few years beyond, were already Presidents and prime ministers, leading new nations and building new worlds.

Vassar

One twilight I came across an old and wrinkled Eskimo sitting in front of his hut in Sondrestromfjord carving a walrus tusk. "What are you making?" I asked him. "It is already made," he said, "it is there, inside the tusk, waiting for me to find it. You wait, and I will find it, and then you will see what it is." And two or three days later, what was already there he had found—an exquisitely wise little witch doctor who looked in many ways like the wrinkled old man who had found him.

At Madison the students carved into the nature of their situation. It was to discover what was already there, a part of the eternal human search for the nature of themselves.

A few years later, as if to reassure the American people after *Time* magazine's discovery of the silent young, *Newsweek* (November 2, 1953) ran its rebuttal through the cover story, entitled U.S. CAMPUS KIDS—UNKIDDABLE AND UNBEATABLE. *Newsweek* said:

Shrewder, more mature than their grandparents, more cautious than their fathers, they worked harder and were more likely to think things through. Socially, economically, politically, emotionally and philosophically, they wanted to conform, they were thoroughly and solidly American. . . . Most of all, they were young and wanted to make a million dollars. And some of them would. . . .

A Princeton senior, pictured sipping his beer in a small bar, was quoted as saying: "The world doesn't owe me a living, but it does owe me a job."

A Northwestern coed, speaking from the back seat of a cream-colored convertible, said: "You want to be popular, so naturally you don't express any screwy ideas. To be popular you have to conform."

A Vassar girl, sitting cross-legged on the floor of her dormitory lounge in Bermuda shorts, put it this way: "We're a cautious generation. We aren't buying any ideas we're not sure of."

Recently the students at Vassar asked me to give a lecture. We met first in some great Gothic hall, where we politely exchanged pleasantries, had a cocktail, and then dinner. I talked in the chapel where the chairman of the board of trustees introduced me. Young President Alan Simpson—a former colleague at the University of Chicago College—was still in bed recuperating from his heart attack, but the president's wife was a gracious hostess and even sat through my talk.

Afterward a delightful young student, dressed in blue jeans and a sweater, invited me back with some others to her dorm "to rap." It was a cold autumn night. The comfortable lounge was warm. She turned the lamps up. From her pocket she offered me a joint, and from beneath the leather cushion on a couch she produced a pint of good Scotch, half gone, from which she poured me a stiff one in a used paper cup. From her notebook, with obvious pride, she handed me a diamond-shaped chart she had drawn, diagraming a new theory of history, from Plato to Einstein, which she herself had created in a brilliant flash of senior insight. She told me what it meant, what it proved, and it meant and proved many things. It proved, among other things, naturally, that technology—apparently the central heating in the dorm and the electrical system which provided the lamps she had turned on—was destroying man's capacity to love, to know his nature, to be himself. And then she said, "Our purposes here at Vassar are now clear. We must reduce this college to the purest form of its absurdity, and when it is there, flat on its back, exposed, we must move on to the other American institutions, whose absurdities must be laid bare on the floor."

I find all this very reassuring, having tenure, as I do now. The disruptions will pass. They are meaningless fevers, and the panty raids will return, even as they did in the spring of 1969 at Columbia next to Harlem. Legal reasoning is still the most supreme—even at Vassar. Or so it seems.

Laughter and Flags

We had barely checked into the hotel reserved for foreign visitors in the middle of Prague when the underground made its contact. The lobby was loaded with official "tourist guides" and plainclothesmen who, we thought, were keeping their eyes on us. But after we checked in and unpacked, I went down to the bar for a warm beer, and while sitting there, a young Yugoslav sailor, offering me one of his cigarettes and asking me for an American one in return, slipped me a piece of paper containing the number of a room at the Polytechnic Institute, and the hour—10 o'clock that night. We had been alerted before arriving in Prague during that summer of 1948. Nonetheless, the classic, bizarre efficiency of the contact was rather impressive. A Yugoslav sailor, yet!

One of the great public landmarks at the University of Chicago down the Midway toward the lake near the International House, is the stony grandeur of the senior Masaryk the great patriot-founder of the democracy of the Czechs and the Slovaks. The base of his statue is one of the places to sit on the Midway, to rest and to think.

I have always been proud of my university's employment of Eduard Benes, the Czech President-patriot, during his exile after the German annexation of the Sudetenland. Benes was gone when I arrived on the Midway, but his scholarship remained—the papers and books in which he never allowed the brilliance of his mind to dampen his passion for man's freedom, a passion which seeped through every page.

In April of 1948, but a few months before we came to Prague, the younger Masaryk had met his tragic death, crushed on the cobblestones beneath his window in the Presidential Palace. The official description of that fall: a suicide leap. But the Czechoslovakians knew then, as they know now, that Masaryk was pushed, and that with his fall their chance for independence fell too. It was a short scene in the drama of the Communist takeover under Gottwald. On the night that Masaryk died and for some days thereafter, the university students of Prague, from the venerable Charles and from the Polytechnic Institute, took to the streets of the city in behalf of freedom's law and order and their dying democracy's due processes. Some joined their leader there, in death. In Prague that year, the fall and winter came in the spring, and the season of rebirth was one of death.

But now, in 1948, it was early July; and summer, outwardly, was transforming the ancient city, its hills and arcades, its grand tree-shaded central avenue. The beauty of the city itself denied the intrigue and the anguish, the life risks seething behind the know-nothing looks on the shopkeepers' faces—the chapel-like hush in the crowded main streets.

The nation, exhausted by the war and sickened by its most recent catastrophe, was preparing to restore one moment of its past happiness. Sokol Slet is one of the great occasions for the Czech people—the time when they, with some of the best athletes in the country and from all over the world, periodically celebrate an ancient Greek inheritance in a uniquely Central and East European style. In a massive demonstration, thousands of gymnasts assemble in a giant stadium, and with extraordinary precision mobilize individual powers into a collective dramatization of the beauty of human physical possibilities. In each city and town, each hamlet and district, clubs of athletes prepare assiduously for the Sokol, to compete in the capital for the pennants and banners, the prizes awarded, not to individuals, but to communities, to cities which honor their youth for the good of the country. Sokol had been a casualty of the war, but Gottwald, disclosing the shrewdness he was to demonstrate for years to come, had decided early in his regime to restore Sokol to the people, and to unite the deep sources of peoplehood-pride with the nation's first Red Army Day. It was a bold maneuver—Masaryk had hardly been lowered into his grave. The people would get their circus—painted red.

The rendezvous at Polytech was the night before the Sokol parade. The city bubbled with the anticipation of the next day. Sokol traditionally began with a monster parade, a dawn-to-dusk march of the athletes carrying the ancient torches of the Olympians to the stadium, where on the following day the competitions would begin. Each city and town, each foreign delegation, marched as a group, led in each case by the banners unique to the place and the pennants won in past victories. People from all over the country converged on Prague for the spectacle.

In one of those gestures of wartime trust or political accommodation, the United States had agreed that the Soviet Union should liberate Prague. The American armies stopped at the nation's second city to the west—Pilsen. To honor its liberation, American battalion and regimental flags had been awarded to ancient Pilsen and were housed in a hall of honor in the center of that city.

The Czech students meant the return of Sokol to mark a popular outpouring of opposition to Gottwald. By plan, the youth of Pilsen, whose Sokol teams were second in number only to those of Prague, and whose city traditionally marched second in the day-long parade, were to provide the signal to the people of Czechoslovakia for the denunciation of their new tyrant. Our flag, the flag of the United States, was to be the symbol of defiance. The American flag in 1948 was to represent for these people and for their Red masters the freedom that had been lost and for which they were prepared to risk everything to restore. Pilsen was to carry the banners awarded by our armies in the parade, and these flags were to rally the hearts and the voices of the millions of Czechs who would see them on the streets of Prague.

Rumors of the plot had swept the city, and that night, as we made our way secretly to the Polytech, we saw the notices the government had hastily pasted on the lampposts prohibiting, as an act of treason, the display of foreign banners by any Czechoslovak delegation in the Sokol.

We were the official guests in Czechoslovakia of the International Union of Students (IUS), whose headquarters was there. The IUS—the federation of the Communist East European national student unions, had arranged for the official American NSA delegation, the three of us, to sit in President Gottwald's reviewing stand to observe the parade. A few rows beneath him, we assembled early the next morning, and the parade began. At the head of the march came the proud athletes of Prague, and behind them the large visiting team from the Soviet Union. The Russian delegation stretched for almost three city blocks, and at their head, for almost a third of their length, a sea of the red flags of their country. The people watched in an electric silence as the handsome Russians, some contingent of their military, marched by. The people, by doing nothing, visibly upset the President.

Then came Pilsen, more than a thousand strong, American war banners at their head, each athlete carrying or wearing some version of the Stars and Stripes, paper U.S. flags pinned to their tunics, front and back. The crowds went beserk! The police cordons broke! Red, white and blue streamers suddenly filled the air. Among the masses along the streets for as far as the eye could see, small American flags appeared from nowhere. And the air filled with the shouts of the people: "Freedom!" "Masaryk!" "Russians Go Home!" President Gottwald, at least for that time, left his place of honor, and disappeared.

Everywhere I turned, the people were crying on that occasion. And, I remember well, I cried too. It is remarkable how few times I can remember crying in behalf of public events in my country. There was the time when Franklin Roosevelt's cortege marched down Pennsylvania Avenue—the hours after that when I walked around and around the Washington Zoo—when all seemed lost. And that unforgettable afternoon, November 22, 1963, when I saw the young cry on Eleventh Street in front of the New School in Greenwich Village for their dead President. But they did not cry with pride, because of what we were, but because of what we weren't. And then there were the moments in front of the television screen when Jacqueline Kennedy and my country needed tears.

It gives me pause. Naturally I worry most about those I teach—what will make them think? But sometimes I wonder if there is any salt left in the tears of the young I encourage to think, or if they can cry at all. Is there anything about their country or their world that makes them cry—the dead lakes—the dying cities—Biafran slaughter —a million Vietnamese dead? Malcolm or Martin King, twitching in their own blood? The flag, our flag, anytime, any place? Forget it. How square can you get? It is not for flags now, or to cry. Not for country, not in public; and maybe, among them, not even for private little things, privately.

It is a time to laugh, not for what is, but for what is not. Laugh. Acid. Laugh, and screw it all. Push it, and laugh. Laugh, not for what it is, but for what it is not. Ask not what your country can do for you. Join the team.

Of course, it is possible I am too old to understand. The country is too old to know. President Nixon—too old, too old. We are all too old. So laugh, and screw it all. And may the Silent Majority, tearless and joyful, rule forever. Maybe our young are too old.

Blood for Ink

In the basement room at the Polytech in Prague, the smell of mimeograph ink was everywhere. The students were grinding out their pamphlets to be distributed, against the law, on the streets the next day. They were to brief us before our formal negotiations with the International Union of Students, and to present to us *their* position, the reasons why we should do no business whatsoever with the Communist student unions in the East. It was a bitter-sweet situation: bitter with the gravity of their plight—sweet in the spirit of their conviction, the intensity of their beliefs, the risks they were prepared to take and were taking. *They were brave and honorable lawbreakers.*

The issue finally was an old one: *What do you do with your enemies, especially when you know who they are?*

It is an issue I have discussed at great length with so many of my black friends lately, and with my student friends who swear by Mao's little Red Book too.

When I studied with Dick McKeon, the chairman of the philosophy department at Chicago, he was the leader of the American UNESCO Commission—wheeling and dealing on practical matters then of great importance. Could intellectual and cultural channels really be reopened among the survivors of the war, among old enemies and new ones, among Germans, Poles, Russians, Japanese and Americans? He preached, in his way, that Plato and Camus, Stalin and Adlai Stevenson could really do business together. He really believed that then. The alternatives indeed seemed very bleak. But then, to the students of Prague, McKeon's philosophy seemed to lead into even bleaker places.

The National Students Association had commissioned three of us to represent its interests in Europe that summer —Rob West, a student at Yale in international studies, Larry Jaffa, a divinity student at Harvard, and me.

NSA's interests were complicated. There were the student communities in the countries we had conquered. Our occupation armies and provisional governments still ruled in Germany and Austria, and the educational systems of those nations, devastated by the war, were our responsibility. Many of their universities had been closed. The simplest tools for learning were in short supply or utterly lacking.

Students in the newer countries of the world, in Africa, Asia and South America especially, were left impoverished after the war, without money or jobs to sustain themselves as students, without books, often without food. The international student relief agencies, centered in the European nations, had lost touch with the traditional sources of their support. The American student body, disorganized, well-intentioned and unaccustomed to leadership, suddenly found itself strategically the richest student community left, but without means or direction in the mobilization and implementation of its wealth, the capacity to focus its strength upon extremely urgent targets.

All of the normal lines of communication in the international student community had been severed during the war. All of the exchanges of materials and people had stopped. All of the summer work and study programs had come to an end. The restoration of the "community" itself was the challenge, and this challenge turned upon the solution of some very hard, nitty-gritty problems. Who would organize and re-establish the programs at home and abroad? Who would provide the ships to transport the students during the summers? About this problem, our own country, which had produced the largest supply fleet in the world during the war, had quickly either decommissioned or given away almost all of our ships. We finally negotiated contracts with the Dutch National Union of Students, which had persuaded its government to allocate three or four ships in order to restore international student exchange beginning in 1949 and 1950. The Dutch students turned out to be, in my estimate, among the earth's shrewdest businessmen, whose negotiations were always conducted in an atmosphere of great levity and good humor, until you sobered up enough to find out what they had persuaded you to sign. I still think, ounce for ounce, that Dutch youth can outdrink the famed Scandinavians two to one, without showing the least sign of wear or tear.

Finally, there was the pervasive problem of how to cope with the East European, Communist-controlled national student unions. Many students in the United States and the West European countries felt it was imperative, as a step to counter the rapidly cooling relationships between the West and the Soviet Union, to enter upon a series of specific treaties with the International Union of Students. The trouble was that the IUS was a severe taskmaster, insisting upon strict control of the programs to be mounted in their countries for Western students, and even a dominant voice in the structure of programs we would plan in the United States for their countrymen. And, of course, they were most interested in the propaganda value of everything they did and said, especially with regard to the youth of the new countries in Asia, Africa and throughout Latin America.

But many students in the West felt that no relationship with the Communists should be established until the European and American students had constructed an international federation of their own to counter the great influence of the IUS. And steps to create just such an agency (the International Student Organization, ISO) had already gone pretty far. The situation was polarizing, and the position of the two main camps was becoming clear. Integrate or separate. Everyone was being asked to choose sides.

We brought our recommendations on these and other matters to the Second Congress of the National Student Association in the late summer of 1948. There were no CIA subsidies for NSA then. Such a relationship would have been unthinkable for NSA and for the CIA. Our proposals were the framework of the principal debates during that meeting, and out of that congress, among other things, came the creation of NSA's international study and travel agency, which for more than twenty years was one of the main instruments for the promotion of student study and travel abroad.

But how we solved our problems then is not the point now. It is the quality and the complexity of the issues which should be noted, and the seriousness of purpose American student leaders brought to these difficulties. Whatever official and empowered student leadership there was on the principal campuses of the nation, NSA brought together. And when they convened their debates were intense, their aspirations far-reaching, and the connections between the global issues and the campuses were, for a while, more than tenuous. The IUS problem had its counterpart in the growing domestic Communist youth movement. Poverty in India reached directly into the pockets of students at Iowa State. The re-establishment of international study programs touched upon a student's credit-hour planning at Georgia Tech. Campus debates instructed delegates to national NSA meetings and were meant to guide their conduct in the decisive votes. The student leaders thought then that what they did might really make a difference. Thinking that they could make a difference, however misguided they may have been, made a difference for them.

After more than a decade of disconnection, I plugged into NSA once again at its National Congress at El Paso in 1969. I guess it was an honor to be invited—one of the three men over thirty (along with Carl Rogers and Edgar Freidenberg)—to speak with the students there. It was a strange experience—how little things had changed, and yet, in one way at least, how much. The issues the young in our country think are important remain much too complex for the old. At El Paso the blacks asked for their reparations. NSA, as always, hovered on the edge of bankruptcy. The Mexican-American youth from California and along the Texas border claimed their citizenship. Pot and acid were talked about everywhere. And sex. Vietnam, and the draft.

But at El Paso, as on so many of our campuses today, I thought I saw something new, both in focus and in form. The real action at El Paso was in the small rooms in the four or five hotels where the delegates were housed. In the small groups there, over pot and beer, people undressed the most intimate parts of their brains, almost compulsively probing the most private inner recesses of their experience, or of the experience they hadn't had. Sex was *talked* about intimately. Experiences with dope were related in the style of the old-fashioned tabernacle confessional.

From things I heard I sometimes thought that the war in Vietnam and enrollment in college had nothing whatsoever to do with killing people or learning something but were simply policy or institutional constructs designed solely to harass people's private lives, to force them into military service or to keep them out. The group dynamics and T-Group approach to life, given the larger issues formally arising at the convention, seemed to lead nowhere and to resolve nothing—except, I hope, they made people feel better and, perhaps, led them to know something through this talk that they did not know before through actual experience. At times it was touching, to hear a pretty coed proclaim with tears in her eyes that she had had a richer sexual experience in the discussion than she had ever had in bed. But how would she translate this into a decision committing herself to something when the blacks tore out the microphones in the general assembly session?

The larger meetings in the gym at the university at El Paso were utter chaos. Shouting and screaming, incompetence in the chair, the crudest kind of legislative proposals and even cruder, primitive legislative conduct. The feelings of camaraderie and love one felt sometimes in the smaller meeting places seemed converted, by the same people, into the most irrational emotion and even hate when they congregated in the larger assembly with the purpose of actually doing business.

The intense use of the devices for self-discovery, it seems to me, have value only when they really lead those who discover something important or new about themselves, to rise out of self. To focus the light-waves of an entire humanity, of a whole planet through the intensifying prism of the most private, inner, subjective meanings of oneself, should at some time, I think, create an intense beam going out of one's innermost recesses back into the entirety of humanity and a whole planet. Otherwise the world comes finally to exist exclusively for oneself, and nothing more. And if this is one's view of the universe, then the meanings of war and of peace, of love, of being black and beautiful, or young, those meanings can never become an integral part of the individual. For, however devoted we may become to the cultivation of our individual meanings, finally, to survive, we must act. And no action by self in this world can long remain free from its impact upon others, whatever our intentions.

In the basement room at the Polytech, the mimeograph ink flowed. But on the streets of Prague, it was blood. And so it was at El Paso. In the hotels the ink flowed, but in the gym, it was blood.

The Ph.D. Language Requirement in Court

When we returned from Prague we brought with us a message to the American students from Josef Grohman, the president of the International Union of Students. Grohman was a professional student, blond and intense, in his late twenties or early thirties, Moscow-trained, a personal history obscure to us. He was one of the ablest and most devoted negotiators with whom I've ever dealt—the sort of man you wished were on your side. Unfortunately, he was not devoted to ours. He wrote:

> The students who love peace and work for the maintenance of peace, for the increase of democracy in all parts of the world, are working for the IUS. The students who must fight for national independence and against oppression by external or internal forces are also working for the IUS. For them national independence is basic not only to the attainment of the right to education but of the right to live in dignity as free men in a free society. Their struggles are in the interests of students in all parts of the world, for peace can only be maintained between free and

democratic communities. All students who fight for democracy in their own scholastic institutions and for the extension of educational opportunities to every strata of society are carrying out the aims and ideals of the IUS.

Grohman knew what he was talking about. He had read the source texts of his ideology and the memoranda he must have received regularly from headquarters several hundred miles to the east of Prague. (He told me he had even studied our Federalist Papers!) In these respects he had an advantage over many of our Maoist students today who have never read Mao or Marx (let alone the Federal Constitution), and over many of our right-wing student activists who seem, sometimes, never to have read anything.

Grohman invited me to attend with him a session of the People's Court in Prague, where university students who had been a part of the resistance—who had disrupted the coup—were brought before a bar of justice to explain why they had broken the law, created disorder and violated the due processes of the People's Democracy of Czechoslovakia.

At the session I attended there were three judges on the bench—a factory worker, a student member of the party attending Charles University, and a third person who was identified vaguely as a functionary in the new government. I heard one case, a Ph.D. candidate at Charles who was accused of participating in an illicit street demonstration and distributing prohibited literature. The student appeared without counsel. He confessed that he had indeed been a part of the action on the street, but he denied having passed out the leaflets.

He was asked if he was sorry for what he had done. He was. He was asked if he would sign, then and there, an oath of loyalty, pledging to uphold the constitution of the People's Democracy of Czechoslovakia. He said he would. He was asked if he would sign, under oath, a pledge that he did not then belong to nor would he ever join any organization subversive to the People's Democracy. He said he would. He was asked if he would identify, under oath, other students who had participated in the demonstration to which he had confessed? He said he couldn't. He was asked if he had passed his language qualifying examinations for his Ph.D. degree? He said he had. He was asked in what language, and he said English. Then he was asked if he was prepared to substitute Russian for English as his Ph.D. qualifying language? He said he knew no Russian, and the court rejoined that this was his problem. He would simply have to begin now the study of Russian. The student argued that he did not wish to do this, since his field did not require Russian, and that it would be a waste of time.

The defendant left the room and the court deliberated briefly. Its decision was in parts: the student was prohibited indefinitely from further work at the university, and the award of his degree was indefinitely suspended; he was ordered to work in a factory in Prague for a period of not less than ninety days where he was also to attend some seminars under the political supervision of the factory's Workers Committee; he was to think very hard about whether he was prepared to substitute Russian for English, and about his capacity to identify cohorts in the demonstration; and after ninety days the court would review his situation and then determine further the disposition of his case.

I returned to the University of Chicago late that summer, exhausted and depressed. I had seen in the German cities through which I passed, in parts of France and in London, the chaotic devastation of the war, streets in the central cities still clogged by the bombs' debris, long lines of people waiting for their weekly allowances of meat and bread, transportation systems still being pulled back together. Only in Rotterdam had the people piled the rubble into neat pyramids and planted flowers on them.

But I was eager to see my student friends on the Midway, to tell them about what I had seen, about my day in court and with President Gottwald, and how I felt. But by the time school reconvened that September, I had grown less certain about what there was to tell. Lawyers in my state were being asked to take their loyalty oaths as a condition for admission to practice. Teachers were signing their oaths to uphold the constitutions of the nation and of the state, and certifying that they didn't belong to any subversive organization. At some places teachers were being asked to renounce their rights under the Fifth Amendment as a condition of employment. And soon students, to get their federal fellowship grants, would also be asked to pledge allegiance once again. It all seemed quite mad and very sad. It had been a horrible war in which millions had died demonstrating loyalty to something, to noble causes, to personal notions of integrity, to cowardice. But apparently the war, which had tried the soul of our civilization so deeply, had left men compulsively needing to know afresh what they could be loyal to.

In Prague, more than once, I was the most loyal American on earth. But back in Chicago, new questions arose, and some of them, even now, remain unanswered in my mind.

The Genius

Among all the loyalty oaths I've been asked to take, some have been taken more voluntarily than others. It is a simple thing to take an oath and not mean it. Depending on the situation, this is often the easiest way to regulate your affairs with society. But of all the oaths I have taken, there is one which has certainly, thus far, turned out to be worthwhile.

While at the university I married a genius—which is something else again to live with, especially for a long time. One of Helen's problems has been her refusal to believe that she really is a genius. About this, and in other matters, she is contrary in the way that all women I know are, at least the interesting ones. When I reassure her that in fact she is a genius, she prefers to be told that she is beautiful. And when I tell her that she is beautiful, she wants to be told that she is a genius. I've tried telling her that she's a beautiful genius—a line she rejects out of hand, accusing me of kidding around too much.

We married during a springtime intercession in an antique orthodox *shul* in nearby Kenwood—a godly house with a balcony into which the females were segregated—a ceremony magically lit by candles and the late afternoon sun shining through stained glass windows in which Moses, stern and heroic, dominated each of the ten frames with a different commandment. Bob Strozier, the university's Episcopalian dean of students, was my best man. The *shul* has since been sold to the Black Muslims, and it serves now as Chicago Mosque Number II, XXXI, XIV, or something.

Our first daughter, Susan, was born early in the eleventh month of our marriage, which meant, given the printing schedules of the *Alumni Magazine,* that our engagement, our marriage and the birth of our first child were announced simultaneously in one juicy item, with all the dates, of course, confused. Helen, even then, had a rare talent for operating just this side of the respectability line, which is one of her enduring middle-class charms.

Immediately after our marriage and a brief honeymoon in Batista's Havana, she returned to her graduate program which included a course with Bruno Bettelheim. It was called "The Orthogenic Husband" or something like that. Anyway, we began the adventure in typical University of Chicago style—out of a book (in this case Bettelheim's)—

with me as kind of overgrown guinea pig with which Helen could (contrary to University of Chicago style) practically do her experimentation at home. Never have Bettelheim's theories been put to a more severe test. Need I add that my wife really earned her A that time.

We established residence in the head counselor's suite in the Burton Judson Dormitory, a place whose intimacy (there were three or four hundred young males living around there too) led me to rig up an elaborate buzzer-alarm system on all the doors and windows, including the one in our private bathroom with the stand-up urinal, which was the biggest room in our suite. We began almost at once to have our babies in the university's Billings Hospital, and brought the first girl home to the men's dorm, a practical living experience which should do Susan no harm when she re-enters college this fall, given the way things are going. Conceiving babies in men's dormitories is no longer a pioneering activity.

Living with Helen has been my most significant co-educational experience. The genius, over the nineteen years we've lived together, has gradually established the principle of equality of the sexes in our family. At last we seem close to the point where she more or less allows me to be the way I am.

Our life together has been a nomadic one, parts of which, until recently, must have been difficult for Helen to understand. She had the strange idea that when you got married, you settled down. But in the course of my academic career, settling down has meant that we have yet to live in one house for more than three and a half years, and our nine years in New York is the longest time we've spent in one jurisdiction. My career crises have added spice, but naturally a female palate tires at times of an unrelieved Indonesian curry diet.

My advice to a young man who aspires to a college presidency, a deanship or even a professorship as a way of life, is to plan for your wife to have some career crises all her very own. One picture is really worth a thousand words, and it has only been since my wife, the assistant professor, went to work a few years ago that after all those deadly teas with gloves and hats, those inane and dull cocktail parties, those hectic, impromptu press conferences, poison-pen letters and noisy picket lines, she has begun to see things the way they really are. This has not necessarily made her happier, but it has made me feel a little better, and more equal.

Still, my wife, being a genius, continues to amaze me with her instantaneous, bitingly insightful qualifications of my own expertise. Working as she does with urban students, she perceives things intuitively I never dreamt about. And then, thinking about her intuitive results, she has come to care about what she perceives as much or more than I. Someday we may write a book together, in which I will state, once again, my formulae for profoundly changing the world forever; and she, in the unassuming way that she puts together an *haute cuisine* dinner, will at the end of each chapter quietly but soundly suggest what we ought to do the next morning. On the royalties of that book we will retire and perhaps, finally, settle down.

The Three-Million-Dollar Caper

During my last years at the University of Chicago, I moved more and more out of the sense and order of the university into the nonsense and disorder of the city. Or, to put it another way, I moved from the reasoned and distorted world of the university into the unreasonable but truer versions of the way most people were existing.

The university, once again, was rapidly growing. But so were the black ghettos on three of its sides. (The lake was polluting on the fourth, but between the university and the lake, the beaches were turning black.) As the edges of these expanding situations pushed harder and harder against one another, almost everyone in his right mind knew that an explosion was coming—everyone, except, apparently, Robert Maynard Hutchins and the university power structure he led. Hutchins, at least intellectually, was unqualifiedly committed to some inner world which would change the outer world. But more and more the real action was in the outer world, which would come, so dramatically, to change the insides of all of us.

Sol Tax, in the anthropology department, was a small man—to look at him, the last you'd expect to lead anything. But he deeply impressed me, because he knew more about the Tama Indians back in my Iowa homeland than anybody else I had ever met. I discovered him first in a curious situation. He was organizing the community *in which he lived* to bring the community *in which he worked* back to its senses. He was against explosions, and he was under the impression that he didn't have much time. As an organizer, he left something to be desired, but somehow, he seemed to get things done. Anyway, I joined his team, and this led me along rushing waters, through channels where I had not been before.

The university, mainly occupying the streets along the northern border of the Midway at Sixtieth Street, was like a huge gray stone dropped into the middle of a polluting pond, the shock waves of its impact spreading out in ever-expanding concentric circles. But beyond, not too distant on the city's surface, especially to the north and south, other jagged rocks, black, were dropping into the pond, sending out their own shocking concentric circles. Ten blocks in any direction from the university's center, the contention of the opposing forces could be seen and heard, a collision of waves whose splashes fell back onto the campus and out into the neighborhoods.

Assuming that the university could be uprooted and

planted elsewhere, it was estimated that its replacement value was in excess of $150 million. In the immediately surrounding ring there were many fine middle-aged houses and multiple-family dwellings occupied mainly by faculty and staff, laced throughout with student boarding-houses, small apartment units and commercial blocks primarily serving the university community—restaurants, bookstores, laundries. But even in this inner circle, pockets of severe deterioration were evident, ugly slum cracks in what was otherwise a middle-, upper-middle-class urban neighborhood.

The circle beyond this contained rows of walk-up apartment buildings, and some exquisite old neighborhoods, elegant mansions built in a grander age, all hovering on the razor's edge of collapse or restoration. A few of the faculty and other professional types had already staked out rescue missions in the Kenwood mansions, hardy pioneers who could not at that time be sure whether their investment risks would pay off. "Integrated" neighborhoods in our great cities are usually transitory phenomena: less places than brief periods of time during which the blacks move in while residents already there are making their arrangements to get out. The apartment blocks were still essentially white, but the blacks were moving in rapidly, and thus for a few years this area had the semblance of integration. The public schools serving these neighborhoods were already predominantly black. Beyond these neighborhoods, the ghetto, unrelieved, stretched for miles, becoming more crowded and dilapidated each month.

Town-and-gown tensions are traditional, but Chicago was (and remains) a classic example of such hassles in the contemporary city. What was happening there was happening elsewhere, but an awareness in Chicago came early (though almost too late) because the events there were happening in the boldest colors. The university was a substantial landlord beyond its own campus, and its own real estate investments (and finally, its integrity) were at stake.

Muggings, armed robberies and break-ins were occurring on the campus with increasing frequency. Prospective faculty members and the parents of potential students were beginning to ask about housing conditions and street security. Finally, the university expected to grow, and was cultivating its postwar appetite for more land, anticipating major new investments in the territory.

Viewed from the streets beyond the campus itself, the university's interests and prowess took on a different coloration. Seen from black curbs, the university did not look gray but almost pure-white—which it was. Seen through the nonacademic eyes of those who needed help, the institution seemed aloof and elitist, disinterested and above-it-all—which it was inclined to be. Measured in terms of the ghetto economy, the university looked as rich as the United States must appear to the Costa Ricans —though, as I subsequently learned, this appearance of affluence was an illusion when measured against the reality of the institution's traditional academic commitments and aspirations. It was perfectly clear that the university and the communities around it were interested in many of the same things, that there were some genuine conflicts of interest here. What was so infuriating and frustrating was the apparent lack of organized leadership —in the government of the city, at the top of the university, or down on the streets in the neighborhoods— inclined to redress the situation. This, of course, changed as events became more compelling.

Professor Tax instructed me carefully, and eventually I succeeded him as the president of the Hyde Park–Kenwood Community Council. From that post, a few years later, shortly after Richard Daley was elected mayor of the city, I became president of the Federation of Community Councils for Metropolitan Chicago.

Two things about that time—the early and mid-1950's —stand out in my mind. First, all of today's urban issues were, of course, already born: centralization versus decentralization of city power, the failure of the public schools for the blacks (and others, too), the growing tide of youth violence, the confused search for the redefinition of what a neighborhood, a community, was, the struggle to put the university and the surrounding territories into some sensible partnership. But the other thing I must state quite honestly is this: in what we were trying to do then, Richard Daley, during his first term of office, was a reasonable and concerned man.

The mayor was the principal speaker on the occasion of my inauguration as president of the Metropolitan Federation. And as I worked with him and his political sponsor, Jake Arvey, over the next few years, I was impressed by the depth of their concern and by their capacity to do business. They were not exactly what those of us back on the Midway would have called "literate or lettered men." They seemed to have their own version of playing the Game. They didn't exactly fool me. I had some idea about how they operated, and of course, officially, I abhorred their way. But in all candor, I think they really cared. They really wanted to do some good—and in some ways they probably did.

But the most remarkable thing about their partnership, and the endurance of it—regardless of my appreciation of their concern and their capacity for doing business—is how wrong, misguided and inadequate the result seems. Together, what an extraordinary monument their careers are to a Missing Piece. Or maybe, maybe what they were up against was—is—really bigger than both of them. In any event, I don't think their failure necessarily proves that Bob Hutchins was right about his university in that city. The mayor *acted* upon the reality as he perceived it, while Mr. Hutchins, talking about the world as he thought it ought to be, ignored this part of the reality, frittering away his own chance to change it.

Then as now, the issues and options were very complex, and the choices to be made cut to the very heart of America's profoundest dilemmas. The decision-making borderline between those institutions devoted to learning and those political and economic institutions expressing the power of our muscles and the compulsions originating in our guts is an explosive frontier along which the main battles of higher education are now fought. How the leader at a particular time and place orders his priorities, decides whether or not to join the fray, determines the balance between right and wrong, is not simple. Indeed, how he does this is a puzzlement, first framed for me substantially in Chicago, and even now not satisfactorily resolved.

About this puzzlement, simplistic and brittle, abstract proclamations serve only to confuse. The danger that the universities might be politicized is not the issue; universities have always been politicized. Their operations have always been conditioned by the politics of their time and place, and have always had political consequences. The defense of the autonomy of the universities is not the issue. They have never been autonomous; they have always been intricately connected to the society which sponsored them. They have always been faced with the problem of making choices about their connections.

Relevance is not a new issue. In the defense of itself, a university, like talented artists, architects, and poets, has always had to persuade its patrons that their support was timely, perceptive and essential—that its relative freedom was worth the cost. Nor is professionalism a novel issue. The professionals have always asserted their monopolistic presumptions, and the objects of their power have always resisted their exclusive claims to fame. Thus, democracy in the university community is no more or no less a relevant issue than it is in any other human community. Obviously, Mr. Hutchins cared about the great issues of World War II, and his caring *was* reflected in his leadership of the university. True, with time he changed his mind—from isolationism and aloofness to Manhattan Project commitments. But he *cared,* and the completion of the first chain reaction on the Midway would have been impossible without his concern. Hutchins had his own personal link to Hiroshima—as did so many of the rest of us.

Mr. Hutchins cared about the Bill of Rights in the United States Constitution, and his caring *was* reflected in his leadership of the university. He was fearless in his resistance to all that Joseph McCarthy stood for, and his bravery had far-reaching political and economic (muscle-and-gut) consequences for the university. (The students adored him, and the donors dropped off.) Indeed, recalling how I, as a student, felt, his courage on this front permeated all of my *classroom* perceptions then. Though I took not one credit course with him, I count him among my greatest teachers.

But the neighborhood situation was unique. It did not require, or so it seemed then, a clear choice between fascists and democrats, between libertarians and tyrants, between resolving the great issues of mankind and what one would do tomorrow morning with the institution's investment and real estate portfolios.

This situation did involve black and white: race. It did involve the status and mobility of large numbers of people on and off the campus: class. It did involve what the university next bought or sold: institutional self-interest. It did involve the city and its future: the shape of American society. Finally, it did involve real people, nearby, and their lives. In other words, it did involve, as a giant laboratory, most of the vital elements addressed in the curriculum of the College and in the courses taught in the graduate and professional schools of the university.

My perception of this was limited then, and to join others to federalize the world or rally against Joe McCarthy were tempting alternatives, perhaps even essential courses of action. One could reorganize the world and save mankind (while getting his degree) without getting his hands dirty on Chicago's Southside, and Senator McCarthy's concerns, for the most part, were directed neither toward the blacks nor toward occupying positions of power south of Sixty-third Street.

I was torn between what Mr. Hutchins stood for and what I was coming to stand for. He embodied ideals I admired. The more I found out about it, the more I deplored what the Southside of Chicago was and my university's apparent indifference to all that. This ambivalence was to haunt me later in Detroit and New York. It shadows me still. It remains as a horrible gap between what I know people should and can be and what they are, between what I want and what is, between what I know should be done and what I can do, between what I think and write down and how I conduct my own affairs from day to day. What haunts me is my credibility —a central theme in my institutionalized, familialized, Americanized existence.

Any man succeeding a Robert M. Hutchins as chancellor of the university naturally would face problems not unlike those any President succeeding John F. Kennedy faced. It seemed to many of us that during the opening months of his regime the new leader, Lawrence A. Kimpton, devoted himself almost too vigorously to his own identity crisis. Mr. Hutchins' failures were catalogued clearly. At the top of this list was the failure to rationalize the university's relationship to its neighborhoods and its city. In due course the main policy planks of Mr. Kimpton's administration were revealed. These included the reversal of the principal educational directions taken in the Hutchins College, and in some of the graduate and professional school programs. The "quiz kid" image of the student body was to receive an infusion of some wholesome American red blood. Fraternal and student social life was to be more aggressively encouraged, countering the leftist or radical imprint of the student newspaper and political clubs. Educationally, it seemed, the university was about to return from its adventure in outer space to a more normal orbit around popular American expectations.

One of the most popular of the American expectations is that everything should progress (including universities), and that physical growth is the most reliable index to progress. Our university was about to grow, was on the threshold of one of its most heroic brick-and-mortar epochs, undergirded, necessarily, by one of its most ambitious fund-raising campaigns. Its aspirations extended, naturally, far beyond new classrooms and science labs. Necessity compelled the university to secure its streets, reassuring the parents of prospective students that their children would at least be safe on the Midway. Faculty demands for decent housing had to be faced. New properties had to be acquired, existing acquisitions redeployed. Something had to be done about the persistent black pressures on the university's perimeters, if for no other reason than the university's own aggressive posture on its boundaries.

At the same time urban decay, the travail of the black ghettos, and subhuman housing conditions in the central cities were rising to the top of agendas in Washington and in the mayor's office in the Loop. New federal legislation defined new powers for the municipalities, offered

some new federal dollars, seeking to encourage a partnership among the cities, Washington and private enterprise
in a first substantial assault upon these problems. One
portion of the new law anticipated the problems of urban
universities, specifically encouraged them to acquire
properties, and in concert with government, participate
in the restoration of themselves and their neighborhoods.
Unknown to me at the time, a New York real estate developer, William Zeckendorf, was first testing the possibilities of this legislation in downtown Brooklyn. As
chairman of the board of trustees of Long Island University, he was acquiring derelict warehouses, garages, bowling alleys and an old theater building in an effort to re-
locate that institution's campus in a rapidly changing
part of the city.

At the University of Chicago under Chancellor Kimpton's leadership, complex battle plans began to unfold.
The university became the driving force in the creation
of a "community" commission through which the resources of the university and the city were mobilized.
Eventually a master plan emerged. The demolition of
buildings, the displacement and relocation of families,
and the blueprints for blocks of new faculty housing,
conference centers, classrooms and dormitories followed.
A clear connection was drawn between slum eradication
and university expansion. Accordingly, it seemed, the
interests of the "community" were defined.

During the course of my own work I befriended a
young Chicago developer, Herb Greenwald. (He met his
end tragically in a New York airport crash several years
ago.) He was doing some work at the Illinois Institute of
Technology, twenty or thirty blocks to the north of the
university toward the Loop. At the time, IIT was facing
problems similar to those growing around the university,
but IIT had begun its assault first. Between the two
institutions was a vast black Sahara, arid and growing

hotter all the time. Aided and abetted by Mies van der Rohe at the institute, Greenwald had a vision. He saw the rebirth of each of the two pivotal academic institutions in terms of a giant irrigation project restoring the desert in between. This meant that the University of Chicago redevelopment could not be based on the premise of the Wall on its north. The two efforts had to flow together, and for this to happen each, in terms of its internal dynamics, had to reconsider what it was doing where it was. Naturally, Greenwald was interested in capturing the University of Chicago job. As things turned out, his main competitor was a New Yorker named Zeckendorf, who was also a man of extraordinary imagination with a reputation for getting things done. Zeckendorf got the job, and after his fashion, he got it done.

As the university examined its problems, it considered what it imagined were its options. Perhaps it could merge with Northwestern. The suburban Evanston campus could become the safer haven for the younger undergraduates; and the graduate centers, whose students presumably were more mature, could live with the risks and perils of the Southside of Chicago. (This was, of course, an absurd option, but one that Mr. Hutchins—I think mainly in jest—occasionally raised, one of his lighthearted and more frivolous ways of confronting the trouble.) Or, perhaps the university could pick up—cyclotron, library, and all—and move itself to suburbia, North, Southwest or West. (This has since become a very respectable and even profitable way for many American corporations and industries to solve their urban problems.) I suspect (without really knowing) that Bill Zeckendorf's greatest contribution to these speculations was to point out how absurd and impractical this option was.

Greenwald was under the impression that Zeckendorf was the inventor of the concept that a little suburban enclave could be created in the middle of Chicago's

Southside ghettos, and that this was the concept eventually bought. But the enclave point of view already deeply impregnated the university community. The implementation basically was simple. To the South, somewhere between the Midway and Sixty-third Street, the objective was to persuade the city of Chicago to build an elevated or depressed expressway moat, protecting the university's flank on that side. To the East was the lake. To the West was Washington Park, already dangerous but potentially a buffer zone if one kept his distance. And to the North, toward IIT and the Loop, a wall of middle- and upper-middle-class high-rise housing, and town houses should be erected beyond the income reach of all but a handful of the blacks but presumably destined to house university and neighborhood professional personnel without regard, naturally, to race, color or creed (anticipating rising salary schedules at the university).

Of course, this drama on Chicago's Southside was unfolded before black became beautiful in America. The idea of consulting the people who would be most directly affected by such plans had yet to come into its own. There was a strong suspicion among those in charge at the university and the "experts" they assembled that these people seldom knew what they wanted, and almost never knew what was best for them. In either event, it was assumed that they lacked the resources and the expertise with which to achieve desirable results. The university, presumably, could mobilize the resources and had the expertise.

There is not too much evidence now that Mayor Daley's political techniques have changed very much over the two decades of his regime. But at the beginning there was very little reason for him to know that the methods in which he had been educated might prove unequal to the problems and constituencies in his future and in the future of his city. And even though, after Mr. Hutchins'

departure from the university in 1951 on the very threshold of these developments, many of his educational in-
novations were summarily dismantled, the old main
theme of the university's relationship to the rest of the
world persisted. It was a theme which first circumscribed
a version of the institution's educational mission, and
then excused the university from the consequences of its
own conduct in the pursuit of that mission. Even though
the university's own conduct was something less than
ideal, its version of itself assumed an ideal world inhabited by ideal men—Plato's academy, perhaps, steam-
heated, electrified and elaborated, in the ghetto.

Not too long ago I had lunch with Bill Zeckendorf and
asked him recollectively what his University of Chicago
engagement meant. That day we saw the premiere showing of a film he had produced, the most recent example
of his unusual imagination. It promoted a fourth jetport
for New York City (one he would develop, naturally)
to be located forty miles to the north on the Hudson, connected to a gigantic new pier astride Manhattan housing
hotels, schools and theaters, by the latest models of a
Japanese or French high-speed train riding on air or
water or something.

About his Chicago adventure, he said, "I wish I'd never
heard of it. I lost three million dollars on that one."
Little enough. There are times when even a Zeckendorf
is a Missing Piece. In the Chicago case, even he did not
think big enough, or could not have cared less.

On the Beaches

The beaches of Chicago were a pageant of the way it was,
stripped down. On a hot summer's day it was all there,
from some of the restricted (No Jews Allowed) rocky

shores of the North suburbs, to the broad yellow sandy ones, segregated, far to the South and East.

A visit to the Sixty-third Street beach was a safari deep into unexplored mysteries—thousands of black bodies in the tropical heat of our August summer. In time the black nomads moved North, first to the Fifty-seventh Street beach, finally covering all the sands far beyond Fifty-third Street toward the Loop. Misshapen, tired and unwanted, my Gothic university clung precariously to the tufts of a deep ebony carpet, a piece of gray lint dropped from some passing civilization's old Brooks Brothers suit.

I spent delightful holidays at the summer house of Helen's parents at Miller Beach, Gary's suburb in the Dunelands. The smoke of the steel mills usually blew the other way, dropping its black smell and black soot on the black neighborhoods to the South. We hiked with our children on the edges of the lake, through the hills of the warm sands. The sunsets illuminated eternity. You could catch fish as far out as you could wade, and with a boat, beyond.

Across the Indiana state border, near the openings of the tubes from which the mills purged their bowels, were the black beaches Gary's whites had fought for, and having won, fought to keep. Hail to the United Steelworkers!

When they opened the seaway, and integrated the salt with the fresh water (in a way God had forgotten to do), the fish began to die. Along the nearby highways, cement supermarket plazas and acres of shingled shacks erupted, angry rashes, from the sick sands. Soon the brown-eyed Susans and the delicate green ferns, the red birds and the bluejays disappeared. Finally, at the battle of the Dunelands, the men defeated the mountains. The corporations belched, and Indiana's politicians said, "Excuse me."

And the final indignity: the dunes they decapitated for Bethlehem they piled onto barges and hauled across the tip of the lake to Evanston, and transformed the winds and the rains forever into a new accredited piece of Northwestern. So it is that the noblest of our tax-exempt causes abets the finest hours of our destruction.

The black skins still do whatever they do in the summer's sun on the beaches. In the Loop's harbor, the new Chris-Crafts are lined up bumper to bumper. Sleek new towers on the North Shore, rising higher and higher into the smog, cast their new shadows on the rows of slums behind them. And along the beaches, Chicago's beautiful beaches, the smell is of death. The dead fish stink in the sun; and at Miller Beach, where beautiful Susan, Laury and Chuck played, where Helen and I built our driftwood fires at twilight and the brown-eyed Susans winked, the dirty dark-green flies swarm.

Being on My Own

By 1957 I had been in Chicago a dozen years—more than a third of my life—the most strategic first part of being on my own. I had crossed the magic line, joined the faculty team, become one of that special breed who taught, taught in the College whose degree I never earned. But the city itself was the real test of being on my own. It forced my eyes open so that the things that came into view—on the campus, in the life of my growing family, on the streets and from the world—began to take a different turn.

My administrative assignments had taken me far afield from the practice of law, sometimes, so it seemed, into lawless fields. In the office of dean of students, I had mastered the landlord's view of dormitory life, management's methods, usually conservative and often reactionary, for containing the most vital extracurricular interests of the corporation's clients. At one point Mr. Hutchins asked me to cultivate the university's international educational programs, and I learned a bit about grantsmanship, the exchange of students and teachers, and the ins and outs of the foreign educational scene.

There were so many parts to the whole—the job, the city, the family, new babies, new wars, riots, inquisitions, MacArthur's parades, McCarthy's hunts, Ike's *non sequiturs*—each compartmentalized part insisting upon its predominance, its pre-emption of my own definitions of the whole. It was the university scene all over again, only more colossal—each academic department aggressively asserting its autonomy, each wanting to impose its own ultimate meaning upon the rest.

The end of twenty Hutchins years at the university was the end of an epoch in American higher education, the finale to an experiment that almost worked, which even in its failure put the future researchers one small step ahead. The few years that followed on the Midway seemed less like the beginning of a renewal than like a retrenchment—an impression perhaps more reflective of my own state of mind than of the realities. For me it was the end of a stage in my own struggle to learn. I grew restless, eager for the unfamiliar, for the changed scene, the proper place to test what I thought I had learned. A dozen years is a long time in one place in America. In the academic world, a dozen years is almost a commitment, usually more to a place than to a process or to an idea.

After the fall of Hutchins, I found myself working in the university's evening and adult education center on La Salle Street in the financial and commercial heart of the city's Loop. But, strangely, though it was an educational place at the center of the city, educationally it was regarded as a remote outpost of the university's empire. Though its four or five thousand part-time "students"

were grown-up people—first-class citizens actually oper-
ationally responsible for the transaction of important
business in the city, men and women often of powerful
affairs—in the university's value structure they were
really second-class citizens. Though powerfully practical
or marvelously idealistic motivations brought these
grownups back to institutionalized learning, mostly at
night and often at great personal expense, the university
received them with a certain condescension, even with a
sense of annoyance. There was a feeling, a mood, that
these people, being older, should already have been "educated." The university, diverted from its main purposes
with the younger, was doing the older a favor, giving
them a second chance, extending to them, as a matter of
rare privilege, an opportunity to retool, to learn later
what, presumably, they should have learned sooner.

Under Hutchins, with the invention of Great Books,
Great Discussions and Great Ideas—one hundred more
or less of each—"Learning for Life" or "Lifelong Learning" enjoyed for a while a high priority on the agenda.
While the university was not yet prepared to reach out
physically and materially into its own neighborhoods, it
was eager to reach out into human minds, even adult
ones, wherever they were. Some of its most distinguished
scholars preferred to teach the businessmen, housewives,
plumbers and lawyers at night in the Loop rather than
suffer with undergraduates on the Midway during the
day. Avery Craven, the great American historian, was one
of these, and Bob Hutchins himself was another. But
just at the time when I was learning about all this excitement downtown, headquarters, back on the Southside,
was deciding that downtown really wasn't very exciting.

Events conspired to persuade me that it was time for
a change—at least of place. Within the university, an
academic return to normalcy reflected accurately the
Eisenhower mood. The long-overdue confrontation with

the immediate community was provocative. But, I thought then—and still do—it takes two to confront. What provoked me most was the attempt to reshape communities in spite of themselves.

Most disturbing of all was the apparent disconnection between the university's domestic and foreign policies, between its inner life—scholarly, academic, intellectual— and its outer operations—economic, political and social. The rich internal life of the academic empire depended, it seemed, upon the rest of the world's conformity to the fragile, often precious imperial values. (It was like fighting the war in Vietnam assuming that the war would have nothing to do with Wall Street or the college campuses.) Finally, Hiroshima, Berlin, Mississippi and Cottage Grove Avenue were all reduced to three-credit courses. Those who ruled would take care of the bread-and-butter issues, releasing the rest of us citizens so that we could just think—which is, after all the main purpose of those who live in a university.

The search for a place to go next took time, but finally, Wayne State University in the middle of Detroit emerged —rough and new, apparently uninstructed and unhampered by deep tradition, eager to discover for itself fresh answers to these same problems. At the moment of truth, leaving the Midway was far more painful than arriving in Detroit. But, a curious thing: after we moved to Detroit and the years passed, the university stood second in the march of my recollections, and the Second City, first. Chicago, the city, was an incredible education; and the university, an essential, indispensable, fascinating course in the city's degree program. I had been disrupted again. The disruption had thrown out new life lines. It was time to cut old cords.

Chapter Five

The First Paved Mile

The Willow Run Caper

Carlo Levi, the Italian artist and novelist (*Christ Stopped at Eboli*) who was exiled to desolate Luciano for fighting against Mussolini's fascist tyranny, and who as a member of his country's parliament still advocates with a deep and abiding passion the meager interests of his poor South Italian people, was due to arrive in Detroit from Rome on a midnight plane. The flight was late. It was almost three in the morning before we, bleary-eyed and slightly soggy thanks to the hospitality of Willow Run's airport bar, eased Levi off his plane. He came out saluting, the middle finger on his left hand rigid and erect, red and swollen, held at arm's length in front of the rest of him. Mysteriously, somewhere over the Atlantic, he had acquired a splinter. We put him into the car and took him back to the hotel room waiting for him near the university. Helen, miraculously finding a needle, a wad of cotton and some rubbing alcohol at that deep hour of the day's despair, extracted the painful foreign body from Mr. Levi's finger. The removal of the splinter from his finger left a cavernous hole in Mr. Levi's stomach. Midday was approaching in Rome, the ancient city to whose pulse he was still attuned, and he was overcome by the desire to eat. Having just arrived in the United States for the first time, he was determined to eat his first North American meal in Canada, across the river from Detroit. Wanting desperately only to sleep, we persuaded our guest to forgo a Canadian adventure at that bleak hour. We retreated to an all-night diner in midtown Detroit for bacon and eggs.

Levi had read somewhere that Detroit had a Frank Lloyd Wright house or two, and after breakfast he insisted we find one and see it. Finally we located the house on the northwest edge of the city, arriving about seven in the morning without, of course, any advanced notice to its occupants. We splashed through the heavy spring dew on the lawn, examining everything from the overall effect of the architectural profile to the unique fittings of the window sashes. Soon the owners of the house, still in their nightclothes, peering at us through the windows, confronted the decision of whether to call the police, to ask us what in the hell we were doing at their front door or to ignore us. Urban discretion overcoming American valor, they more or less ignored us until we went away.

Levi, back in the car, his feet thoroughly soaked by the dew, his energy surging in giant throbs now, wanted immediately to see how a Ford was put together, and thought that Walter Reuther was in charge of that sort of thing, personally waiting somewhere in Detroit to show him how it was done. We pacified him by driving past Solidarity House on our way back to the hotel. Meantime, in Rome, siesta time was approaching, and our guest, creature of habit, was persuaded to do privately for a while whatever Italians do during siesta.

The man's passion for his mission was powerful, and so it remained throughout his visit. When he accepted my invitation to come, he wrote that since he had never been to America before, he was especially grateful to be asked to Detroit. For Detroit, he had heard, *was* America, and it was America—all of America, Detroit—he would want to see. We can forgive him, I guess, his small errors—like looking for the United States first in Canada, or thinking that the chief officer of the UAW was in charge of the giant motor corporations. These are the kinds of mistakes that even the natives sometimes make. Helen and I had been in the Motor City for almost two years, but when we finally approached a nap later that afternoon, we were beginning to think for the first time that Detroit indeed might be the most American place of all. It had monuments that distinguished foreigners came to see, like Canada, a Frank Lloyd Wright house, and the factories where Fords are put together. And we had forgotten to tell Mr. Levi the most uniquely American thing of all. The University of Michigan, capitalistically nonprofit and tax-exempt, owned the airport on whose runway his plane had touched down. He was on utterly American soil from the beginning.

Respectability

Levi and his Italian colleagues who joined him from Milan and Turin came to the city that spring as part of one of the first festivals of the Detroit Adventure, a citywide cultural and adult education enterprise we had launched the year before.

According to our design, the Adventure, in addition to its activities around the calendar, was to reach a climax each spring in the intensive development of a single theme—a central problem or idea to which each of

Detroit's principal music, theater and ballet companies, museums and universities would make sustained programmatic contributions. About thirty-five institutions had joined in the creation of a master corporation to develop the cultural and artistic life of the city, and during the year before, with the help of the banks, the department stores, the mass media, the automobile companies and the UAW, they had succeeded in mobilizing thousands of new participants in their programs and educational activities. By accepting our invitation that spring, the Italians revealed an ignorance about Detroit almost equaling my own at that time. They were eager in a healthy, optimistic way to share our hopes.

Milan, of course, had been one of the great productive centers of the Renaissance. Together with nearby Turin, it was situated in a region of beautiful lakes, like Detroit. Detroit and the Italian cities had grown to about the same size. The North Italian industrial hub produced most of the country's automobiles. There were a few dissimilarities. Milan had a great opera house. Detroit did not. Milan's universities and museums were old. Detroit's were not. Milan had had a Renaissance. Detroit was hoping for one. It was these vague connections and disconnections that brought Detroit and Milan together that spring. Two great urban adventures were to be examined and compared. One had happened, and the other, hopefully, still might.

Each of the Italians expressed a special interest in the part of my invitation which said that Wayne State University was meant to be by, for and of the people. They were all men whose lives, in unusual ways, had been devoted to their people. The poetry of Salvatore Quasimodo, who had just been awarded the Nobel prize for literature, sang of the sad but irrepressible spirit of the common people who had fought so hard and suffered so long, first under the tyranny of Mussolini's Black Shirts and then under Hitler's. He and Levi were soul brothers, and their devotion had been of the kind which led the poets to risk their lives in the streets with the people.

Enrico Perisutti, Milan's great architect, built his sensational towers for the rich and the powerful to enable him to turn his talents onto the horrible slums in which the destitute emigrés from the South were huddled near the factories to which they had come for work. And the social conscience of Adrianno Olivetti was a far greater part of his fame than the giant industrial empire he had created. Tragically, he died unexpectedly the week before he was due in Detroit, but his brother Dino came in his place.

Wayne State had indeed sprung from humble origins close to the most urgent educational needs of the people. Beginning with only limited municipal support and housed first in a now-decrepit former high school building, it had grown from a modest teacher training center to a university with more than twenty thousand students— law, business, medicine, pharmacy, Ph.D. programs, nursing, social work, and even a school of mortuary science. Like all great American universities, Wayne was ready, willing and able to prepare the young both for life and for death. Not too long before I arrived, the university had reached a climactic moment of its truth: designation as a unit in the state system, a thick new pipe line to the rich untapped pools of statewide tax support and the unexplored regions of Statehouse politics in Lansing. It was to become the third crown jewel, along with Michigan State and Ann Arbor, in the glittering tiara of public higher education in Michigan.

It was the summertime of Democratic power in the state. "Soapy" Williams and the Reuthers—the party and the union. Equipped with a cooperative Democratic mayor—Louis Miriani—Detroit seemed to have a chance, and so did Wayne State. More than 85 percent of Wayne's students were first-generation collegians, right out of

United Automobile Workers homes. And of course Wayne, unlike Ann Arbor or East Lansing, had Detroit —a contemporary base for a contemporary and sensible center of learning.

The university was in a curious state of transition, puzzled about what its new status and wealth might mean. It was rapidly moving from the improvised storefronts, handsome old brownstones, leased garages and ware-houses, into the new buildings which Detroit's famous architects, Eero Saarinen and Minoru Yamasaki, were creating. Yamasaki had just been designated campus architect and planner, and his first building there, the McGregor Conference Center (which has turned out to be his best), was already approaching completion. The campus plan was unfolding like an ancient Japanese gar-den: the white gravel sculpture courts, the reflecting pools and splashing fountains, all, ultimately, to be forti-fied from the black ghettos, so close, with giant peripheral parking lots and new expressway moats. On one of its sides the university was flanked by what is called in De-troit, somewhat optimistically, the Cultural Center—the location of the main library of the city, the Art Institute, the International Institute, and the School of the Arts and Crafts Society. The university began its new era as an enclave within the Cultural Center, itself an enclave, both pressing up hard against the expressway and ghetto borders.

The students, too, were in transition, from what their fathers had been, to what they hoped their fathers' bosses were. For most of them Wayne State was a magic box, inside which they might be transformed from "on the line" to inside the executive suite. The university stood for economic upward mobility, if nothing else, and represented (it still may) a very serious threat to the future quality of UAW leadership and rank-and-file support.

Politically, most of Wayne's student body was conservative. In pursuit of what they thought they wanted,
the students would have done anything the university
asked, taken any credit-hour combination, conformed to
any code of conduct, jumped off any bridge. So many of
them were hellbent on moving up, and who could blame
them? And so was the university—onward and upward—
but to what, with what purpose?

There was much talk about the "uniqueness" of the
situation. Suddenly Wayne was one of the few and largest
state-supported urban universities in the country. It
would "find" itself "uniquely" in connection with its
city. To do this Wayne State would have to be "innovative" and, naturally, "creative." Wayne would be "different" because, obviously, its circumstances were "unique."

Shafting Knowledge

At international conferences about higher education
where Americans are sometimes asked to explain their
system, they very often respond, with great pride, that it
can't be done. With almost three thousand colleges and
universities of various kinds and with various purposes,
we have produced a higher-education network that defies
description. *Everything* is "unique, creative, innovative
and experimental." From Parsons to Princeton, Harvard
to Hunter, Wayne to Wittenberg, and Staten Island to
Syracuse, nothing is normal. There are private and public
schools, Catholic ones and nonsectarian, liberal arts colleges and technical institutes, large universities and small
junior colleges, institutions serving farmers and the small
towns, and others city-bound. They are governed every
which way, built in infinite architectural styles, and of
course, all are on varying verges of bankruptcy, from New
York University's "almost" to Harvard's "not quite yet."

For several years we have been delivering new colleges and universities in this country at the rate of almost one a week, and of course, each new one is born uniquely different. I have been one of the midwives during at least five of these births: during one of the endless revisions of the Hutchins College at Chicago; during the delivery of the Monteith College at Wayne State; during the preliminary gestation stages of the Senior College at the New School for Social Research; during Bedford-Stuyvesant's attempt to create a new college for itself; and now, hopefully, during the rebirth of the Staten Island College, to which I am attached. Strange thing about these collegiate nativities: shortly after their delivery, you wouldn't have the slightest doubt about their common parentage. Their very first hospital bulletins describe certain genetic combinations which lock up forever their personality potentials.

Inevitably, a college begins with the designation of its campus. A campus is a continuous space devoted exclusively to what a college does. If the college is to begin on a potato patch on Long Island surrounded by other identical potato fields for as far as the eye can see, the first step is to build a fence around one potato patch and ordain it a campus. If the college is to begin in the middle of Brooklyn or Detroit or on the edge of downtown Denver, everything that stands in the way must be torn down and the people relocated, so that in the middle of the city there is created something which resembles a potato patch but which can be called a campus. No open space, no fence or no wall— no college.

Once the collegiate space is defined, collegiate time coincident with that space must be established. Everywhere in America, everywhere, a liberating undergraduate education is Four Academic Years big. Half of such an education can be obtained in the junior colleges, but "half" is defined in terms of four. In mature civilizations a special significance is always attached to certain numbers.

With the Chinese there are the Two Principles, the Four Forms, the Eight Trigrams, the Three Kingdoms, the Six Dynasties, etc. In Tibet there are the Eight Glorious Emblems, the Seven Gems, the Twelve Animals and the Five Elements. In our own we have the Three Graces, the Nine Muses, the Ten Commandments and the Four Academic Years. An undergraduate educated in less than four is not getting full value; if he takes longer to get educated, there's something wrong with him.

A campus, therefore, has not only a spatial but also a temporal size. It is so many acres and Four Academic Years big. It has been so for a long, long time. The fences have remained practically unaffected by lesser developments such as the changing quantity and quality of human knowledge—the split of the atom, Freud's birth or God's death, computers, automobiles, TV, pictures and rocks from the moon, or the rise and decline of civilization, Vietnamese or Black.

Maintaining the purity of the campus concept is, of course, complicated by the changing quantity and quality of knowledge. And the longer our species endures, the more knowledge there is to change. We have been recording in some form or another what we know for almost six thousand years now. Each passing year adds more and more to the pile of what we know. Some of the increment may not be worth knowing, but generally the bigger the heap gets the more of it we need to know to get along. No matter—the sun will rise, the sun will set, and the education of our college young will take four academic years.

The inevitability of the campus concept confronts American collegiate education with a classic economic situation—*a supply and command dilemma*. The supply of knowledge is growing at an algebraic rate far greater than the command of the time and space required to accommodate the supply. Given what there is to know, and the intensifying connections between knowing and surviving, how can the campus, fixed in time and space, contain it all?

This dilemma is solved by *shafting knowledge*. Everything that we know is neatly classified, and each classification is packaged in a vertical shaft of its own. Chemistry, physics and biology, history, economics and psychology, literature, philosophy and art—all neatly packed, each in its own shaft. The shafts are then arranged in a row, side by side, across the campus square. Each shaft, however, contains not only its peculiar knowledge, but also the *people* who claim a special wisdom about that knowledge. The people, assembled in their respective shafts arrayed across the campus square, represent the political dimension of the campus community. Some system must accommodate their relationships. The politicalization of the campus is achieved by the departmentalization of the knowledge shafts. Each shaft is empowered. A leader is designated for it. People are judged and ranked inside of it. It is budgeted. The people inside it may punish and reward, hire and fire, admit and expel each other. Finally, and most important of all, through this system the shaft may define its own meaning.

Success in the politics of shafted knowledge requires mastery of a fundamental operational procedure. The campus square is entered—by student, teacher or administrator—at the thin and tenuous top of a knowledge shaft. As the applicant approaches he proclaims loudly, publicly, his ignorance. He wants *in* because he "knows nothing." Once in, over the officially prescribed time, he quietly descends into the shaft. His success will be measured by the depth to which he sinks. The richest knowledge lodes, the finest promotions, the most precious rewards are all to be found near the bottom of the shaft. On the way down, one is gradually prepared for the pressures at the greater depths. Finally, at the very bottom of the shaft, one may be ceremoniously ejected, or specially commissioned into the shaft's lowest (i.e., highest) place of honor. Tenure in the highest rank may be awarded, or a parchment may be issued stating that the candidate has sunk so low that he qualifies as "educated" within the terms of that shaft. In either event, at this point the candidate is expected to proclaim loudly, publicly, his learning. He "knows something."

The growth of knowledge adds more and more shafts onto the limited campus square. And as the relationships among them, all trying to squeeze into the limited time-space, grow more crowded and complicated, the shafts become narrower and narrower. The greater the jam, the more intricate their political relationshps become. Which shaft should an ignorant student enter first? During the time that he has, should a student do some sinking in more than one shaft? How deeply should he sink in one shaft before he moves over to start sinking in another? How much should he know about how little? How little need he know about so much? Answers to these questions are called a *curriculum.*

A curriculum is an elaborate *treaty*, negotiated in mandarinlike fashion among the various shafts. The treaty regulates economic competition within the campus realm. The campus economy is based upon a common-currency system. Four Academic Years (the size of Fort Knox on the campus) is divided up, more or less, into one hundred and twenty monetary units called *credit hours.* Credit hours are things that students must earn to get educated. Students earn credit hours by sinking in their shafts. The lower one sinks, the more he learns. Once one hundred and twenty of these things (more or less) are earned, a student may cash them in at a specially designated place for a dividend-bearing bond called a *diploma.* This document proves he is educated.

Each shaft possesses a limited number of credit hours which a student can earn in it. The political (and educational) importance of a shaft is determined by how large its supply of earnable credit hours is. (At Wayne, where more than two thousand courses, most worth three credit hours each, are listed each semester, the total supply of available credit currency exceeds six thousand.) The larger its supply, the more people a department must engage to supervise the dispensation of the supply to the sinking clientele. The more people it engages, the larger its budget must be. A shaft's influence in the campus community reflects the size of its budget, which is generally assumed to be a valid index of the importance of its knowledge. As the number of shafts has grown pursuant to the proliferation of knowledge, the competition multiplies and aggravates the political relationships among the shafts. If a shaft is ambitious and aims to grow bigger, it can only do so at the expense of some others, because the overall currency supply available to any one client is limited by the time-space of the campus. (This is probably why, incidentally, so many faculties without much hesitation happily voted to abolish ROTC. ROTC is a low-prestige little shaft, pre-empting a small but vital share of the currency. Its abolition releases a new piece of political action. With such a limited overall currency supply, even a small piece is worth fighting for. The abolition of ROTC takes nothing away from those who feel they really belong to the club, but potentially, in the reclaimed credits, offers something to everybody. Politically, matters of principle are often resolved this way.

To prevent a suicidal bloodletting in the competition for the coin of the realm, the shafts accept several *horizontal operational principles*—rules meant to apply with equal justice for all and malice toward none of the shafts as their clientele maneuver across the lines, horizontally across the campus square. There are commonly accepted rules establishing who cannot enter the shafts at all. These are the *admissions and employment criteria* for the college.

All agree to observe common standards for judging the performance of those who get into the shafts: how students are to be graded as they sink; how faculty may earn promotion, tenure and other rewards as they, too, sink. All agree to refrain from taking actions which might inflate, and thus reduce, the value of the credit-hour currency. Knowledge is made available in all the shafts through courses of a given length of time, and course time is imbued with a common credit value (three credits per course, three hours per week, etc.). These rules are the Geneva Conventions regulating the process for making the treaties which result in a curriculum.

The politics of the campus community run up and down the departmentalized vertical-knowledge shafts, and horizontally, from side to side, in the campus square. The combination of the vertical shafts and the horizontal bars convert the campus square into a rigid grid, a mosaic of little boxes. Happy survival in this grid requires a psychological pitch which welcomes being boxed in. The curriculum is meant to box in the student. The politics of the shafts is meant to box in the faculty. The greater the boxing-in capacity of a campus grid, the more respectable it is. The disruption of this system consists of a failure to conform to the flow of events as described. Resistance to being boxed in is disruptive. A disrupted campus is not respectable. Consequently, to build a "creative, unique and innovative" educational experiment on a solid and respectable foundation (Maintaining Standards and Quality), one must first acquire a time-space campus like this, and develop within it an intricate rigid grid. Once everything is securely boxed in, then the creative, unique and innovative effort may proceed.

Except for these little things, American higher education really is too diverse, open-ended, variegated and free to be described. Except for its grid, it really defies description.

Urbs Shafted

Inside the campus grid, where knowledge is shafted, only a few engage in decision-making conversation. Small oligarchies, possessing great decision-making powers, emerge out of the grid, are produced by it. The oligarchs talk with one another, but not very much with others. The others find out what the oligarchs mean through the memoranda, directives and occasional manifestos they issue. So it is among a large population, claiming to be a city, among whom power has been shafted.

I am still not quite sure what Detroit is or intends to be. We settled in a northwest suburb without realizing that we were still not in Detroit. Inside the city almost everyone has some grass to cut, and the population of power lawnmowers must exceed that of the people. The city is uniquely defined in terms of the car. Without the wheel, life would really be quite impossible, for work, for play, or even for a loaf of bread. Given the way it is, two cars per family are hardly enough. Out on Woodward Avenue, six or seven miles from the palpitating commercial heart, the cars may be seen during the morning or evening rush hours, creeping bumper to bumper along a stretch between two bronze plaques celebrating the First Paved Mile in the United States. From where has this road come—from Waterloo gone insane? And where is it going—to its own version of Chicago or New York? Who knows? But as one drives the length of Woodward, from the river along the Canadian shore to the plusher outer limits of this giant suburb where the second- and third-level executives in the automobile companies live, Detroit may be seen as it is. And from what is seen, the suspicion grows that for those in charge of it all, the first mile has been paved for a long, long time.

Detroit's streets are not always smooth, and sometimes,

despite the precision with which the traffic lights are co-ordinated, traffic gets horribly snarled up. After the bitter-cold and snowy Michigan winter, when the first warm spring sun begins to melt the debris, ugly cracks and pot-holes crop up. And in the intense summer heat that can be generated toward the middle of our continent, some-times the tar melts and bulges, and dangerous unexpected obstacles erupt even in the principal avenues.

In addition to its automobile-making prowess and its professional athletic teams, Detroit was famous for its race riots long before 1967. About the automobile-making and rioting, it is very difficult to know what they mean, if anything. After the race riots and the crises in the auto-mobile industry happen, a powerful committee is almost always formed—usually of the same powerful citizens each time—which in due course issues a powerful memoran-dum, directive or manifesto stating what the occurrence meant. But after a while, after the automobile sales go back up or the barricades go down, the committee usually quietly dissolves, and you are left wondering. Only one thing is for sure: a lot of profit is made in Detroit out of selling and maintaining cars and cleaning up the debris from the riots, and sometimes out of baseball and football, too.

Once, about a decade ago, I made a list of all the members of the governing boards of the main educational and cultural institutions in the city, including the uni-versities, the opera association, the symphony, the Art In-stitute, etc. There were almost three hundred names on the list, including two Negroes and less than half a dozen Jews and Poles. There was a lot of overlapping, and once I eliminated the names that appeared on more than one list, the total was less than two hundred. Of these, making allowance for the wives of the important, for figureheads and fluky appointments, I figured that fewer than forty actually occupied really powerful positions in the economy of the city. And of these, six or at most seven families, often represented by more than one member, clearly were essential. There were three (perhaps four) of these without whose collaboration no effective decision could be made, especially if the intent was to affect more than one of the institutions involved. Finally, the Fords were in a class virtually by themselves.

At moments of crises in the life of the city—like during or after the race riots or the strikes at the car-making corporations—or at times when traditional and essentially noncontroversial civic endeavors were pursued—like the annual united philanthropic money-raising campaigns—established or improvised forums, staffed from among the essential decision-makers, transacted the necessary business. But between crises and annual campaigns, civic conversation was rare in Detroit. The perception of common civic interest was limited to narrow or immediate conflicts of interest, or to broad and consensus-laden objectives. The same people talked with each other over and over again. As for the rest, they were talking, but they were not heard.

I discussed these matters with Clarence Hilberry, the president of the university, toward the end of my first year in Detroit. Just for fun, we decided to go into the street-building business together.

Saturn

I had not been asked to Wayne State to build streets, but for a very different construction job. I was asked to Wayne to help Lloyd Allen Cook build a Graduate Division of Instruction and Research.

Lloyd Allen Cook was a scholar, deeply respected on his own campus and beyond, even though he came out of the College of Education. He was nearing the twilight of his career, dreaming more and more about the little house facing the Pacific on the Washington coast where he planned to write his great book. He was one of the few men around the university whose stature gave him a fighting chance in his special mission. He who would build a Graduate Division of Instruction and Research in a university where none had existed before had better know how to handle a whip, the chair and a six-shooter before he goes into the lion's cage. Beyond that, he had better be a fearless man, prepared to show the lions beyond a shadow of a doubt that whatever their antics, he will not turn and run.

As it turned out, building a Graduate Division of Instruction and Research was not the most stimulating venture in which I have engaged. Of course, starting anything new can be fun, even if others have done it before elsewhere. It can always be done "better," and it is being done for the first time *there*. But the world of graduate education, I imagine, is what our whole planet would be like if the "best" products of the academic Establishment ever took over. It is a world not quite to be believed—like, say, Saturn. It is a thing of beauty to behold, with its spectacular research-and-publication rings, and its rainbow-hued grantsmanship and reduced-teaching-load surface. But insofar as we know, it is wholly unfit for human habitation. A nice place to visit, I guess, but I'd sure hate to live there.

Education at the graduate level is one of the most sophisticated and refined ideas our civilization has yet produced. Dr. Cook, in his occasional mellower moods, used to refer to the graduate part, ideally, as the cutting edge of man's mind. And so, sometimes, it really is. He who undertakes a critique of American higher education must account for its incredible production of specialized and professional talent and new knowledge. The graduate part is the main factory, and in some fields the outcome is the earth's best. True, the production process is often so inefficient as to border on downright corruption. But education at any level implicitly defies efficiency. All this is on the one hand.

On the other hand, the ethics of academic organization, the ultimate "goods" that academics value and revere, and the way-out things that they will do finally to secure those goods, all come to focus in the graduate part. It is like Napoleon's civil service distilled into the essence of Kafka's nightmare. Trade unionism gone mad. It makes one wonder: To realize the best in ourselves, must we indulge the worst?

One of the essential objects of formal education at any level is students. Ernst C. Colwell, Mr. Hutchins' president, greeting the new students entering the University of Chicago, told us that though the university didn't have the best of all possible faculties, it undoubtedly had the best that there were. Insofar as was humanly and administratively possible, the students were kept out of the faculty's hair. Students, Mr. Colwell pointed out, deter the faculty's performance. The university would really be great, he said, if it didn't have to bother with students at all. He concluded that we were there as a matter of privilege, and cautioned that it was in our best interest to do as we were told. Keep out of the way and don't bother the faculty! (It was, of course, important that we pay our tuition on time.)

The less a professor has to do with students, the greater his prestige and status in higher education. In graduate education, the prestige and status are highest. The national norm, not yet achieved everywhere but universally sought as the proper situation, is that those who teach in the graduate school should officially meet with students not more than six hours during a workweek, and preferably less. At worst such a schedule is arranged so that the professor is obliged to be around for a while on two or three days of the week. But in well-ordered administrations, everything can be arranged on one. Moreover, the fewer students one meets, supervises or in any way sees, the more distinguished one is likely to be.

Time is of the essence for such scholars. They must supervise the students' theses, write books and articles, and commit research. And if they know a great deal (and they always do) they really do have a responsibility to share with others what they know, i.e., "consult." (Commanding large consultation fees is an additional prestige index.) Time spent with students, especially in direct teaching relationships, is time subtracted from the other essential pursuits. Among the other pursuits, research and publication are the most essential. Consequently, the fewer theses one has to supervise, the better. Of course, the really accomplished scholar connects what his students' theses are to be about with his own writing and research interests. The greatest honor a graduate professor can pay to his student is to allow the aspirant scholar to perform slave labor for his senior colleague. The idea of the apprenticeship, generally held in low esteem throughout most of higher education, is curiously reversed at that level where the profession replicates its own kind.

Successful publication or research depends upon successfully finding someone to publish what is written or pay for what is to be researched. A very well developed art has arisen in this field which sometimes has something to do with the merit of the idea to be published or studied. As graduate education has grown so spectacularly, there is a keen competition in most fields for the attention of prospective publishers and grantors (though in some areas there is a surplus of available support in view of the paucity of talent to pursue lines of inquiry). Grantsmanship reaches its most sublime climax when the applicant succeeds in obtaining a grant which sets him up as an almost independent fiefdom back at his university home-base. Knowing of his institution's eagerness (and the funds usually built in to accommodate the institution's administrative override), the grantee can expect to be given an unbridled head. Successful graduate faculty members often act as if they were Richard Burton or Maria Callas or both. Being a stableboy to a long line of tense, overbred, pure-blooded Kentucky race horses is enough to make a nervous wreck out of anyone. And it almost made one out of Lloyd Allen Cook.

On the administrative track, the jockeying for position among such types is intense and even vicious. The competition is keen for the preferred teaching schedule, the best office accommodation, the perfectly equipped laboratories most loosely accounted for, and of course, for the "brightest" students. And the graduate students have become a serious complication as they have come to feel more and more aggrieved by the way the system works. They bitch about irrelevant language requirements, the assignment of thesis topics which are absurd if not wholly uninteresting, improper instruction and supervision, and the isolation the system enforces upon them, separating their keenest interests from the places and pursuits which might bear them out. Finally, the university in which all this happens naturally views the outcome as its most conclusive proof of respectability. The graduate part is the best evidence that in fact a university really exists.

Dr. Cook presided over the departmental feuds, the posturings of the prima donnas, the little contests for control and power with great equanimity. He was Solomon most of the time, handing down decisions aimed at keeping the baby alive. But every time he had an idea of his own, an idea which transcended departments or personalities, born out of reason and aimed conceptually at what he imagined was the good of the whole, he was chewed up into little pieces. He was not, unhappily, independently funded. His research was into the researchers, which is the most dangerous kind of all. Actually, there was little I could do to help him, except to provide a friendly shoulder to cry on and to make as noble an effort as I could to execute some of his splendid and absolutely rational schemes, so many of which were doomed to abort.

In retrospect, for me this time produced two questionable claims to fame. Every respectable graduate operation must have a respectable graduate journal. I created a journal for Wayne—*Graduate Comment*—which survived for a decade in spite of the fact that we never quite made it respectable. It was, instead, rather interesting, and even published the thoughts of people who, having achieved something in realms beyond the graduate schools, were not a part of this game. And I can point with pride to my supportive activities on the money-raising front which led to an increase in annual research income from $1 million to more than $4 million, and all that in less than four years. Now, don't ask me what it means. Frankly, I still don't know. But I sure met some fascinating money givers in the process along the streets of Washington, Detroit and New York.

Preparation for college admission now determines much of what goes on in our high schools. And preparation for graduate study now reaches deep into the senior, junior and even sophomore and freshman knowledge shafts, prescribing in a very substantial way the character of collegiate education. There is usually a direct relationship between the strength, the traditional solidity, the respectability of a university's graduate school, and the need for its reform. At Wayne the primary goal, as it was then seen, was to prove strength, solidity and respectability. It was no time for reform or innovative departures in graduate studies. It was instead a time to emulate those very models most in need of revision. There may be an operational truth proved by all this. Perhaps the education of new academic institutions, like that of little children, must be addressed to the accepted social norms rather than to the subjective personality potential, the release of the peculiar talents of the individual. Perhaps the new starts in American higher education must be born out of the urgent desperation, the corruption and the breakdown of the old, established situations.

Anyway, a few years of these rituals and games at "new" Wayne State were quite enough. My interests began to veer in another direction.

Ant Hills and Beehives

Charles Blessing, director of the City Plan Commission, was supposed to make sense out of Detroit, out of what it was becoming. It took Wayne State an unconscionably long time to invite Mr. Blessing to teach a course or two in its respectable Graduate Division. But in his office at his drawing boards, surrounded by his bright young staff, or on the streets, surrounded by Detroit's dull old slums, Charles Blessing was one of the city's most important professors. In one respect he is different from most other professors. He is compelled to translate what he thinks into actions which commit him and the future of his city. Unlike the scientist in the lab, his mistakes do not simply waste material and equipment, creating a little mess that some technical assistant can clean up in preparation for the next day's experiment. His failures waste the lives of people and decades of time, and for better or worse, he knows it and cares.

After I was well into my own Detroit experiment, Charles once said that his operations concentrated on the bones and sinews of the city, while mine aimed at the heart and life-giving bloodstream it pumped. Clearly we needed each other, but we were both in the same bag. As it has come to pass, everything in a great city—its bones and muscles, its heart, its brain and even its soul—everything

is institutionalized. This profoundly important fact sometimes confuses those who look at the urban mess and decide
they want to Do Good. It misleads them to prescribe
remedies applicable to beehives, ant hills and insects rather
than to neighborhoods, communities and people. It leads
them into the misuse of both the technology and the
institutions.

It is true that we are born, most of us, institutionalized,
in the hospital. And in death we are institutionalized
forever in the modern burying or cremating places. In
between we will be institutionalized for working, for
learning, even for regenerating our spirits—but not necessarily like ants or bees. It is important to maintain, at least
for the sake of argument, that there is still some small
difference between a prison and a university, between an
insane asylum and the international headquarters of the
General Motors Corporation, between the modern hospital and the contemporary cemetery.

As I saw it then, Detroit's cultural, artistic and educational institutions incredibly underestimated the capacities and longings of the majority of the city's people. The
blacks were practically nowhere, nonparticipatory in the
key centers of the city's life. The huge unionized middle
class sometimes sent their children to the universities, to
the concert halls, etc. but seldom went themselves. At the
top, the governing caste seemed small and ingrown. Both
the audiences and the sources of philanthropy were very
specialized essentially middle-, upper-middle-class, representing a select and overlapping cut of the corporation
executives, the lawyers and the doctors in the city. Many
of these institutions were constantly on the tightrope,
balanced between bankruptcy and barely getting through
the next fiscal year. But worst of all, viewed from Charles
Blessing's office, they all shared the same sinking boat—a
fact of their existence practically none of them perceived
down on the streets where they were. Within each insti-

tutional frame, the same people talked with one another incessantly, mainly about the same things.

These intense internalized discussions invariably defined abstract external villains. The problems were never a consequence of what the institution had done or not done. The problems were always the result of popular ignorance, indifference and incapacity, or the rapacious and subversive activity of some competing institution. When the whole city shut down, as it did during a strike, the Fords and the Reuthers conversed. But in between strikes, and about the rest, too little and usually too late.

The view from the streets was somewhat different. Black leaders wanted "in," but many of them saw engagement by their wives and their children dependent upon gaining a piece of the control at the top. I never entered a UAW home (homes financed through work on the lines) whose walls were devoid of pictures, whose rooms were empty of the sound of music, or whose aspirations did not extend to higher opportunities for the children. The quality of the art, the music, the literature and the aspirations may, according to some standards, have left something to be desired, but not the human expressions and impulses, and for all I knew, capacities. The city contained an impressive number of young painters, musicians, architects, aspirant actors, dancers and writers struggling to find someone, something to talk with. In the universities there were even some academics, eager to go beyond their classrooms to share with others what they knew, some even in the expectation that the "others" might teach them something too.

Finally, throughout Detroit, from the top on down, there was a hypersensitivity about the city's potential for brutality. It was not that Detroit lacked "culture," one was told; somehow what it had just didn't seem to come out right, civilized. In the Motor Bar in one of the principal hotels downtown, the décor exalts the city's principal industry. More than once Detroiters have told me at that bar that the hotel's management, based in another city, had a very distorted view of Detroit. They sounded like New Yorkers I know who, when they see the latest versions of the automobiles, disdainfully point out the distorted outlook of the Detroiters who design and produce them.

Detroit's plight, I thought, represented a terrible frustration and a waste. For a failure among its people to make the right connections with one another, there was much talk and very little conversation, too much noise and too little action. From an educational point of view, precious talents, essential to the task, remained immobile, unused, uninspiring and too often uninspired. More than ever now, people learn in terms of *where* they are— I mean physically, as well as state of readiness. Learning systems and urban systems are more rather than less coincident than ever before. The problem is how to invent new institutional forms, employing the technology and respecting the actual capacities and innate decency of the people, to make better use of the urban environment as the central learning scene. To do this, obviously, the ancient lines drawn among the various functions of different urban institutions must be redrawn, and in many cases erased. This means that some sophisticated environments for "working" and "living"— neighborhoods, clinics and hospitals, offices of government, etc.—are the proper "departments" of the future learning institutions. But we have yet to figure out how to organize and implement this situation, using without fear the ultimate weaponry systems the technology and institutional know-how represent: the computers, closed-circuit television, the more skillful use of human talent. In other words, we must soon stop thinking in terms of the campus and the school, the museum and the theater, the places of work and for play, and start thinking in terms of learning-and-enjoyment environments, new combinations of talent and of places that relevantly bear upon the perfection of living in the city. Our views of who can teach and who can learn, of who want to learn—and where and why—are as old-fashioned as the Model-T. So many of our places of learning are trying to blast off to the moon in Model-T's. No wonder they've got problems.

Clarence Hilberry brought a great sympathetic understanding to the conception of the problems, and he was excited by the chance to do something about them. He had come to Wayne State's presidency from the department of English literature, a move many felt was a tragic mistake because he was known as a brilliant teacher of Shakespeare. But Dr. Hilberry enjoyed his presidency. He told me once he had come to see it as another, unexpected but potentially powerful way to teach Shakespeare.

The Adventure

After the very substantial private funds had been pledged for the construction of Yamasaki's exquisite McGregor Conference Center, just as the building was nearing completion, university authorities began to worry about what they would do with it, and how its operations might produce the forty or fifty thousand dollars a year required to maintain it and keep it open. The construction costs of new university buildings, difficult as they may be to marshal, are really less difficult to handle than the annual operational charges each new building adds to the budget of the institution. There are some academic institutions that have virtually bankrupted themselves by successfully raising money for the construction of new buildings without anticipating the operational consequences of having them. Having invented a magnificent building for communicating, Dr. Hilberry encouraged me to think about what messages we might send. The immediate problem was how to launch the new building, how to program it through at least its first year. It became the de facto headquarters for the Detroit Adventure.

Minoru Yamasaki—like all very talented artists, I guess —was not an easy man to live with. (He is now doing the giant Trade Center Towers in Manhattan.) The McGregor Center was his baby. Once he had conceived it, he was determined at any cost that it be born right. On the university's side, naturally cost was a factor. I am sure that Yamasaki must have felt that the academic administrators were a bunch of artistic idiots. I know that the administrators involved came to feel that Yamasaki, unchecked, would convert the whole budget of the university into the McGregor Conference Center. Yamasaki, like any good architect, not only designed the building, but supervised in detail putting it together. I mean, he personally picked each living plant to be placed in the grand lobby, and selected the silverware that was to be used in the dining rooms. If he did not like the flow of the grain in the wood on a banister, that wood was ripped out and replaced. Yamasaki would argue with God about the configurations of forms He had pressed into the marble slabs.

When Yamasaki first took me across the threshold of his finished creation, my eyes instantly went up, up the full height of the building to the jeweled, mosaic skylight, which runs the full length of the main hall. I was standing, I discovered later, on a flawless marble floor. Yamasaki smiled, for I had fulfilled his Pavlovian intention. "I meant," he said, "when you walk into this building for you to do what you have done. What is inside of you is supposed first to reach up. Inside of this building you are meant to reach for the sky."

Clarence Hilberry, too, was a man of some talent. Whatever he really felt about Detroit's ghettos, he knew where some of them were and something about how they worked. It is remarkable how he knew just who the right forty or fifty people were, that he got them in a room together, gave them lunch, and then, in less than two hours, persuaded them and the twenty-five or thirty institutions they governed, to embark upon the Detroit Adventure, with all of its budgetary, corporate and other implications—most of which were little understood at the time by either Dr. Hilberry or me. But Dr. Hilberry understood how Detroit worked—its own special version of "democracy." And I think he understood that we intended to make it work against certain aspects of its existing version of itself, i.e., *for* itself. As he said after lunch: "Only in Detroit could things get done this way. Isn't it a wonderful place?"

In the following months, whatever the cooperating institutions had agreed to led them to reach out—to one another and to the neighborhoods of the city—in new ways. Teams of musicians from the Detroit Symphony gave concerts and lectures in the classrooms of the public schools. Institutional activities, art exhibits, concerts, performances, lectures were decentralized, staged in shopping plazas, civic centers and libraries in the neighborhoods. Young painters found themselves both teaching others and exhibiting (and selling) their works to newly discovered audiences. Thousands of people who had never undertaken adult studies found themselves being taught, in single courses, by faculties combining talents from several fields and organizations. Ordinary citizens began to explore the intricacies of urban planning—the plans for their own city. Groups formed to study their own neighberhood problems and to act upon them. Classes were convened on airplanes, from which the teachers and the students could examine the topography of what they were studying. The arts and education began to move from obscurity or small items in the inner sections to the front pages of the *News* and the *Free Press*. Questions began to arise about who ran what, about what the institutions should be doing, about their relationships with one another, and about Detroit—not only its cultural life, but through that, about aspects of its political and economic life and aspirations. Institutions began to mobilize and plan the use of their resources together, in pursuit of common program goals. They collaborated in publishing a monthly calendar of their events, which the automobile and utility companies distributed in tens of thousands to their employees in paycheck envelopes. And together, for a few weeks each year, they celebrated themselves in a climactic conference and festival of their talents—staged throughout the city, in the civic center and in the institutions. And the year that the Italians came was, in many ways, the best of them all.

But all of this was not without its own internal tensions and paradoxes. In the cause of breaking through institutional walls the Detroit Adventure, Incorporated, had been created. To decentralize and make contact, a new centralization was, for some purposes, required. To help solve the fiscal problems of the cooperating institutions, the new mechanism was created, adding new budgetary demands of its own. And, naturally, as the participating institutions came to know more about one another, they also discovered better-informed reasons to challenge, question and compete among themselves. Still, in little more than a year and a half, almost fifty thousand people, most of whom had not been involved before, were connected through the sustained and continuing programs of the Adventure, and tens of thousands more were added to the audiences of the special events. The new approach gained great visibility in the city and was a new source of civic pride. And finally, when Governor Williams established one of the first statewide commissions on the arts in the country, he asked me, as its first chairman, to translate what we were beginning to learn in Detroit into programs serving the whole state.

The Smell of Lilacs

About the time that the Nobel poet laureate came to
Detroit with his fellow Italians, *Time* magazine ran an
article on the university entitled "Rare Days at Wayne,"
which concluded by quoting me as saying: "These are
rare days here. The people of Detroit are graduating . . .
Wayne is no longer a factory-town university because Detroit no longer considers itself just a factory town."

I remember well my excitement upon receiving Salvatore Quasimodo's acceptance of my invitation to come to
Detroit. I rushed into the faculty club at Wayne with the
cable to share my excitement with the faculty there. There
was no excitement, because no one had ever heard of the
Nobel poet before.

The university issued a routine press release, and almost at once I received a special-delivery letter from
Harold Hartley, a carpenter and cabinetmaker in Detroit
of Scotch-English descent. He begged for a chance to meet
Quasimodo. Quasimodo, he wrote, was one of Italy's greatest freedom fighters. He had read all of Quasimodo's
poems, including the ones cited on the occasion of the
Nobel prize. (Quasimodo's work had yet to be translated
into English.)

After the Nobel laureate came, he met the carpenter. It
turned out that Mr. Hartley wrote poetry. He wrote a
poem in honor of meeting the Nobel-prize winner. Quasimodo was touched, and asked to see more of the man's
poetry. Impressed, Quasimodo arranged for the carpenter's
poems to be published in his own journal, *Inventario,* back
in Milan. Intrigued, the newspapers in Detroit asked the
carpenter: How come you, a man who makes his living by
making things out of wood, write poems at night? And
Hartley replied, "There must be many people in Detroit
—automobile executives and union leaders, doctors and

businessmen—who, when they go home at night to relax, build things out of wood in their basement workshops. When I go home at night, I write poems."

For the Italian poet, the Detroiter wrote:

> But yesterday I heard Quasimodo.
> And today; how proudly sway the
> Poplars, sprinkling infant green
> Upon the ground,
> While arctic born, a flickering
> Arrow northward homes—
> And yes, Oh yes,
> I smell lilacs!

When the riots raged in 1967 all around the boundaries of Wayne State's campus, not a building there was burned, not a window broken. Its models may be all wrong; its timing horrible. But for Americans from the most unexpected places and of the most unexpected kinds, Americans who still have not been admitted, Wayne and places like it still represent an unexpected hope.

Wayne grows ever bigger. The Detroit Adventure is still there, now primarily a coordinating and promotional agency for whatever its member institutions represent. And now, after those violent nights on the streets of Detroit not so long ago, what do they represent? When a city burns, the institutions which represent its potential for greatness are lost in the clouds of smoke, and the poets flee from the streets. A burning city illuminates the failures of those institutions embodying its highest hopes. In Detroit and in many other American cities, the peace is fragile and the time is ticking away.

Chapter Six

New York, New York

Anatomy

I sat once in my office at the New School overlooking
Twelfth Street in Manhattan and watched the construction of a new residential tower across the street. One day
the workmen stripped away the thick skin of cement walk
in front of the new building, and there, just beneath the
surface of the Manhattan street, was a duplicate of a drawing I remember in my high school biology text of a human
hand with a triangle of skin neatly folded back to show
what was beneath. There, each in a different color, were
the complex and interweaving networks which make the
machinery of the city work—the blood vessels and veins,
the nervous system, the pads of cartilage linking the bone
structure, the bands of muscle which lift and extend each
part. I saw the multicolored cables, the twisting pipes
weaving around one another, some carrying water, some
gas, the ventilating lungs which let the Sixth Avenue sub-

way breathe, the nodules of energy which warmed the towers soaring above.

We have built something of our own intricacy beneath the skin of the city, and if the skin is cracked and wrinkled, weather-beaten, dirty, aged, spit upon, disfigured and scarred, these are the wounds we inflict upon ourselves. These are true marks telling honestly what we are.

East

I suppose if a young man is born and grows up in the Middle West, the only place for him to go is West or East. When I was sixteen I spent a day in New York City between trains en route to a summer camp in the Catskills. I suspected even then it was the only place to be. When I was invited to New York to be dean of the New School for Social Research, it was the strangest thing of all. For strange as New York appears from the distance of the Middle West, the New School appears even stranger.

President Hilberry thought I was insane, and he told me so. Our enterprises were booming in Detroit, and as he saw it, after all the hard work getting things in motion, it was a time to relax, consolidate and begin to enjoy what was happening. I did not see it quite that way. Detroit Adventure's deficits had grown substantial enough to prove to me that its potential was really significant. It was clearly a time to take new risks, to escalate, not to consolidate. Sometimes a man in his thirties and a man approaching sixty do not see things quite the same way.

There is a certain symmetry to each academic year. School opens in the fall and closes in the spring, and in between there are the official holidays, tests, social festivities and routines. A few times around the track, if one is not careful, and it can all become rather boring. It wasn't that I was bored in Detroit at all, but what others were beginning to regard as an achievement seemed to me the most tenuous of beginnings. I have since learned, still imperfectly, the importance of being patient. It is a very difficult thing to accept. Money never entered the question, for Dr. Hilberry graciously played the academic game played on such occasions, offering to match whatever the New School would pay. Actually, the New School offered me no additional money. It was something else—some inner force which simply, powerfully said, "Go East, young man, go East."

So once again we packed, sold the house, put the children and the plants in the back of the station wagon, and drove to New York. On the morning of our departure, just after dawn, my friend and housekeeper, Mrs. Josephine Jett, appeared on our steps with her bags packed too. The day before, we had said our farewells. Mrs. Jett had come to Detroit as a young woman from somewhere deep in the South. Now somewhere over sixty, she said, "Dr. Birenbaum, I've changed my mind. I'm going with you. It's Harlem for me. That's the place to be."

Chapter Seven

An Affair in the Village

Revolution in Menopause

The New School for Social Research was over forty years old—older than its new dean. In fact my predecessor, Clara Mayer, had served in that office a term almost equal to my age.

In standing up to Nicholas Murray Butler's version of Columbia University, Charles Beard, Thorstein Veblen, James Harvey Robinson, and others, made the birth of the New School a noble celebration. They celebrated a human mind capable of renewing itself regardless of age and previous state of uncredentialed servitude. Later, in the rescue of Hitler's intellectual victims, Alvin Johnson and his supporters showed how noble the human enterprise can be. If the New School in its graduate operation is now basically indistinguishable from Columbia, if Columbia in fact is its secret model, the midwives at its birth cannot be blamed. And who can explain the School's lack of passion when the mainland Chinese, the

Hungarian, Cuban and black refugees knocked on the door of the Rescue House and found no one at home?

Revolutions are made, not born. And once a revolution succeeds, once the Southern plantation owners, the Boston merchants, the commissars have a success to defend, the revolution is probably lost forever.

The "Greatness through Bankruptcy" Principle

I distinctly remember being told, when the board committee bought me a very expensive lunch at Charles French Restaurant on Sixth Avenue, that the one thing I would not have to worry about, should I accept their invitation to become dean, was money. The new dean would be expected to worry about *education*.

Clara Mayer, the School's first and only dean, was retiring against her will at something over seventy. Though the School had used up two or three presidents during the few years since Alvin Johnson had retired, at almost ninety years of age, for all practical purposes he and Dean Mayer had been it. They had been great, but now it was time for a change. Everything had to be re-examined, aired afresh, sunned, renovated. Obviously a new dean couldn't do all that and worry about money too. The board member telling me these things was one of New York's most respected financiers. It just never occurred to me to ask to see the School's books, to talk with its accountants. Accepting their invitation to be dean, I was prepared to think exclusively about *education*.

In one of his war books Winston Churchill tells how *he* put together the giant flotilla for the North Africa invasion, how *he* issued the directives assembling the battalions, how *he* multiplied, added, and divided the fire power, ordered the necessary aircraft, and how *he personally* checked off the supply requisitions—the bags of potatoes, the kegs of rum, the crates of mess kits, the tubes of toothpaste required to sustain the great campaign. Being younger then, I did not think of wars in this dimension. It never occurred to me that the troops would need some toilet tissue, or that if they did, I would have to be concerned about that too. I came to this campaign with grand battle plans sketched out on global maps, more in the image of MacArthur wading ashore in his hundred-and-fifty-dollar English boots than of a Pentagon flunky checking off lists of BVD's. The lavish luncheon at Charles's fortified this image of how it would be.

My battle plan became a little unsettled during my first week in office when I discovered, quite casually while in the process of deciding some little thing, that the School was virtually bankrupt.

Such a discovery would never surprise me now. From the University of Chicago through City University, I have yet to be employed by an academic institution which was not balancing precariously on the brink of insolvency. Bankruptcy is not only "normal" among such enterprises, it is one of the basic indices of respectability and of educational strength. Bankruptcy is a significant part of the definition of "nonprofit." Nonprofit, I have discovered, does not mean that those employed by the institution do not profit. Quite the opposite, it means that their rate of profit is so great that the corporation as a whole is not profitable. The closer the institution comes to complete fiscal collapse, allegedly the more expensive and thus qualitatively superior is the educational activity it conducts. The trick in this trade is to come as close to collapse as one can without collapsing. The point is always to spend more than what was originally intended so that the various philanthropists backing you are properly impressed by the importance of what you are doing. An educational institution, by law, cannot be profitable for those who fund it. For everybody else, except perhaps the students, it is strictly for profit.

The New School, traditionally supported mainly by tuition income, had been caught for several years between a stationary student enrollment and a rapidly rising cost of operation. Its educational reputation was soaring, i.e., its deficits annually had risen to an impressive part of its total operating costs. The graduate part of the operation, magically somehow, always seemed to cost more than it took in. This meant that the small and struggling new upper division college and the large adult and evening programs had to earn "profits" so that the graduate faculty could continue to maintain its peculiar way-of-scholarly-life.

Deficits now ranged respectably between $300,000 and $500,000 per annum. And these dollars, graciously, had been supplied each year largely by a few dedicated friends of the School on its board—like Jacob M. Kaplan, the Albert Lists, whose interests veered toward the arts and scholarships for African students, and by Dean Mayer herself, whose family's philanthropy had mounted to about $100,000 in gifts to the School annually. A dean-in-office who also represents major philanthropy to the institution the dean administers is a unique phenomenon in American higher education. It carries with it not only the proof of an extraordinary dedication to the cause, but also some challenging administrative complications. In my own case, I had to prove my dedication in a different way—but a way equally complicated administratively.

But now, as the dollar gap was growing, a new restiveness had arisen among the gap fillers, the philanthropic dentists. This led to a second surprising discovery during my first week as dean of the New School. Henry David, the School's new president, was in an escalating state of warfare with powerful elements of the board which had appointed him. He had been president for only a few

months when he called me in Detroit. His newness, his declared desire for change, were a big part of the enticement
of the situation. To be a new dean, harbinger of change,
to serve an old president would not have been realistic.
But under a new man, himself eager to pursue new courses,
there was a fighting chance—or so it seemed.

A continuing state of some tension among a faculty, its
administrators, the students, and their governing boards
is, I am sure, a sign of institutional health, a part of the
constitutional harmony required for an educational institution's corporeal and psychological well-being. But open
warfare between a chief officer and those to whom he is
responsible is quite another matter.

This case was complicated by the fact that Clara Mayer,
my predecessor, did not approve of Henry David's presidency, which meant that, sight unseen, she disapproved of
the young twerp from Detroit he had chosen to replace her.
She made an honest effort to provide me with a conventional "briefing," but for reasons I did not understand at
the time at all, she was as cold as the icecap in Greenland
and indecently proper for a New School dean, even a retiring one over seventy. At the time, Dean Mayer was not
speaking to President David, nor were they visiting each
other's offices. It was a rather novel situation in which to
promote the free trade of ideas and all that.

The School's pressing fiscal crisis compelled a reconsid-
eration of the tactics for educational reform. The president's difficulties with his board in part turned upon his
own strategy for coping with the crisis, for "turning the
School around." Henry David was a scholar of reputation
who, before coming to the School's graduate faculty, had
taught at Columbia's School of Business. There was some
difference of opinion in all sectors of the School about
where its future greatness was to be found. Dr. David was
developing his own versions, some of which, I thought,
were at least worthy of debate. It seemed to me that he was

prepared to take great risks to improve the School's quality, according to certain conventions of Morningside Heights. But after all, he was president, fully entitled to promote his own solutions to the problems and to expect the support of his executive staff in the process. The unusual part of President David's approach was that the greatness he sought was to be achieved more or less instantaneously, and certain aspects of achieving this goal required at least doubling the scope of our operational deficits more or less instantaneously, albeit, it was alleged, temporarily. This meant that at least for a while, generous donors should be prepared to donate even more generously.

This part of his solution left some members of his board a little less than overwhelmingly enthusiastic. To the extent that any of them thought beyond the personality part of the conflict at all, some of them believed that the future of the School was being hung on a dichotomy. Either the place might be converted quickly into a unique little Columbia in Greenwich Village, or the whole thing might quickly be washed down the Twelfth Street drain. These are not exactly the kind of options big donors like to face. Faculty members whose jobs are involved are likely to be a little wary of such formulations too. The president in his own way was thinking big—the only way for a president to think. But down in my office, even during my first week, we were estimating student enrollments in the five hundred adult and evening courses we offered, multiplying that by the tuition charges, dividing that, course by course, by our faculty salary obligations, subtracting from that a factor equal to the cost of heat and electricity, and hoping that the grand result would be something a bit more than even so that a reasonable contribution could be made to the graduate faculty payroll.

It was a delicious way to begin a reform movement, to move forward a little bit the meaning of our civilization. My introduction to educational politics in New York City convinced me, a young adult, that I needed some intensive adult education. Having been taken in by the great university-in exile, I started out feeling desperately the need to be rescued.

Bronx Cheer

The New York *Post* reporter was charmed by the fact that I had arrived in New York, she thought, from Iowa. Consequently, when the paper devoted its profile column to my arrival, it reduced all of my brilliant achievements in Detroit and Chicago, about which I had talked at great length with the reporter, to an obscure line or two, featuring instead the patent absurdity of the situation: a New School dean harvested, literally, out of a corn field in the remote West somewhere. The reporter gave me the impression that Greenwich Village had never taken in an Indian before.

I fell neatly into her trap, for my ignorance of New York was from her point of view amusingly stupendous. She asked me where I had decided to settle, and I was, fortunately, aware of the fact that there were five boroughs and that the one in which we had rented an apartment was called the Bronx. Which part of the Bronx, she asked? As my terrace commanded a spectacular view of the Jersey Palisades, and as I was acquainted with the city's map revealing that this was as far west in the city as one could go, I replied that we had settled on the west side of the Bronx. How far north? she asked. Turning off the Henry Hudson Parkway to go home, I used the 236th Street exit. Armed with this additional fact, the reporter, smiling, informed me that I didn't live in *the* Bronx at all. I lived, she said, in Riverdale, the part with the high-rise apartments rather than the high-status single-family houses; my rent was undoubtedly so many dollars a month; my children undoubtedly went to such and such public schools; and eventually I would no doubt join this synagogue or that temple; and did I have a swimming pool on the premises? She made it perfectly clear that I had chosen a low-camp neighborhood, quite unfitting for a New School dean, but perhaps rescued by a spectacular river view, if I really had one, and the swimming pool, if there was one.

It was an amazing performance on her part, an incredible series of Sherlock Holmes deductions. But I have subsequently discovered that New Yorkers peg one another with great precision this way. Give a person your street address, and they can tell you immediately whether Jews are encouraged to live on that block of Park Avenue, your annual total income after taxes, the name of the butcher with whom you do business, and which television programs you are likely to watch. The nature of one's citizenship in this great city is intimately connected precisely to where one lives. To a very great extent the city is a mosaic of residential ghettos from which many other things follow. Naturally, its educational institutions, higher and lower, tend to reflect these important facts and to define their own ghetto meanings accordingly.

As a matter of fact, other occasions were provided in the beginning for me to examine my barbarity in a completely fresh light. I knew, of course, at the New School on the graduate side, that most of the professors who had been rescued were great Jewish scholars out of a rich German cultural tradition. But I was not quite prepared for the party one of them gave to introduce the new dean to distinguished scholarly colleagues in the city. His apartment on the East Side of Manhattan was held up by floor-to-ceiling bookshelves containing a stunning array of rare and precious tomes mostly in the German language. The soiree was full of distinguished-looking gentlemen and no-nonsense middle-aged lady professors, all talking German among themselves, drinking dark beer or some other concoction out of ornate steins, bowing from the waist, hand-kissing and clicking their heels at one another. Now, I had read Louis Wirth's discussion of Jewish pecking orders in his wonderful little book on the development of the Chicago ghettos, but neither in Waterloo, Chicago nor Detroit did I have occasion to try out my conversational German at a cocktail party full of rescued Jews. I suddenly realized once again how wise my grandparents had been, acquiring this German-type name of mine, en route from the Polish ghetto to this American one in which I now found myself. It was an amazing demonstration of how cosmopolitan New York really was and how much this cowboy had yet to learn.

Orozco's Drawstrings

The New School was a place to which you brought your latest idea whose brilliance had been ignored everywhere else. If everywhere else had said no, there was a good chance that the New School would not only say yes but also present you publicly, put you in a room where your idea could be conveyed to others, and dignify, somewhat, your insanity. This used to be the New School's greatest strength, and within a certain range of subject matter regarding the implementation of such insanity, Dean Mayer was, in my opinion, one of the most brilliant educators in the world. Within the ranges of her interests and background, she had a deep and abiding sensitivity to what ought to be encouraged. Accordingly, our faculty was one of the strangest assemblages on earth, and my daily appointment book—the people who came in off the street to see the dean of the New School—was like a Rudyard Kipling adventure story.

I found myself being invited to buy theaters, convert the School into an Esperanto publishing house, reform

New York through yoga or have classes on stock investments conducted in subway terminals. I found myself in
the middle of the Velikovsky controversy, or discussing
lecture fees with Robert Lowell or Max Lerner, or trying
to find Marianne Moore's house in Brooklyn so that I
could deliver her to the Sculpture Court to read poems. I
found myself learning more about actors' methods than
there are actors. If all the aspirant painters' portfolios I
looked at were hung end to end, New York would be converted into a giant museum, which might not be a bad
idea. I actually met a man who had really discovered not a
fountain, but a gurgling pool of perpetual youth somewhere slightly south of Biloxi; and an Austrian inventor
whose machine, burping on my desk and connected to my
wall with a purple extension cord, would teach me Japanese or Icelandic while I slept or read the morning's
Times. The educational opportunities that came my way
were not only higher—they were slightly out of sight. At
least at the end of a typical day, I felt rather orbited.

In time I was conditioned so that nothing that came
into my office really surprised me. But in the beginning
there were some wonderful surprises. One day, for example, during the first few weeks after my arrival, a small-
ish man, well over seventy, appeared in my office and announced that he was Mr. Irving Berlin. He told me that
he had been in and around New York for many years and
had never seen the New School's famous Orozco murals.
He happened to be in the neighborhood, and he wanted
to see the frescos. But he had been told by some functionary down in the lobby that only the dean possessed "the
keys to the paintings," and only the dean could show them.

The New School has decorated itself with some marvelous art, most of it displayed in clear public view. There are
the Ecuadorian Camilo Egas's magnificent murals,
Thomas Hart Benton's monstrosities, a splendid Noguchi
slab in the sculpture court, Cadaret's riots of abstract

color. I had heard about Orozco's work, reputedly the most controversial thing of its kind in the city, and indeed, one of the rare examples of his talent in New York. But I had yet to find time to see the paintings, and I didn't have the vaguest notion that I possessed the keys to them, whatever that meant. But I did. They were in my secretary's desk, and having obtained them, I escorted Mr. Berlin to what was supposedly the faculty lounge.

We unlocked the door and turned on the lights to behold four walls draped from ceiling to floor. The drapes were on drawstrings, and the drawstrings had little padlocks on them. Additional keys were produced, padlocks unlocked, and the drapes drawn. We had penetrated an elaborate security system to get down to the art.

Orozco had meant to portray twentieth-century revolutionary ferment, particularly in the parts of the world yet to be overcome by industrialization. One wall was devoted to the artist's native Mexico, showing a great pyramid of Yucatán, a dignified grouping of peon slaves, and the face of the revolutionary hero Carillo Puerto, properly shown in a frame of the revolutionary banners of his time. Another wall told an Indian story. There, magnificently, sat Gandhi, his challenge to British imperialism contained in his mournful, patient, bespectacled eyes. He, together with representatives of British business exploitation, looked upon a raging scene of colonial violence, raised sabers and bayonets, uniformed white forces repressing the peasant slave masses. A third wall celebrated the Russian Revolution. There, beneath a massive poster of Lenin, marched heroic Stalin and his multiracial cohorts, off to build some great new society. On a final panel sit the races of man at a peace table, a large book open before them, its pages blank, on which, Orozco said, mankind could write its own future. About this wall an official art guide issued by the New School reads: "Much criticism of a racial character has been directed against Orozco's peace table, with representatives of colored races honored equally with the whites." But those authorized to speak in behalf of the New School continue in a calm and scholarly manner: "The idea is gaining currency that some such union of races will be necessary if peace is ever to be established on a firm foundation." All contingencies, with dignity, must officially be provided for, possibly.

Before World War II and the great Russian resistance to the German invasion, Orozco's murals had apparently agitated various and sundry leftish factions, particularly the Trotskyites who resented the glorification of Stalin. But it was after the War, under the heat of Joe McCarthy, that the board of the New School, in the name of protecting valuable art from hostile defacement, ordered the walls draped—I think with the help of Macy's.

But now it was a decade after that, and the academic processes being what they are, even at the famous New School in New York, the murals remained draped, padlocked—rare gems hidden in the locked lounge. As the School's little art catalogue says: "American conservatives were almost equally bitter, being addicts of the quaint notion that American morale is so weak that any suggestion that progress of any kind may be made under another system is likely to shatter American faith in the American way of life." The faith of the board of the New School seemed equally fragile and quaint to me. So, early in my career there, I performed quite ceremoniously what was probably my most profoundly significant educational act at the New School for Social Research.

After Mr. Berlin left me I sneaked back up to the lounge alone, and borrowing my secretary's scissors, cut Orozco's drawstrings. It was late afternoon, and I retired then to the bar at Enrico & Paglieri's across the street on Eleventh. And quietly I explored my puzzlement, pondering these profound differences between Waterloo and New York.

What in the hell was going on here? I'm still trying to figure out the answer to that.

"Dear Dean, Sir"

I think that in the later years of its respectable success, the things that the New School had done to rescue people embarrassed somewhat some of those who were rescued. It also embarrassed some of those who inherited the tradition and the necessity to reinterpret the mission.

I have met some arrogant people in the course of my professional affairs, some even on the faculty at the New School. But more degrading than the kind of fear and ignorance which makes for arrogance is the kind of fear or cowardice that makes for obsequiousness. Imagine me, out of my background, in my mid-thirties, confronted by a man more than old enough to be my father, author of five or six learned books, heavy German accent, addressing me as "Dear Dean, Sir." I do not mean in the salutation of a letter: I mean sitting there, across my desk, speaking to me this way. Every salary negotiation is an indignity unless the man arguing in behalf of the value of his services is not confused by false professional notions about prestige and by the need, at some time, to talk about money. Among the great German university traditions for which the New School once stood (but has now abandoned) is to pay men for a course of lectures on the basis of a direct relationship between salary and the number of tuition-paying students the course attracts. Both the evils and the merits of such a system have been thoroughly discussed by Max Weber in his perceptive essay "On Science as a Profession." It is an un-American alternative to the trade union option.

But there is a certain European mentality that exaggerates the worst in the bureaucratic constructs we invent to regulate decent human intercourse. Ever since I first knew him and to this day, this fine European professor insists on calling me Dear Dean, Sir. I tried once to ask him not to do that, but I knew, the moment I asked, that I had made a mistake. It was a case in which there was no possible retreat from mutual insult. He resented talking to me the only way he could. And I resented being talked to that way. His past and mine did not fit together too well, and although we always reached workable results, neither of us was happy. He was an extreme example of a larger problem. It is not nice to be saved by something one feels is inferior to oneself. In fact, it is as unpleasant to have to be saved at all as it is to have to save someone.

There were superb European professors teaching in the evening programs at the New School who expressed, in one way or another, a deep disdain and contempt for the quality and purposes of the students they taught, whose tuition was so essential to their livelihood. What a curious quirk that this raw and rough American society should turn out to be the best-equipped to help save some of the finest remnants of an older, if not of a superior, culture.

In theory the most beautiful thing about the New School was the reasonably equitable division of knowledge, expertise and wisdom in any classroom where students and a professor met. As most of the students were grown-up people, surviving in New York City one way or another, they all came to the situation knowing some things the professors did not. Men were teaching French to bank presidents and corporation lawyers who knew things the French professor desperately wanted to know. But, unhappily traditional presumptions too frequently got in the way, frustrating the honest implementation of fair trade. It is in the nature of our profession, I guess—at least until recently—that the poorer shall teach the richer. It is unfortunate that those who claim to know more by definition turn out to be those who teach the ones who know less, even while being dependent upon the more ignorant for their own survival. It is a curious fate, a terrible injustice that worldly success is not always achieved in direct proportion to the state of one's knowledge and refinement. No one really likes to be called "culturally disadvantaged" or "underdeveloped," even when calling him that is meant to be for his own good. This is simply the reverse of the other resentment.

There was a very huge gap indeed between what the renegades from Columbia had in mind when they started the New School, and what the European professors made of it after it rescued them. About the time I came there, due to retirements and death, professional mobility and resignations, there was an almost even balance between the Europeans and the younger Americans coming in to replace them. It was a situation which should have made for some heroic controversies in which the best and worst of the European approach to the mind could confront the best and the worst of the American. But there were no real controversies because everyone ultimately wanted the same thing. It was neither the Platonists versus the Aristotelians, nor the applied versus the theoretical. In psychology, of course, and elsewhere, there were sects and feuds, but finally, everything was neatly ranked, departmentalized and tenured in a manner clearly understood by all. I thought that after the School got over being bankrupt, then we might devote ourselves to some really significant institutional crises. But it didn't work that way at all. Once the enrollments began to increase and the deficits were turned into handsome new surpluses, all the attention turned to the redivision of the larger pie.

After a year or two, the graduate faculty asked me to address one of its learned seminars. They assembled to hear what I thought and, hopefully, to find out what I might be planning to do. We all started out historically, but it ended up rather hysterically. We were referring to different parts of the history. I reminded them of what the School had said about itself in its earliest bulletins. One of the first, issued during the Great Depression, said:

> Technical progress is transforming the basis of our economic life. The relations of our country to the world at large are assuming new forms. Our legal and political institutions are being subjected to unprecedented strains. The physical sciences move restlessly forward. Modernism is advancing rapidly . . . Confronted by the bewildering problems of the time, men and women take a harshly critical view of their earlier education which failed to prepare them adequately. . . .

And in the School's official catalogue for the fall just before we entered the war against Hitler, the introduction read:

> The New School was founded . . . in a time of great confusion of economic, social and political ideas . . . There was widespread acceptance of the notion that study and thought were essentially futile and ingenuous. What was needed was enthusiasm and action. Fortunately this form of obscurantism is disappearing. In the life of certain European peoples we may now observe the effects of impulsive and irrational political action. They are not such as to inspire emulation.

These weird and alien nonacademic statements, so unlike the way Harvard, Columbia, Yale or Chicago presented themselves were not what my distinguished colleagues wanted to hear, even though such words may have said what they really wanted to practice.

Morris Cohen, whose memory I revere, once wrote: "The liberal views life as an adventure in which we must take risks in new situations, but in which there is no guarantee that the new will always be the good or the true." He was right. But it is not "new" that I would emphasize here, but the problem of taking risks. About those we have abused the most, what risks do we seriously expect them to take? And if the ghetto is the only way of life we have allowed the blacks, the Jews or the professors to know, then when they are set free to build the new life should they not, naturally, build new ghettos in our own image? In the first instance it has not been the minorities in our country who have advocated the ghetto. The ghetto is really the majority's invention here, as it always was in Europe. The minority advocates the ghetto after it's in it. Such advocacy, then, is a way of surviving.

Orchestrations

Eventually President David's ship sank in the stormy waters where he sailed. And Robert MacIver became acting president of the School.

MacIver was an astonishment. Of all the men I have served, none has been more decisive than he. Or more skilled in making it clear to others where he stood. Or more courageous in standing up for his convictions and his decisions. Or, given the brevity of his regime, more productive. The Center for Urban Affairs—probably the most important new venture at the New School in more than a decade—was essentially Bob MacIver's achievement. And he was the way he was on a two- or three-day week. When it was necessary for him to be there, he was there, but when he was there, he *was* there. He was writing still another book, and he loved his walks in the woods in the Palisades where he lived, along the trails where he discovered the magic mushrooms about whose identity and living habits he was truly an expert. One of the great adventures on Martha's Vineyard in the summer was to assemble at Menemsha's country store to join Bob MacIver on one of his mushroom safaris.

MacIver clearly thought that the progress of the School was important, but he had lived long enough to know that to promote the interests of the institution well he had to respect carefully the composite of self-interests which defined his own humanity. For the most astonishing thing about Bob MacIver was that he came to his presidency nearing his eightieth birthday.

MacIver and one other man caused me to consider with very meticulous care what the word "New" meant in the title of the New School for Social Research. When Horace M. Kallen, who was among the original faculty of the School, asked the young new dean to teach a seminar on educational philosophy with him, he too was on the threshold of his ninth decade of living. Dr. Kallen's challenge, frankly, frightened me half out of my wits. By reputation the man was a monument: Santayana's student, editor of his *Some Problems in Philosophy;* disciple and honored student of William James, author then of twenty-eight books, elder statesman of adult education—a living legend, ancient enough to be revered for his survival capacity, if nothing else. It was the combination of his stature and age which made the prospect of sharing a classroom with him so frightening. I *knew* that the gap between him and me on the main issues could never be bridged, and that to be true to myself in any dialogue with him I would have to expose the distance between us. One can disagree with the past and still respect it. But in the presence of a group of students and in the heat of debate, to be true and gentle, firm and respectful was an assignment I approached with trepidation. To even undertake the assignment was probably insane. It was the same feeling I had conjured up in law school just before a final examination about whose subject matter I was not completely sure.

We gave alternate lectures, each beginning by commenting upon and criticizing what the other had said the time before. By the third week of the course I had begun *my* ninth decade of life. The gap was there, but Kallen had utterly outflanked me. Prematurely wise, his gentle but rapier-sharp youthfulness exposed my pompous antiquity on almost all issues. He was taking space walks and going to Mars, leaving me in the shade of Athens' ancient groves or on the curb of Twelfth Street. It was an extraordinary reversal of roles. As I bravely tried "to be true" to myself, I came to realize how uptight I had become.

It is no accident that what Kallen has said and thought since the 1920's turns out to be now what so many of our brightest young people mean. His revolution is in progress and unfinished. While we are busy building our educational kettles bigger and bigger, and while the fires of America beneath the kettles are burning hotter and hotter, Kallen reminds us that the process is not meant to melt everything down into some common base metal. When he points out that a drum is different from a fiddle, and that only out of the defense and mastery of the uniqueness of each can a great masterpiece successfully be orchestrated, he is saying what any great city should say to its citizens, what those students I admire most now are saying to me in their fumbling efforts to harmonize their own existence.

When his friends and colleagues celebrated Kallen's last lecture at the New School not too long ago, Kallen apologized, at eighty-seven, for nothing. In his short speech that night there was a sentence, spoken without any special emphasis at all: "I am identified with the pragmatic method, which is the scientific method—not for reconciliation, but as a way of living together." There he stood, the consummate demonstration, the test tube bubbling over with the final proof of what he meant.

Kallen was not born in this country, whose meaning he epitomizes so perfectly. His heritage is German-Jewish.

When I left the New School to go to Long Island University, I asked Kallen to join me there. He did. He packed up his books and his belongings, and with his wife, Rachael, he left his comfortable apartment near Columbia to move into LIU's tower on the perilous streets of downtown Brooklyn. Unafraid, he moved to the wild frontier, and soon, hearing aid turned up on high, he picked up an axe along with the rest of us to chop down some trees and build a log cabin out there on Flatbush Avenue. There was so much I didn't know then. I didn't know then that long before, Kallen had been rebuffed by Harvard's faculty, which earlier had awarded him its magna-cum-laude degree, or dismissed by Princeton's, or kicked out by Wisconsin's. I didn't know what Kallen knew: that in the process of becoming an American, you have to be kicked out a little. Neither Kallen nor I knew that I was on the verge of getting kicked. A bit later, we both got a little more Americanized at Long Island University in Brooklyn.

Warming LeRoi Jones

LeRoi Jones's application for a job at the New School was typical of many. He had no credentials, no prior teaching experience and no one to vouch for his potential except himself. He said he would make an absolutely superb teacher of creative writing, and besides, he desperately needed the money, however meager, such an engagement might provide.

Mr. Jones's first book had yet to be published, but I had read poems and critical articles he had written, and sitting there in my office, he wrote a very clear impression of himself. In my profession, if you're any good at all, you develop a keen intuition about people, a capacity to judge them in terms of themselves on the spot. I have made my mistakes, but in the longer pull my batting average has been pretty good. Unfortunately, a man's official credentials often do not rise to the level of his talents, and in my profession such a disparity creates a presumption difficult to rebut. My profession prefers official credentials to which a man's talents may seldom rise. We hire such men all the time, and once they get tenure, they help the profession repeat and perpetuate the mistakes they represent in the cases of many others. But a dean of the New School had no such problems. He was relatively free to make mistakes, and as there was no tenure in the adult education faculty, he could correct his mistakes in due course without too much stress or strain. Mr. Jones left my office with the job and a modest salary advance to boot.

The addition of LeRoi Jones to the faculty was a departure from the New School's style at the time. Orientals—especially the Indians teaching their various and sundry kinds of philosophy, and a Chinese or two in calligraphy and the language—were present on the faculty. There were some bona-fide African students around. But except for a few very decidedly Greenwich Village types enrolled in the art or drama workshops, there were virtually no home-grown blacks in any of the institution's categories: faculty, student, administrative, clerical or secretarial. I think I found one Negro on the faculty, and there were none on the graduate side. It was not that the School was wholly disinterested in this part of our population. It was just that whatever interest there was, was abstract, conjectural. Blacks were something one occasionally thought about, like Hopi Indians, of which the School also had none.

LeRoi probably doesn't realize even now that his employment really began the process of "integration" at the New School—wherever it has gone since and whatever that has come to mean. Mr. Jones (who has since adopted as his name "Imamu Baraka") developed a student following,

which at the New School more or less secured his continued employment. And in 1963 his first book was published, identifying him on its jacket as a member of the
faculty of the New School, an advertisement I am sure he
approved. *Blues People: Negro Music in White America,*
was dedicated to "My Parents . . . the first Negroes I ever
met." "White," of course, is a very ancient controversial
word. But "black" has yet to complete its first decade in
the special dictionary of our time, in LeRoi's dictionary or
even in mine.

There was a group in the New School called The Associates, who came as close to being an alumni organization as
the School could produce. Its members either attended or
were enrolled in courses. Many had been with the School
almost from the beginning. They were a hearty, middle-
class, reasonably affluent, mostly Jewish and almost entirely over-fifty bunch. They sponsored their own special
lectures (Max Lerner was their Richard Burton), organized art exhibits and contributed sums of money to the
School which the administration always felt were too
small. The ladies, many quite stylish and very bright,
dominated the organization, having a surplus of time and
energy to devote to such things. Hair was frequently
bleached, but skins, all, were naturally white.

One of the most decent and imaginative things the
ladies of The Associates did was to conduct book-warming
cocktail parties to honor the new publications of the faculty. Over martinis, Manhattans and highballs, shrimps,
cheeses and assorted nuts, usually in a room decorated with
flowers and art and lit by candles, the president of the
School, the dean, faculty colleagues, the author, his friends
and publisher assembled to pay homage to the man and
his new creation. These were lovely, thoughtful affairs, a
hundred to a hundred and fifty large, during which the
author sold and happily autographed several copies of his
new book under utterly proper, convivial and friendly cir-

cumstances. Authors showered with such attentions invariably responded, however biting and acrid their written
theses, with the most sentimental and heartwarming little
speeches, thanking their hostesses and the School for the
kindness.

Though anxious to get his first book selling, LeRoi was
not so sure he wanted his book warmed at the New School.
I had to sell him the idea. And the ladies, though anxious
to keep their dean happy, were not so sure they wanted to
warm LeRoi's book. Who was LeRoi Jones? A *first* book?
About jazz? Etcetera. I had to sell them the idea. (One of
the main functions of a dean is selling. His potential
customers surround him everywhere: his president, his
board, his faculty, himself.) Once finally sold, the principal
parties held a conference to negotiate the crucial details
of the proposed affair. What day? What friends did the
author propose to invite? Would the publisher be available? Copies of the book? Unfortunately LeRoi, having
decided to be warmed, was a little bit too cooperative. His
guest list exceeded three hundred. He wanted no cocktails
—only beer, beer only out of kegs. (There had never been
a keg of beer in the New School before, and the keg proposal almost led to the breakdown of negotiations.) He
wanted no speeches. The book, he said, was about black
jazz, and he wanted jazz (black)—a little group he personally knew and would provide. About the hors d'oeuvres,
he had his own ideas about what went well with jazz
and beer.

To the ladies' credit, though shocked, dismayed and
unsettled, they acquiesced after a heroic struggle. To antic-
ipate the unexpectedly large crowd, the affair was moved
from their more genteel, art-laden headquarters to the
much larger Martha Graham dance studio in the basement of the Alvin Johnson Building. There had never
been a party in the room, which had the distinction of
being perfectly round—Miss Graham's contribution to

the design of the School when she taught there. The beer was rolled in, and on the appointed day not three hundred, but six or seven hundred of the most extraordinary-looking people in New York appeared. The combo was deafening, and by six-thirty that night the New School was virtually paralyzed by the mob and the noise. The beer flowed, indeed it flooded into the gullets of the guests and onto Miss Graham's carefully waxed floor. The ladies, dutifully chapeauxed and gloved, did their best to pass around the sausages, celery stalks and potato chips, and to turn the spigots of the kegs on and off in the proper rhythm. By seven we were dancing in the studio meant for that sort of thing, and by eight things were getting slightly out of academic control.

At some point, to the blast of a trumpet and a crescendo of drums, an order of sorts was momentarily achieved. The dean and LeRoi's publisher each briefly praised the occasion for our gathering, and it was LeRoi's turn to respond. He had said "no speeches," but at the moment of truth he raised his arms for attention, motioned everyone out of the center of the room, and then with great deliberation walked slowly around the circular floor, the inner circumference of the crowd. He smiled in a kindly way upon each of us there—his dean, the black, tan and unlikely assemblage, the Village refugees and the Harlem adventurers, the ladies from the East Side and Westchester. And after one complete circuit in silence, he said; "You have just seen a young Negro in action. Now go home in peace." And so we almost did.

Before we left that night LeRoi introduced me to his mother and father—a dignified couple, he in a black suit, a red tie and a white shirt with a murderously starched collar, she in a fur wrap and very happy. They told me how proud they were of their son, though they wished that when he was asked to speak, he would speak up a bit more.

As he left, really quite pleased by how the evening had

gone, LeRoi gave me a copy of his new book which he had inscribed:

For my dean at the end of a long, long speech

It had been perfectly clear to me from the day I first met him in my office that Mr. Jones would do some creative writing, and could teach others to write creative things too.

X-ing Malcolm

In the fall of 1963 and the winter of 1964 we began to turn some of the School's attention onto black things. Black teachers were recruited and black subjects began to appear in the curriculum. We met with a group of twelve black Southern colleges at a retreat in Virginia, and began to detail plans for an interregional consortium through which numbers of students and teachers from the South could pursue their study interests in New York, while specialized talents, sources of dollar support, and unique city resources could be mobilized in New York, with the guidance of the Southern schools, and sent there. A black writers' conference was talked about, and a public presentation of leading black spokesmen of different persuasions was planned. In this connection, invitations were extended to Elijah Muhammud, Martin Luther King, Roy Wilkins, Whitney Young, Malcolm X, and others. Malcolm had broken with Elijah. He accepted our invitation, but the leader of the Black Muslims did not.

After Malcolm and the others had agreed to come, but before they were scheduled to appear, President John F. Kennedy was shot. Malcolm made his intemperate remark about people getting what they deserved, about chickens coming home to roost. Everyone was outraged, but the board of the New School concretely expressed its disapproval. It directed its dean to un-invite Malcolm. No chicken-roosting advocate was to enjoy the hospitality of the New School's platform. It was a very upsetting situation. I was cut to the quick by the Kennedy tragedy, as I was to be again but five years later when my boss, Robert Kennedy, was shot. But our faculty planning committee and our advisers in the black communities felt strongly that Malcolm X's participation was essential to the credibility of the future programs we had in mind. They thought it unfair to judge a man on the basis of one remark, and they saw in the board's action a serious threat to the freedom of the School, to faculty prerogatives, etc., etc. This sudden discovery of the limits upon the New School platform was indeed somewhat of a shock.

But under such circumstances, what do you do? The intense emotions of the time were at war with reason. And about what reason was, one could find staunch and respectable advocates on twenty different sides. If you accept the power of an office an institution provides, you exercise that power "responsibly," i.e., you subject your own intelligence to some abstract collective will, or you get out. Finally, in its own way for its own purposes, the institution wins. In this case I argued passionately for honoring our invitation to Malcolm X. Losing, I set about un-inviting him.

It was not a mission I felt I could implement through a letter, so I called and arranged to meet Malcolm at his Harlem place to explain the situation. He listened to me calmly and without any particular expression. If he felt any indignation or anger, he made no effort whatsoever to let it out. He nodded once in a while to let me know he understood my formulation of the problem. His attitude toward my dilemma was terribly unsettling. Finally he offered me a cup of tea to calm me down, and then, with great sincerity, gave me a little lecture pointedly designed to relieve me of the embarrassment I obviously felt. In the necessity to do things sometimes that I felt were wrong, he compared me with himself. He assured me that he understood such situations very well, but that sometimes events were bigger than any of us, and that perhaps we should relax a little bit about some of these things we have to do. He said he appreciated my consideration for having taken a subway all the way uptown to explain this situation. He hoped that someday we might find some common interest we could pursue together. I had come filled with concern about his feelings. I left clothed in his concern for mine.

A Little Too Old

Alvin Johnson, the Emeritus president, whose office was down the hall from the dean's, had taken a very special and sympathetic interest in my progress at the School. Many an afternoon we drank sherry together while he lit and relit his pipe, telling me the history, warning me of the pitfalls, guiding me through the intricacies of the personalities and politics of the place as he saw them. I think he liked my spirit and appreciated my hard-nosed approach to the economic survival of the School during my time there. But he thought I lacked patience and told me so, even on the afternoons he urged me on to solve quickly the pressing problems of the budget, to get the urgently needed curricular renovations under way. "We'll be shopping for a new president by-and-by," he would say. "Cultivate the graduate faculty a bit . . . be patient."

Alvin Johnson was a giant oak who grew from taproots sunk in a Midwestern field. I have seen him on a blazing hot summer's afternoon, over ninety, cutting the tall grass behind his Nyack house with a scythe, honest Nebraska sweat pouring off his brow. Dr. Johnson, I think, changed New York more than New York changed him. But it was the wrong time for a scythe at the New School, or perhaps, the New School was cutting in the wrong field. Its graduate faculty had been cultivated more than a bit. It has prospered. Its enrollments and classrooms have multiplied. Its pay scale for faculty has topped Harvard's. Now it is one of the largest graduate schools in the city, and to the extent that it still allows—over the objections of some of its faculty—New Yorkers to pursue their master's and doctoral degrees on a part-time basis harmonious with their adult-life commitments in the city, it performs a unique and valuable function. Through its adult programs the School continues to be a vibrant and exciting life line connecting its essentially middle-class clientele with life-long learning opportunities.

I had come to New York ready for an adult's education. I learned that it is not only the time and place but, until he is dead, the student's attitude that counts. At the New School my attitude changed somewhat. The youngest spirits I found there were all over eighty—Kallen, MacIver and Johnson. For me, they were new—not the School. Then, in 1964, on the threshold of its first half-century, the New School for Social Research seemed, prematurely, a little too old.

Somehow the murder of John Kennedy had left attitudes within the New School strangely untouched, or so it appeared. Nineteen sixty- four was the year that Berkeley blew, the first spring and summer of widespread rioting in the streets of our cities. European friends on the faculty recoiled from these events, or drew ominous parallels between them and what they had known in the thirties in Central Europe. And so many of the young Americans coming in to replace the older Europeans as they retired or died spoke a language that neither I nor many of the Europeans seemed to understand. They were bright, technology-oriented scientists—in some ways, I thought, more careerist in outlook than some of the German academics they were replacing.

In retrospect the New School looks like a disconnection or an interlude between what I had experienced at Wayne in Detroit and what I was to face later in Brooklyn and beyond. Perhaps somehow then I sensed that. Now, in the prosperity and success of its older age, in the full flower of its most recent researches, the New School may yet be new again. It may rediscover what it is supposed to mean. But during my last year or so there I had gotten mixed up with a place called Long Island University in downtown Brooklyn. By the summer of 1964 I was ready to go there, and I did.

Chapter Eight

The Battle of Long Island

The Graveyard of the Moths

Once upon a time at Long Island University on the front porch of Brooklyn's black neighborhoods, diverse personalities, like moths around a front-porch bulb in the middle of a black summer's night, converged on some powerfully hot issues. Mysteriously they appeared out of the emptiness of the night, some on wings fluttering nervously, timidly exploring; others unafraid, big and bold. Some flexed their wings like peacock's tails, glistening, iridescent jeweled fans; others spread faded grays and browns, heavily powdered like the cheeks of old ladies.

By the dawn's early light, when the man who had carelessly left the porchlight on all night came to turn it off, a magical democratic process had transformed the bold and the beautiful, the ugly and the timid into a perfect state of equality. It had been a momentous night, for together they had all seen the light. Together now, in the cool morning, they shared the insect garbage heap there on the slats of the front porch. Like all places of the dead, the graveyard of the moths makes one wonder. This flight of death, this single night's debauche, what did it mean? This sterile bulb, now cold and alone, once bright and hot—off and on, a mere whimsy?

The moths are so stupid, knowing little more alive than they do dead. These fragile insects, so trivial and irrelevant in the magnificent master scheme of solar systems and galaxies, why must they dirty up the porch? Consider our board of trustees, dedicated and neutral, its articles of incorporation austerely indifferent to the carnage! Today, like yesterday, it serves the public still. Consider the chancellor of the corporation, conjurer of the switch, idly fingering his magic medieval medallion certifying exactly what he is. Today, like yesterday, he turns it on and off, off and on, as it suits his whim—without regard to race, color or creed, light or dark, life or death.

This pile of seared antennae and fragile wings burned crisp, these dead things, did they really live last night? In some perfectly round office high in a Manhattan tower on Madison Avenue, connected by orbiting satellite to Albany instantly, they have decided to redevelop the front porch, throwing in the house for fun. According to the Law of Model Cities and Instant-University, Sections 301 to 723, amended by the acts of 1967, 1968, 1776, and A.D. 2012, they have decided to burn it all down, sweep it all up, and replace it with a plastic superblock, landscaped with rubber orchid vines and lit by their automated neon lights. It will be the Harvard of Flatbush and win HEW's Finchley prize and five honorary degrees from St. John's. And crowds of people will come to see from faraway places like Bedford Avenue and Kappock Street and exclaim: "It is the Taj Mahal for the Brain! The Anti-Ghetto! The United Nations Plaza of the Future and a Cure for City University's Drug Addiction!"

But what about moths? This disturbs the redevelopers;

they want it all to be so natural. High in their Madison Avenue tower they have called in an expert from Pratt Institute on the edge of the black neighborhood to help them design a moth that flies, and according to the schedule announced in the official bulletin, dies each night. The redevelopers, having called up the Ford Foundation and talked with the man in Albany, still can't even make one little grubby insect that flies and neatly on schedule dies. They are very upset, and perhaps, deep in their hearts, a little sad. For in the wreckage of the moths, they may see a glimmer of the truth, and they are forewarned of their own doom.

The moths did what by their nature they had to do. But on Madison Avenue, on the morning after, the God of Choice, bankrupt, reigns supreme.

Moral: *For every flock of moths, there should be some balls.*

Jocks in the Powder Room

I have found that men—and institutions, too—who are unsure of themselves and of what they are supposed to be often caricature expertly what they are. Ugly ducklings who think they are swans are ludicrous. Ill equipped to perform swanly acts, they sometimes are hilariously funny. But like all high comedy, such caricatures contain a delicate pathos which, if mishandled, can abort, becoming either very sad or just plain maudlin.

At Long Island University's Brooklyn Center in Flatbush, the door to the chancellor's office was but a few yards from where the provost, who was supposed to run the campus, held forth. Both rooms were in the office tower of the old Brooklyn Paramount Theater building. Both commanded spectacular views, beyond the battered Texaco station across the way, of Junior's delicatessen restaurant, one of New York City's better kosher corned-beef and dill-pickle dispensaries. Flatbush Avenue, always choking with trucks and cars, a continuous symphonic performance of rumbles, horns and occasional backfires, was the campus walk. The tree that grows in Brooklyn was nowhere to be seen. Around the corner, beneath Flatbush's perpetual dusty, fumy pall, the soccer field bravely committed photosynthesis, simulating a campus green. The whole center was enclosed with fences. Its gates could be locked, and for a while after I left, they were.

Wall to wall with the chancellor's office in a converted bowling alley-garage, the registrar punched the eight thousand students' IBM cards, and the bursar collected each semester a $700 or $800 tuition check from each student, or a reasonably contrived excuse in lieu thereof. Across what was optimistically called "The Mall" was the old Maltz warehouse building, a white elephantine ugliness in which, before Bill Zeckendorf helped the university acquire it for future growth, a printing company was housed along with outfits which manufactured dolls and lampshades. It was now being converted into a place for the manufacture of the Humanities for future student customers.

Piled nine stories high on top of the chancellor's head, the students convened in offices originally made for insurance brokers, dentists, chiropodists, collection agencies and other essential community activities, now all efficiently transformed into crowded classroom slums. And in the Old Paramount's main auditorium itself, right there among the ghosts of Eddie Cantor, Fannie Brice and Rudy Vallee, was New York City's most fabulous collegiate gymnasium, the famous basketball boards of the Blackbirds, once a national powerhouse until the fires of bribery and scandal left its fame in ashes. But remnants of past glories remained: the tattered plush red velvet curtain separating basketball from the gymnastic apparatus backstage; the chipped, gilded cupids winging their way around the theater's sensational old organ tubes; the rococo, Neo-Renaissance glass light fixtures dimly illuminating the mezzanine, the upper balconies and the peanut galleries. Even after it was converted, more than three thousand students could still be jammed into the rapidly deteriorating stuffed seats in the room, if there was ever an occasion to get three thousand of them there. It remains one of my favorite rooms in New York, a marvelous and unexpected carnival of things to look at, an excitement of circus smells, animal sweat and wisps of grease paint. The coaches of LIU put on their jocks and sweat suits each day in a carpeted former ladies' powder room, now fitted with lockers and a shower stall, concessions to the cosmetics of the sporting life.

It was, in other words, an absolutely perfect setting in which a *chancellor* and a *provost* might meet, exalted officers of an ancient fiefdom, feudal barons of the academic freedom lands, empowered by the various symbols and seals of their offices to transact the most important affairs of higher learning's medieval realm. Thousands of the peasants came to the place each morning, emerging in columns of four from the nearby subway tubes. The provost usually walked to work from the elegant federal house the university provided for him in nearby Brooklyn Heights. But Chancellor R. Gordon Hoxie rode to this magnificent castle each morning on a prancing, gay black charger, a uniformed coachman driving four hundred Cadillac horsepowers, a carefully groomed thoroughbred out of his C. W. Post stables (the university's Nassau County Campus in Old Westbury on Long Island).

Even before I met Robert Kennedy I had acquired the habit of working in my shirtsleeves. But not when the provost entered the chancellor's throne room next door. On a hot July day the year before, he had explained to me the protocol governing such audiences. So when his secretary called and said the chancellor wanted to see me immediately, I put on my jacket and wondered, "What now?" There were plenty of possibilities, for the issues outstanding between us had multiplied like the dormitories and deficits at C. W. Post and the Southampton Center way out on the end of Long Island, the third LIU outpost for the higher learning.

R. Gordon Hoxie, chancellor of Long Island Multiversity, maintained between Southampton and Brooklyn four offices that I knew of, each equipped with hot-and cold-running secretaries and the latest-model electric typewriters. At least in this respect he made very clear what was what to the chairman of his board, the real estate tycoon Bill Zeckendorf, who seemed to get along with only one office. But Gordon's offices were all square, while Bill's was round. Gordon had at least sixteen corners he could back people into. Bill just chased things around in circles, terminating conferences at whatever point he decided was the end. Sitting at his round desk in his round office served by a round elevator tube going up to his private dining room, he was fond of saying; "Wherever Caesar sits, there is the head of the table." Geographically at least, Rome was a drop in the bucket compared to the Empire, and Caesar's proconsul necessarily was a man on horseback.

But of all of Dr. Hoxie's offices, his Brooklyn room was the grandest. It must once have been the headquarters for the Sol Hurok of Flatbush. Cavernous, dark, it was like a perpetual theater lobby, meant to impress but somehow never giving the impression of being the real scene of the action. One entered there expecting to get his ticket punched so he could move on to some inner sanctum to see the real show. The chancellor sat in there behind a huge mahogany desk, enthroned on an altar about one mile in from the door to the room. When you came in you had to wave or shout in order to let him know you arrived and spotted him off in the gloomy, oak-paneled distance.

On this occasion, in February of 1967, the chancellor was unusually cordial, walking the mile from his desk to award me an especially firm handshake. This unusual friendliness immediately alerted my inner antiaircraft artillery stations. Sirens began blaring, and inside me I grabbed my helmet and began running for cover. We sat down at his huge empty conference table, the two of us alone. And then he said, as sweetly as he had ever addressed me, "Bill, I think you'd better resign now and start writing that book you've been talking about. Of course, if you don't want to resign, then I'll have to fire you. Now let's discuss the details."

And, in due course, we did.

"So Jump Already!"

About a year before the chancellor summoned me to "discuss the details," a great international writers' conference was assembled at LIU in Brooklyn. It was an unlikely show for the Old Paramount on Flatbush—forty or fifty literary figures from around the world were on stage. Most of them had grown up during World War II and had emerged in print during the age of the Cold War, Vietnam, global race riots, student rebellions and space walks. Thousands of New Yorkers as well as students and teachers from around the country came. The debates and discussions raged for more than a week around the theme of "Alienation and Commitment."

The voices of the writers reflected the dissonance of their various purposes and places and of the times. The Czechs, the Hungarians and the Yugoslavs came, but at the last moment the Russians and the East Germans did not. From East Berlin poet Gunther Kunert wrote: "I'm very sorry, more than sorry, but I didn't get permission to depart. I can't come. And I don't understand why not. The refusal is motivated with one nebulous sentence: 'There are many heavy political, cultural, moralistic reasons which speak against the journey.' That's the damned fact I can't change. So I wish my fellow writers a great success. With melancholy, Kunert." The shadow of a sad silence was cast upon the conference at the outset—of a silence imposed upon a man who wanted to speak and felt it his duty to do so, but couldn't.

But George Steiner, then a Cambridge don, opened the debates stating a case for a *self-imposed* silence. "The question of whether the poet should speak or be silent, of whether the language is in condition to serve his purpose, is the real question . . . Has our civilization by the bestiality it has wrought or condoned—for we are accomplices to that which leaves us indifferent—forfeited for a time its claim to that indispensable luxury we call literature? . . . The poem unwritten may speak very loud when the words in the city are full of savagery and lies."

Later, the unthinkable thought of self-imposed silence having been rejected by most, a different problem arose sharply—a problem between the young and the old, about what to say, about what there is worth saying. In a heavy Yiddish accent Isaac Bashevis Singer, grandfatherly wise, read a new short story he had just written, an old formula for a new tale. And then he said, reacting to some of the things the younger were saying; "Writers who don't know who they are, are read by people who don't know who they are either, and together they get no place. A young man wants to know why I don't write about the Vietnamese war and how come I fall back on mysticism and hobgoblins? If I knew maybe Mr. Johnson would read what I write, then maybe I might write about Vietnam. I am an old man and I remember how after the revolution in Russia they were making a new literature and it didn't work, and now they are more traditional than the traditionalists and haven't even found their way back to tradition. At least the hobgoblins don't disappoint me. You cannot get away from who you are, just as a man cannot run away from his accent!"

Jakov Lind, who had grown up in Hitler's insane world and survived, rose in anger to respond to the older man. "Mr. Singer is so sure of *his* identity, he knows who his parents and grandparents are. What about me? What about the young people who don't know? Are we going to keep on telling the same old stories in the same old way?"

Isaac Bashevis Singer raised his voice to reply. "I do not reject anybody. I welcome work that is real work. But I am sick and tired to hear the young man who says, 'I'm going to jump! I'm going to jump!' So jump already!"

On the next day my own participation in the conference was interrupted. A young man from the Middle West who had not attended the conference had found his way to the roof of LIU's dormitory tower and jumped. It was my duty to call the father off his tractor in an Indiana field and summon the parents to New York. Early the next morning we sat together in my office—nothing left to console or explain our tragedy except a short note. It recited briefly the young man's alienation, but gave not the slightest hint of the commitment beyond the leap to nowhere.

"Urbi et orbi"

Almost a year before I ever thought of joining LIU I got involved. Bill Zeckendorf called me in my New School office to ask if I would meet with John Howland Gibbs Pell, the acting chancellor of the university. There were organizational problems, he said, involving the multicampus structure and operation of the institution, which had grown to more than fifteen thousand students at its four campus centers.

John H. G. Pell had been acting chancellor for little more than a year. As a member of LIU's board, Mr. Pell had been asked by his colleagues to step into the breach created by the airplane tragedy which unexpectedly claimed the life of the preceding leader, a retired admiral who had led the university during the decade of its rapid growth. Pell was a consummate gentleman, a decent man who had never worked in the academic world before. He was a Wall Street investment man of both means and reputation—director or trustee of a half-dozen banks and international corporations, and director of the restoration of the Fort Ticonderoga historical site. Episcopalian, he was a commander in the United States Naval Reserve, and the author of a fairly good study of the life of Ethan Allen. His book and his work at Ticonderoga gave him some claim to a historian's status.

Decisions had become painful for John Pell because those he had made as acting chancellor seemed to please no one, and he was a gentle man, convinced that people should get along together reasonably. He was a man determined not to hurt people at a time and in a place where, it seemed to him, everyone was bent on hurting everyone. Under these circumstances it was fair to say that Mr. Pell was not exactly cut out to be the acting chancellor of LIU.

I met with Mr. Pell and agreed to undertake a study of the university's main campuses in Brooklyn, Old Westbury and Southampton. Almost immediately I found myself in one of the strangest and most intriguing zoos imaginable. Once, after my mission was known throughout the university, I was visited by a dozen deans and directors from the Brooklyn Center who presented a top-secret memorandum they had sent to Chancellor Pell. It recited the most outrageous allegations concerning the management of their campus: telephones were being tapped; offices were being bugged; wastebaskets were being searched. At C. W. Post, where Gordon Hoxie was then provost, a group convinced that the administration was spying on the personal lives of the faculty and assembling damaging dossiers for future use, had organized a counterespionage agency to look into the personal affairs of the administrators. When the officers of the various campuses gathered in the chancellor's cabinet meetings to transact the policy business of the university, the name of the game was to make no decisions. Each of the three provosts, it seemed, and perhaps a few others —in view of Mr. Pell's temporary status—was convinced that he himself ought to be the new leader. Each time the acting chancellor gently approached a conclusion designed to make reasonable men live together reasonably, a multitude of complications expressed in long, haranguing orations led the group inevitably to indecisive dissolution. Such was life in an institution which worshiped at the temple of man's mind. To laymen, unfamiliar with the flow and disposition of power in the academic institution, all of this may sound a little extraordinary. But versions of such situations are commonplace. The academics, being a cautious breed, long underrewarded and abused by a society sensitively dependent upon them, are finely skilled in the art of mounting giant campaigns and mandarinlike maneuvers aimed at little things.

But all this stalking and slinking through the underbrush was merely a preliminary. Big educational game really was at stake. During my consultancy Mr. Pell brought me a proposal submitted by one of his top officers to solve all the problems of the university by renaming each college in a way to make it clear that the whole really was more important than its parts. But the problems here went far beyond mere nomenclature. Each part, in pursuit of its own interests, had a version of itself it wished to impose upon the whole. And among these versions, with a few exceptions, the gamut of some of the more depressing options in American higher education was present.

Southampton College, the newest in the chain, was centered, like C. W. Post, on a beautiful abandoned Long Island estate. It commanded a magnificent view of Southampton Bay from a rolling hill, a setting (across the road from the Shinnecock Indian Reservation) which, in its later years, it was to deface with a Neo-Colonial architecture suggestive of a medium-class motel. The rich who summered at Southampton were supposed to appreciate the university's effort to bring learning and culture to that region, and to contribute large new sums for its development. Unfortunately, the people there were a little slow in expressing their gratitude. Consequently, this new college, with less than a thousand students, had an annual operating deficit of several hundred thousand dollars. As the university was sustained almost entirely on tuition income, at rates even then more than $1,500 per student annually, Southampton had to acquire more students, any students, quickly in order to reduce its unpopular call upon the earned income of the other campuses. It welcomed all the students it could get (housing them in motels along the highway while new dormitories were being negotiated on federal funds). Most of these students, while they could afford the prices, could not obtain admission elsewhere. Southampton was attempting a general education curriculum, trying to avoid the traditional rigid departmentalizations common in most liberal arts colleges. But its basic experiment was in economic survival more than in educational innovation.

C. W. Post had in less than a decade grown from empty potato fields to a Neo-Colonial hodgepodge of four to six thousand students, depending on how you counted them. Whatever else might be said about R. Gordon Hoxie, he had—with strategic help from some others—made something out of nothing. The campus was his monument. He had personally hired most of the senior faculty, and personally presided over the style and construction of every building, every program and everything else.

I am not sure whether Harvard or Iowa State Teachers College was Dr. Hoxie's model, but he had a passion for size (it had to be big to be good), for doing everything (a campus had to provide every imaginable expensive graduate and professional option in order to be a real university), and for a certain style, ranging from an annual deficit-laden horse show for the local Long Island gentry to a rapidly growing deficit-laden football operation which had begun to produce a few fellows on whom professional teams had taken options. Having instantly done C. W. Post, Dr. Hoxie was hellbent on instantly adding more and more dormitories to his campus (commuting was low camp), a law school, an oceanographic research center, countless Ph.D. programs, an interfaith chapel and an enlarged football stadium with an air-conditioned viewing box for the chancellor and his party.

After he became chancellor, Dr. Hoxie added some other goodies to his list. In his inaugural he announced a plan to develop a new $31 million campus at Brookhaven —"a little MIT on Long Island." And within a year and a half thereafter, he actually built a new million-dollar headquarters for the university at C. W. Post, centralizing in one place many of the operational functions of the various campuses, and increasing the annual allocation for central administration from about $600,000 to almost $2 million in less than two years. (Each campus was assessed a prorated share of this cost. Brooklyn's price went from $125,000 to almost $1 million during this period.)

Under certain educational circumstances, quite apart from money, the realization of all of these things might have made sense. But these circumstances, unhappily, simply did not exist. Neither did the money. At that time, to

Southampton's deficit, the Old Westbury campus added almost a half million more each year, however the accountants might compose the books. At the same time, the giant public educational systems in New York were rearing their beautiful heads. Near C. W. Post, the State University had already developed a large undergraduate and graduate program at Stony Brook with overtones of a little MIT approach. Actually adjacent to C. W. Post's campus, the State had begun to build its new college at Old Westbury for ten thousand students. And in New York City it was perfectly clear that City University was on the threshold of a major expansion, directed especially at an urgently needed accommodation of minority group youth.

The Brooklyn Center was the parent campus of the university. Founded by a group of downtown businessmen in the 1920's, it was intended, they said, to equalize educational opportunities for the young people living in Brooklyn. The charter of the university granted in 1926 reads: "The University's established policies are that it is independent, non-sectarian and democratic, and that it stands for free enterprise in education as a way of life." Soon after its birth it adopted the motto *"Urbi et orbi,"* linking on its official seal its destiny to the fate of the city.

By the mid-sixties LIU had grown to seven or eight thousand students, having survived the recurring crises in its history—the Great Depression, the Great War and the Great Basketball debacle. I was its fifth provost in less than a decade, none of the preceding four, including James Hester, now president of NYU, having survived more than two years in office. Nevertheless, despite continuous financial and leadership crises, the Brooklyn Center had prospered, and in a more or less honorable way. Over the years thousands of middle- and lower-middle-class young people, out of Flatbush and Bay Ridge, Red Hook and the other neighborhoods of the borough and the city, had been educated there. Most of its student body was Jewish and Italian or Irish Catholic, more than 80 percent of whom were the first members of their families to go to college. (Fewer than 3 percent were then black or Puerto Rican.)

The Brooklyn branch contained the university's most solid graduate programs, and its most adequate library, developed by one of its most creative faculty members, Nathan Resnick. Resnick represented a thin but strategically critical line of faculty talent in the Center. He had been with the place almost from its beginning, and after more than thirty years he still believed passionately in its mission, its unrealized potential. But just as important as his dedication to the institution was the fact that he actually read many of the books he imported to the library—an unusual thing for a librarian to do. Moreover, he was an accomplished artist in his own right, and no mean scholar of Walt Whitman, especially of his Brooklyn days. Resnick was disdainful of the privileges and benefits of his rank and seniority. He did not punch a time clock, and he even liked students. There were some others around the Brooklyn Center like that.

Moreover, Brooklyn's surpluses were between $400,000 and $1 million annually at this time. But these surpluses, accumulated mainly from tuition income, were not readily available for the development of the campus. They took the form of paper credits to some undisclosed future account, for the actual dollars were urgently needed elsewhere in the university. Given the Center's student clientele, tuition rates at the level of almost $1,600, and what was happening to the surpluses, a moral problem as well as a budgetary one was raised. We were not uproariously happy with the chancellor's proposal to raise tuition to $1,676. Our staff had planned a modest cut.

Almost all the students worked part time. And as massive federal loan programs were not yet available, the

Center appropriated (before surpluses) about $1 million of its own for student aid. (Dr. Hoxie questioned this allocation. Compared to C. W. Post's provision of $400,-000 annually for this purpose, he felt the Brooklyn sum was grossly excessive.)

There were other storm signs in Brooklyn. The undergraduate programs, involving over three fourths of the students, had not been re-examined comprehensively for more than twenty years. With tuition rates approximating Columbia's, there were serious questions about the value our students were receiving in return. Throughout its history, but especially during the last decade, the neighborhoods surrounding the campus had changed dramatically. Large numbers of Puerto Ricans and blacks had moved into the Fort Green Park area. They were on the streets and their residences could be seen from the campus. And of course, just beyond, half a million blacks resided in Bedford-Stuyvesant. These changes were having an impact on other institutions in the area: Pratt Institute, the Brooklyn Hospital, the Brooklyn Academy of Music and the Art Museum. Unfortunately, in its faculty, its programs and its student body, LIU did not adequately reflect these changes. It had lost touch with its most immediate neighbors, with the reality of its most immediate urban neighborhoods.

Dr. Hoxie, it seemed to me, was either disinterested in or a little restive about our tentative and exploratory probes on these fronts. We had thrown out lines to several community leaders and groups in Bedford-Stuyvesant and Fort Greene. There had been a great receptivity to our interest. Several hundred new black and Puerto Rican students enrolled in the Center. A few pilot programs had successfully gotten under way. More ambitious ones were on the drawing boards. But our efforts required the invention of new ways for sharing decision-making power, new kinds of personnel to implement the programs.

Finally our thinking led to major permanent commitments by the university. Plans had been drawn for a new library which in an unconventional way would be a joint university-and-community resource. Programmatic plans would put some of the university's efforts on a continuing basis out on the streets of the nearby neighborhoods. We had about reached a point of no return. To this point LIU brought the advantages of being a couple of steps behind Wayne State University in its redevelopment, and several laps behind the University of Chicago in Hyde Park. Wayne State had already begun to abandon its converted brownstones and garages, to expand its enclave, further disrupting its city streets and buttressing its walls. And Chicago, at least physically, was irrevocably committed to apartheid.

But at LIU the Old Paramount theater, the Maltz warehouse awaiting its renovation, and the converted garage, bowling alley and office tower represented well over half of all usable space. The investment was too great to abandon. Though the cement mall and the soccer field held the buildings together, giving the semblance of a traditional superblock campus, the main buildings opened onto Brooklyn's downtown streets, shared sidewalks with restaurants, barbershops, clothing stores and taverns. As it was, LIU was irrevocably committed to city streets. As it hoped to be, the Brooklyn campus was still relatively free to decide. Looking at itself, its part of New York City, its nearby sister institutions and its future student clientele, LIU could still fearlessly walk the streets, blending its mission with the city's in exciting new combinations. LIU had some of the drama and feel of the circus come to town. As urban education was going, LIU could have pitched some intriguing new tents.

Two other sharp differences arose between the thinking in Brooklyn and the chancellor's. We were living in the backwash of the Berkeley uprising, and one did not have to be very bright to understand that we were entering a new era of student participation in the conduct of higher education. Some of Brooklyn's faculty were uneasy about this, but we were nevertheless actively searching for ways to accommodate constructively this exciting new development. But Dr. Hoxie, adopting without quotation marks a sentence written by a conservative professor named Lewis Feuer in a *New York Times Magazine* article, delivered a speech at a college in Michigan, condemning the student slogan "participatory democracy," and saying, "If, as at Berkeley the year before the uprising, a middle-aged Socialist librarian could have given in an evening school a course called 'Ten Revolutions That Shook the World' and if the one hundred students who attended that course believed that at Berkeley they were making the Eleventh Revolution, in retrospect their nihilistic ideas are impotent by contrast with the positive force which is yours (here at Makinac College) . . ." The chancellor erred somewhat in the assumption that Brooklyn's students read neither his speeches nor the *New York Times Magazine*. In this case they read both.

Finally, there was the inevitability of City University's expanded fulfillment of its public, tuition-free responsibilities in LIU's Brooklyn territories. The economic competition would be intense. All LIU had was some unique experience and a little time to get ready—and even these meager assets might not be enough. I saw what little hope there was in a rapid movement in new directions. But beyond the downtown campus, the university's leadership seemed to view the urgency of the situation differently. I gathered from a few enigmatic remarks Bill Zeckendorf made about this time that the thought of selling LIU to City University, or merging it, had already been put on somebody's agenda. But of all the solutions available at the time, knowing the spirit and the aspirations of Brooklyn's faculty, students, alumni, and community friends, this option was the least acceptable.

So Chancellor Hoxie and I had a lot to talk about on that afternoon when he summoned me into his office to discuss some "details." Exactly a year before, the Office of the Commissioner of Education in New York had written the chancellor commending the leadership at the Brooklyn Center for its efforts to strengthen its undergraduate operations, consolidate and improve its existing programs, and extend its resources in new ways into the communities of Brooklyn it aimed to serve. But the same letter warned that no university, least of all ours, could simultaneously create new law schoods, new Ph.D. programs, new "little MIT's," and long remain in business. The commissioner wanted to know if we had some "secret nest egg," some magic formula for adding all these great new things in the absence of greatness to begin with. But there was no secret nest egg, no magic formula, and at the chancellor's conference table that day, there was to be no discussion of these issues.

Strike!

The chancellor got right down to business. Brooklyn would raise its tuition. Architectural planning would all be centralized through the C. W. Post headquarters, including the development of Brooklyn's new library. Student decorum at Brooklyn would be "upgraded," and plans for graduate expansion would be pushed. Obviously, he pointed out, I was not the man to implement these policies. Accordingly, he produced the draft of a letter he had thoughtfully prepared for my approval, and he asked me to approve it then and there. The letter stated that I wished to resign to complete the book I was working on (which later appeared as *Overlive: Power, Poverty, and the University*), that I agreed to certain terminal salary and housing arrangements, and to a press release the chancellor would eventually issue expressing his regret upon my departure, but reluctantly accepting my resignation. It was the last day in February 1967, and I was to vacate my office at the end of my contract on June 30.

Approve it, the chancellor urged. If I did not, he would simply have to dismiss me, in which event, he assured me, there would be no terminal accommodation. The remainder of our talk centered on whether I would be compelled to choose between my two options on the spot, or might be given a little time to think things over. Generously, he allowed me four or five days.

The next day I assembled the faculty senate and the executive committee of the Student Government to tell them of my options and to seek their advice. (We had developed the habit of consulting together about important matters.) Their advice came quickly, and was predicated upon one basic premise. The job at stake was mine. But the loss of it brought into sharp focus issues that were theirs. It was to be their fight, and fight, they decided, they must. As for me, they advised me to sign as generous a terminal agreement as I could secure, and to submit a resignation they would battle to rescind. It was my duty, they said, to join them in the struggle as it unfolded at a time and in a manner yet to be decided. On the following day I adopted their advice, much to Dr. Hoxie's satisfaction.

A few days later the faculty and student leadership called a council of war in my office. While they were meeting, a *New York Times* reporter called. He said that the chairman of the board, William Zeckendorf, had just issued a statement that I had resigned to write a book and had agreed to serve the university as a consultant on urban affairs for a year. Was this true, I was asked, or was it true, as the reporter suspected, that there were some other problems? Asking the reporter to hold the phone a minute, I reported to the group assembled in my office what had been said. Leo Pfeffer, chairman of the department of political science and a distinguished civil rights lawyer, immediately picked up a pen and wrote a sentence. "This is your statement to the press," he said. And so it was. "My resignation was not voluntary."

From this moment on the fat was in the fire. The students, about to leave for a week-long Easter holiday, decided to strike the Center on the day of their return. The faculty resolved to respect the student picket lines. A committee was established to open negotiations with the chancellor and the board. The chancellor responded within a week by evicting me from my office and banning me from the campus. The story broke in the metropolitan press, where it was to remain very visible for weeks to come. It was the opening of a four-year struggle to change the course of the university—a struggle still unresolved.

Huck Foxie

L.I.U. STUDENTS STRIKING

The first student strike in the history of Long Island University was expected to send thousands of students into the streets around the downtown Brooklyn campus today . . .

Under the guard of a 30-man detail from the 11th Division, picket lines formed at 7:30 at the main entrances on Flatbush Avenue.

Charles Isaacs, President of the Student Government Association, said the boycott would cripple instruction at the Brooklyn Center. Sympathy demonstrations are possible at the other L.I.U. campuses. The overwhelming majority of the faculty members are expected to honor the picket lines and not show for classes.

Tactics and picket line assignments were worked out at a Sunday-night meeting in the cafeteria of the Brooklyn dormitory—New York *Post,* April 3, 1967

Horace Kallen, then a Distinguished Seminar Professor at Long Island University, dropped in on the students' meeting in the dormitory. "They were having serious pleasure in what they were doing," he said. "So many of them are the first generation of their families to go on to a university. Each of them seemed to be standing up for himself, in terms of a principle."

Chancellor Hoxie told the New York *Post* that if there is any disorder or property damage he would hold Isaacs responsible . . . "the University over which I preside," he said, "is a community of scholars, not a loose council of Indian tribes."

As to any disciplinary action that might be taken against Isaacs, Hoxie said: "After all, he's posing as a young adult, and the action would have to be appropriate to the consequences of his action."

Charles Isaacs was some revolutionary. In fact, he was a typical child of Revolution—the American one, that is. A senior in mathematics, an honor student, before the strike he was bent toward business administration.

"L.I.U. is not in business to deal with children who can't pay tuition"—John P. McGrath—banker and real estate developer, and trustee of the University

Charles Isaacs' family could afford to pay his tuition. They were decent professional folk, who like so many residents of Brooklyn and Queens had sought some refuge from the trials and tribulations of the city in a Long Island bedroom suburb.

Isaacs was one of the better-known student politicians on the campus. But because he seldom dressed like 99.9 percent of the others, some of his peers thought that he was a little odd—certainly different. Charlie, always clean-shaven and neatly cropped, invariably wore a shirt and tie, and a suit, usually with a vest.

> "I've never threatened to close the University. I've simply said that if it's forced upon us by an anarchistic action on the part of these children and certain members of the faculty, we will have no choice except to close that school . . ."—William Zeckendorf, chairman of the board

Charles Isaacs was no "militant activist." Clean-cut American boys who not only honor but really like their mothers and dads, who join and vigorously engage in fraternity life, who organize Red Cross blood drives and try out for one of the varsity teams, though extraordinarily active, even militantly so, are not, in the popular parlance, "militant activists." *Militancy* and *activism* are not the essential ingredients in the definition of the term. (Nothing is more "militant" than a football player in action, or the student mob in the last quarter of a tight basketball contest.) What really counts is the thrust, the direction of the human energy and enthusiasm. Every college provides established channels through which the animal vigor of its students may properly flow. The ports at the end of these rivers are Happy Times, unpolluted by political sludge. The "militant activists" are the ones who paddle their canoes against the current, or stop along the bank and walk away, or propose insane schemes for redeveloping the port.

Isaacs, along with several other able students, organized and led one of the most effective and longest student strikes in the history of American higher education. Their efforts utterly paralyzed, virtually closed the largest campus of LIU, and "disrupted" all the others. Eventually, as a result of what they did, the chairman of the board of trustees and the chancellor of the university resigned. And though it is not at all clear that the goals for which they struggled will be achieved at LIU, it is clear that the university has abruptly changed its course and can never safely return to where it was before they struck. The goals they sought—campus autonomy, community involvement, the integrity and distinctiveness of an urban educational center, and student participation, are now the official policies, if not the perfect practices of LIU in Brooklyn.

The two weeks of the strike were a kaleidoscope of strange, hectic events. The official buttons of the student cause erupted on campuses all over New York City—one reading "EDUCATION—NOT EXPLOITATION: THE APRIL 3 MOVEMENT," and the other elegantly proclaiming "HUCK FOXIE." There were the incessant calls from the press at all hours of the day and night, endless meetings, secret conferences and public rallies, intricate negotiations and rumors of reprisals and of possible occasions for violence. A command headquarters was established in the library of Professor Pfeffer's home in one of the University Towers adjacent to the campus. There the forty or fifty student and faculty leaders met daily and on weekends into the early morning hours.

It has been less than two weeks since it became known that L.I.U. Chancellor R. Gordon Hoxie had forced Birenbaum's resignation as Provost of its Brooklyn Center. Since then deans who had been almost strangers to each other have become eternal friends. The President of Student Government found himself, with no loss of respect and no embarrassment, calling a dean by his first name.

P.T.A.'s from Bedford-Stuyvesant and Fort Greene have wired their protests to Zeckendorf . . ."—Murray Kempton in the New York *Post*

The liquor and the telephone bills at the Pfeffers were horrendous. There was one occasion when Charles Isaacs, backstopped by three dozen others, conducted long-distance negotiations on two telephones simultaneously with Mr. Zeckendorf, Dr. Hoxie, and Congressman Ogden Reid (one of the few board members who vigorously supported the student-faculty cause) all on the other end of the wires.

But the board remained obdurate. Finally students who had already paid their exorbitant tuition fees for the semester, who were approaching examinations and were dependent upon the university's certification of their status to defend their exemptions from the draft, received an ominous letter from the chancellor threatening the worst. A giant rally of the student body was called to decide what to do next. It was rumored that Mr. Zeckendorf or Dr. Hoxie might attend the rally, and faculty and student leaders were worried about the potential for violence.

At eight on the morning of the rally, a committee of the faculty visited me in my home. They had been magnificent in their support of the students and the cause, virtually risking their own jobs in the courageous course they had followed. Later that morning they reaffirmed their support for my reinstatement, and even suggested the organization of a university-in-exile, all other options failing. But now they too were worried about violence, and they urged me to make a surprise appearance at the rally to help calm the emotions they knew would run high. They also posed a very serious moral problem for me. I held tenure in the rank of professor in political science, and they argued that I should claim my tenure and return to the university in that role to continue the struggle. But this was something I felt I should not do. As I saw it, under those circumstances my days at LIU were over. I had tried, done the best I could. I was sure that my continued presence there would have been an adverse and divisive influence. If a cause depends too much upon one man, it is not much of a cause.

I agreed to do what I could at the rally, but since I had been banned from the campus weeks before, I insisted on a personal invitation from Mr. Zeckendorf before I would set foot in the Old Paramount's auditorium again. Time was running out, so we decided I would proceed to my office-in-exile, the bar at Junior's restaurant across the street. Finally the invitation came, and a delegation of forty or fifty faculty members and students arrived to escort me to the auditorium. As we walked across Flatbush they bombarded me with advice: "Urge the students to keep the strike going"; "Tell them to go back to classes"; "Say you will come back and teach"; "Keep them calm. They're hot."

More than three thousand students jammed the Old Paramount to capacity. The students were hanging over the balcony rails and standing shoulder to shoulder amid the tennis nets on the basketball court. The air was charged with emotional electricity. Earlier that morning the faculty had voted overwhelmingly to back the students in whatever they chose to do. Faculty members had already addressed the assembly, telling the students that their stand was right. But many of the students were obviously worried about their academic standing should they decide to continue the strike.

Shortly before I arrived William Zeckendorf, flanked by a phalanx of Burns guards linked arm in arm, had made a surprise entry into the hall. It was the kind of dramatic act for which Bill Zeckendorf had a certain zest. After the catcalls and boos subsided, he addressed the crowd. It was time, he said, for him to have a "heart to heart" discussion with the student body. "It may well be," he observed, "that your action will in the long run be the greatest thing in the history of the university. You will accelerate by years radical change on the various campuses."

Mr. Zeckendorf told the students that the individual campuses of the university would receive far greater autonomy in the future (which, in fact, they subsequently did). He said that the trustees had authorized a committee of board members to hear student and faculty views (which they did), and they would give "prompt action and sympathy" (which, as things turned out, they did not). Finally he declared that in the future the financial surpluses of the Brooklyn Center would not be used to develop newer units of the university. (Shortly thereafter, the Brooklyn Center entered a period of sustained deficits.)

This was to be Mr. Zeckendorf's last address to the students as chairman of the board of the university. A few months later, in July, he resigned the post he had held for twenty-five years.

I followed Mr. Zeckendorf at the microphone, and he stood by my side as I spoke. The students' welcome was unsettling and I do not remember exactly what I said. But according to press accounts—

> Birenbaum told the students that . . . "the risks are no longer viable . . . There are practical questions of graduation, mid-terms, and even the draft facing many of you." His voice seemed to crack slightly, but he continued. "You have already risked all. I can't ask you to risk more." —*Seawanhaka,* April 13, 1967

> Birenbaum . . . urged the students to get on with their studies while seeking "alternative levels of weaponry."— *New York Times,* April 13, 1967

When the shouting died down, the strike came to an end. The students and faculty at LIU began the arduous job of building a new university—a task unfinished still. Whether they "won" what they fought for is still not clear. Most of the institutional issues they raised remain unresolved. But they did make clear that LIU's survival critically depends upon facing these issues.

Of the hundreds of letters and visits I received during and since these events, a large number have come from these students, their parents and their teachers at LIU. They strike a common theme. These young people, many of them for the first time in their lives, stood up and were counted for what they believed in. They took substantial risks for a cause beyond themselves individually. They were proud of themselves and of one another.

And over and over again they have said that during those few tumultuous weeks that spring, they learned something new and important. It was an essential part of their higher education.

And of mine.

Dunkirk

On Brooklyn's Heights, three blocks from the house LIU provided for its provost on Pineapple Street and even closer to where I live now on Willow, there is a plaque marking George Washington's headquarters during his battle for Long Island. From that spot one can see past New York City's oldest bridge, the Brooklyn, and beyond, the spire of the Empire State Building. In the other direction, past the Statue of Liberty, you can see on a clear night the lights of the city's newest bridge, the Verrazano joining Brooklyn to Staten Island across the mouth of the port. It is one of the most spectacular vistas in New York.

Washington's battle line ran from this point near Montague Street, off and on to what are now Fulton and Willoughby streets, over Flatbush and through the lobby of the Old Paramount into Fort Greene and the Bedford-Stuyvesant. The Sons of the American Revolution have dignified the Paramount lobby with a bronze marker adding the ghosts of the Revolutionary Army to the others floating around there.

There are eyewitness accounts of the Americans' evacuation from Brooklyn Heights after their defeat in the battle of Long Island. Several thousand troops under the command of Alexander Hamilton mobilized a Dunkirk-like flotilla to escape to Manhattan's safety across the bay. Brooklyn Heights was even then a Tory hotbed. Commandeering every fishing boat, barge and sailor in sight to provide for the escape of his men, Hamilton did not endear the Revolutionary cause in the hearts of the local townspeople. They bid adieu to the tattered remnant of the retreating army with bouquets of rotten eggs and overripe tomatoes, pelting the exhausted American troops with the garbage of the day and certain unmentionable obscenities. Such is often the way of those who defend the morals of the time, standing up to the obscene, the irreligious, the rebellious fringes who would upset the established comforts, the order of the realm.

Ironically, Hamilton's forces made their way safely to a part of lower Manhattan near what is now the Battery, where little more than a decade later the inaugural barge of General Washington landed. One can see in one sweep of the eye these points of defeat and triumph from the Promenade in Brooklyn Heights. The first President's barge was rowed by oarsmen clad in white satin, a torch at each rower's place reflecting a glistening light on each man's fine tunic as the barge appeared off Jersey's shore. A coach drawn by eight gallant white horses awaited General Washington's debarkation.

We can only wonder whether General Washington re-called, amid such triumphal splendor, arriving for the trip up to Wall Street, the misery and confusion of that night not too long before when Long Island was ceded to the enemy. There must be many spots on the planet fertilized by the irony first of defeat and then of victory, or first of victory and then of defeat. Time is the crucial element—time, and a point of view.

About a year and a half after Dr. Hoxie requested my resignation, his puppeteers requested his. On the day before the chancellor complied, the *New York Times* reported that "there has been a growing feeling among Board members that Dr. Hoxie is not attuned to the needs of today—'especially in the ghetto.'" The paper quotes Dr. Hoxie: "'If I go tomorrow, unwittingly it will be a Birenbaum triumph. The ironic thing about it is that we were from the same hometown—Waterloo, Iowa.'"

Poor Waterloo: it was not the irony at all. The irony was that in less than two years the threat of "a Birenbaum triumph" had utterly ceased to be a threat at all, if it ever had been. What was the triumph? Some men, each motivated by his own notions of honor, justice and the common good, may have some small influence upon an institution's fate, but finally an institution's fate will be its own.

At the time, LIU seemed like my Dunkirk. It tried to disgrace me publicly. It evicted my family from where we lived. It withheld my livelihood. Before it all hap-pened, and during it, I was not confident I could survive such a thing. But we learned we could survive. For this lesson, I am deeply in the debt of R. Gordon Hoxie and members of LIU's board at that time.

But about LIU's survival—the issue, sadly, remains in doubt. For those who understand how great the city's problems are and how limited the resources available remain, the potential of an LIU is impressive. Even now, as its unsolved problems mount, it is the right place at the right time. But somehow, even after all this, it has yet to arrive.

The highest service an educational institution can perform is to help the people who come to it find and realize themselves. Self-discovery, self-realization are not always happy events. No matter. In finding ourselves, if we do— whatever we find—we should acknowledge with humility a modest debt due the institution which threatens, because of its own needs, to crush us.

Chapter Nine

The B.(edford) S.(tuyvesant) Degree

Joe

I missed my father's presence and advice throughout the Long Island University adventure. He would have brought a certain gusto to the battle, and as a matter of principle, he would have enjoyed the fight. But he had died a few years before.

Joe was fairly relaxed about winning and losing. Naturally, he preferred to win, but losing did not dampen his audacity, his devil-may-care boldness. For Joe, to live was to dream, and the thing he criticized me most for was the limited canvas of my dreams. It was my mother, female nature, who emphasized getting things done. Joe too wanted things done, but he understood the importance of knowing what there was to do, and of attempting the exceptional. Joe had a passion for what might be, and this more than anything else enabled him to survive and to encourage those near him to try.

A Hole in the Wall

One of the most extraordinary developments in the LIU affair was partially reported in the New York *Post* of March 25, 1967:

> Spokesmen for the Negro community, clergymen and leaders of anti-poverty agencies said Birenbaum had taken steps to revitalize the area around the Brooklyn Center of L.I.U. and they feared his ouster would isolate the school from the people around it. They sent wires and letters to the L.I.U. Board of Trustees....
>
> The Ingersoll Tenants' Association embracing Fort Greene and the Navy Yard area told of his work in setting up a reading clinic. Mrs. Olivette Thompson, president, said Birenbaum's exit "will terminate the hopes of many families." She said his activities "helped take Fort Greene out of the Middle Ages," and asked if his departure means L.I.U. now intends to "build a cultural wall around the community?"
>
> The Reverend Vincent Foley, Chairman of the Clergy Concerned for a Better Fort Greene Community, sent a wire to "strongly urge" Birenbaum's reinstatement. "He has been most active in our area and has tried to involve the University with the community."
>
> The Central Brooklyn Coordinating Council said Birenbaum . . . had changed L.I.U.'s image from "one of invisibility to one of involvement . . ." The Council cited his work in developing a Small Business Opportunities Center to serve the area, his involvement in Bedford-Stuyvesant anti-poverty programs, his work on a plan leading to the designation of Fulton Park for an urban renewal project.
>
> Mrs. Allan G. Richtmyer, president of the Willoughby House Settlement, said Birenbaum supported a remedial reading program now serving 214 Fort Greene families . . . They are being taught by L.I.U. students as a part of a teacher-training course.

"This marriage between an institution of higher learning and the surrounding community is proof of how to
begin to face up to the challenges of education today,"
she said.

Here was a rare case, if not an unprecedented one in
recent American higher education, where not only a
faculty and a student body united around issues in support of campus-level administration but where the neighborhoods of the university joined the academics in common cause. And the communities involved were mainly
black and Puerto Rican, while most of the faculty, students and administrators were not. In the spring of 1967
—a year before the uprising at Columbia—a university's
active engagement in its urban scene was an idea so new
that LIU's feeble efforts were in some respects pioneering.
And feeble those efforts were, which made the community's response to the situation even more amazing.

LIU was insensitive to or ignorant of its immediate
city. There was more competence and knowledge on
faculty concerning poverty in India, the struggling efforts
to establish some semblance of representative government in Korea, and the literature, art and culture of
Italy than there was about poverty, self-government or
the cultural problems of our own neighborhoods. The
"ghetto" was an academic concept, studied academically,
even though the university itself practically lived in or
was one. It was very difficult for an academic community
which knew so little to be helpful to another community
which needed so much. It started out as a case of the lame
leading the blind. Of course, this academic situation is
true, far beyond LIU, even now. Some argue, because
of this very fact, that a university has no business getting
mixed up in the dirty problems of its immediate city
neighborhoods. A university cannot do everything. It is
not a social welfare agency. It has no moral commitments

or obligations beyond its professional ones. It should not attempt to do what it knows so little about, what it is so ill prepared to do.

But this argument leaves unanswered some very basic questions. Granting that no one institution can do everything, how does a university decide what it will do, the objectives and purposes to which it will devote its resources? This is not simply a question of whether institutional *action* is academically proper or improper, or whether all academic activity must be confined within the campus walls to be proper. Education is often an *active* process, and universities often, routinely act beyond their own walls. They commit economic, political, and cultural acts of great significance beyond themselves. What off-campus action is legitimate? Does only the exclusive pursuit of institutional self-interest legitimatize such action?

LIU's unfolding efforts in the mid-sixties were tentative and exploratory, frankly and expressly based on our expectation that the institution, its faculty, students and administrators would undoubtedly learn in the neighborhoods at least as much as they would teach or do for others. This expectation was absolutely correct. On the other hand, the formal, organized educational situation in the neighborhoods was pretty desperate. Hardly more than a third of the youth of graduating age received diplomas of any kind, academic or vocational, in the high schools serving the very large populations involved. Fewer than 2 percent of these were going on to college. NYU was raising both its tuition fees and its traditional admission requirements. Columbia, Fordham, St. John's, Pratt Institute and the other private institutions were prohibitively expensive, even if admission thresholds could be overcome. Brooklyn College, the closest four-year public campus, was then about 94 percent white.

The two-year colleges were not much better, and these schools were popularly viewed as mere extensions of the clearly inadequate high schools.

Beneath all this was a junior high school and elementary public school system notorious for its tendency to reach conclusions about the learning potential of its students very early in the game. Youngsters were often pegged by the third grade, for all practical purposes tracked from that time in one economic-educational direction or another. The majority of the teachers did not reside in the community and possessed but a modest feeling for or knowledge of the realities there. And many of these were among the least experienced in the system's teaching force. Most of the student decisions to drop out of school, we discovered, were made long before the secondary level, even though they were often implemented a year or two after they were made.

New York's giant public school enterprise enjoyed a virtual monopoly in the communities. There were few private schools in Bedford-Stuyvesant, and these were either church-based or virtually bankrupt or both. The resources and capacities of the community for the creation or maintenance of optional formal or informal educational situations were practically nil.

When LIU began to make its first serious probes on this front, we weren't even familiar with many of the basic facts I have just recited. All we really did know was that the youth and their families in these neighborhoods and our own institution increasingly shared the same territories. One did not have to be brilliant to know that our destinies inevitably would be linked in some manner, to some extent. Beyond this, sincerity, genuine modesty, and a demonstrable capacity to learn carried us about as far as we could go. It wasn't until our own moment of truth that we began to understand how far that was.

Planned Failure

Upon the collapse of the LIU strike, a large number of people and organizations in Bedford-Stuyvesant and Fort Greene joined in a public invitation asking me to assist them in the design of a new college to serve their communities. They had in mind an institution which would from the outset have an impact on the training of teachers for their lower schools, and which would reach out through practical educational programs to the adult population, as well as provide for the higher education of the younger people. It was a quixotic invitation, colored by some sentiment, though addressed to what was an urgent, practical situation. There was no money, and virtually no chance to produce any. Moreover, on almost every other front of the public life of the area, there was an acute shortage of funds, and the competition for whatever there was, was so intense that it was almost immoral to even think of adding another snout at the trough.

During the preceding year, in connection with what we were trying to do at LIU, I had repeatedly attempted to get through to Senator Robert F. Kennedy. The senator had staked out a very special interest in the Bedford-Stuyvesant territory. He was attempting to organize some kind of semiprivate agency, some center of leadership and resource for a frontal assault on the problems of jobs, housing and neighborhood planning in this vast Brooklyn black community. But the senator's efforts had been entrapped in a complex web of personality and political problems in the area. Even being Robert F. Kennedy did not ensure an open-arms reception in a community as large and volatile as this one.

Within days after the public invitation to design a new college, I was called by the senator's New York chief of staff, Tom Johnston. Preliminary conversations were followed by the development of a proposal to buy a year's time for an intensive design effort. The problem was: Where and how to attack? Education was in disarray at the preschool, elementary and secondary levels, and virtually nonexistent beyond. Battle lines for community control of the public schools were already drawn, and Ocean Hill–Brownsville, which became the ultimate symbol in this struggle, was a part of this territory. The polarization of races, which became so acute during the battle between the teachers union and the community in the year to follow, was already well advanced.

There was a very strong and reasonable tendency to start at the beginning. The higher educational problems sensitively attended the secondary school failures, which related back to the junior high and elementary school chaos, which opened up the whole preschool situation, which led eventually back into the homes of the children and other critical aspects of the community's life beyond the formal educational systems. The senator was intrigued by the possibility of launching a semiprivate, autonomous lower school system to compete with the monolithic, failing public monopoly. Many thought that the best way to cope with the massive problems of dope, unemployment, adult despair and four successive summers of street rioting and violence was to develop new educational programs for new generations to begin at the moment they emerged from the womb. Unfortunately, this approach did not come to grips immediately with the tens of thousands in their teens and beyond who, having been born and grown up the way they had, faced the immediate problems of making adult lives for themselves in the Bedford-Stuyvesant American setting.

Daniel Moynihan once said that since it took three or four centuries to create the American race problem, it was reasonable to expect another two or three centuries to pass before we begin to emerge from it. Patience, born of the exercise of the intellect, however accurately guided, is not exactly helpful when one is on the front line working with people who do not seriously see the future in terms of two or three centuries, but who are worried about a job, where to sleep and what to eat the next day. Confronted with an extremely critical, potentially violent and revolutionary situation, policy-making in America is still not couched in terms of nonviolent revolution. The persistent assumption that we may yet "evolve" solutions to these problems, an assumption fortified by the nation's material and technological success, may very well be our undoing. The question the brightest college students I know ask me over and over again is: How come you're still in the Establishment? Working with and through their system? Playing their game? Being corrupted by their notions of power? I tell them I am still committed to reform, and some of them laugh at me.

The tenuous line which separates the young and dedicated reformer from the young and dedicated revolutionary in contemporary America is probably the most fragile line in our society just now. It is a twilight zone through which many of our ablest young people pass back and forth, often tentatively, exploring. People like me deserve to be laughed at unless we can demonstrate, practically and quickly, the capacity of the system, the Establishment, our power to produce nonviolent, just solutions, which, given the problems, will probably have to be revolutionary. But this places an almost unbearable, perhaps unrealistic, burden on the Establishments, requiring them, peacefully and without reluctance, to devote substantial portions of their power to change themselves, perhaps fundamentally and irretrievably. Both Bedford-Stuyvesant and Capitol Hill find themselves in quite a predicament. We all are in quite a predicament.

The essence of competition is the ability to compete. One of our most serious problems is our expectation that those whom we have not allowed to participate in American life should now participate, playing the game according to our rules of competition (law and order, due process, etc.) knowing that *our* past failures load the dice against *them* at the outset. People who according to every social index available realize they are regarded as failures are not especially eager to play a game again in which another failure is preordained.

Of course, such rigging often has nothing to do with the good intentions of those in charge. There are ample collegiate examples of this point. For most of the urban blacks we are now admitting into the colleges, the campus is the first predominantly *white* community in which they have ever had a sustained working or social experience. We admit large numbers of them conditionally. We make it clear to them that they are "deficient," i.e., inadequately prepared academically, especially in math and English. We also admit large numbers of white middle-class youth who in the same respects are "deficient." Usually we say to *them* that until their "deficiencies" are corrected, they will not enjoy complete student citizenship. Their curricular choices are severely circumscribed and extracurricular activities prohibited until they "get off probation." For most white students this situation, however much disliked, is accepted as being the way the game is played. It is better than not "getting in," in a social context where "getting in" is the only thing to do.

But for the blacks, the perception is often very different. They arrive knowing that they are, of course, different, i.e., black—a fact underscored by the strange whiteness pervading the whole. They arrive knowing they are "deficient." We tell them that clearly, through the terms on which we admit them. Naturally, our normal approach encourages an equation between being black and being "deficient." Our desire to be helpful aggravates feelings of inferiority and inadequacy among those we want to help. Key to any learning program is the excitement of the student's will to learn—his motivation. Essential to a student's motivation is his degree of confidence in himself. Many of our black students arrive with a sophisticated and superior political acumen, often born of experience in the city streets. Many are superb athletes. Those very areas of collegiate activity in which they might demonstrate a superiority, a capacity to compete successfully, are often circumscribed by our well-intentioned but archaic campus approach.

We are in similar curricular boxes. In the two-year colleges, to which the majority of our black and Spanish-speaking youth are now being directed, the applied technology programs (nursing, mechanical engineering, computer programming, etc.) have been especially designed for them. ("Being educated" almost exclusively means "becoming employable.") In these programs not only are the liberal arts choices we routinely provide for white middle-class youth practically nil, but the introductory *applied* math and science requirements are in some respects tougher than the more conceptual courses the "higher achieving" white, liberal arts students take. While the liberal arts student usually is not required to make a professional or vocational choice until his sophomore or even his junior year (we assume he must be exposed awhile in order to make a reasoned choice), the technology student must make his choice—an almost irrevocable one—during his first freshman registration, before he has attended a single class. Knowing the least about his options, presumably least prepared for college-level math and science, he is compelled by our good intentions to choose first and to engage almost at once in studies where failure is often probable, if not certain.

To these professional, vocational decisions, the white student brings the experience and understanding of the conditioning he has received growing up in middle-class

America. This conditioning is full of imperfections and antieducational bias, but it corresponds far more accurately to the tone and temper of the typical campus than the conditions with which the black or Spanish-speaking student is familiar, growing up in the typical urban neighborhoods reserved for them.

Perhaps there is no more formidable competitor in all of New York City than the public educational system. Anyone aiming to establish an alternative to it is really taking something on. By size and jurisdiction its monopoly is almost unassailable. Serving more than a million young people, and spending, apart from capital items, more than a billion dollars a year, its administrative and bureaucratic machinery rivals that of the Department of Defense, without enjoying whatever decision-making clarity a military hierarchy imposes on such a situation. Its more than ninety thousand employees are virtually all unionized, from floor sweepers to teachers. And the score of contracts with which it lives confuses and diffuses managerial, decision-making powers hopelessly. In some ways it is hypersensitive and vulnerable to popular passion and the grossest of political pressures; in others it is utterly unresponsive to the democratic political process and the constituencies to which it ought to pay attention.

Taking all this into account, we proposed to develop inside Bedford-Stuyvesant an institution unique to it— a college. A few years earlier, City University had declined to do this. A college would not fall under the jurisdiction of the Board of Education. Establishing one would avoid the head-on challenge involved in setting up a competing elementary or secondary system, but through a strong teacher education program—and perhaps, eventually, the creation of its own model lower school—a college could immediately move into some of the difficult areas of concern in the public system. The design and launching of such an institution was proposed to Senator Kennedy—

with a price tag attached. Eventually he bought this strategy.

Between Planes

I actually met Senator Kennedy for our first discussion rather late in the development of the proposal for a new college in Bedford-Stuyvesant. By this time the arrangements for the implementation of his own plans in the black community had taken shape. Two corporations were to be organized. One, all black, was to be based in the community, governed by a black community board, and directed by an able young black man, Franklin Thomas, a Columbia Law School graduate and former basketball star, and a deputy commissioner of police appointed by Mayor John Lindsay. The chairman of the board of this corporation was Judge Thomas Jones, a Democratic politican, who like most others in Brooklyn worked through the Steingut machine, one of the few remaining examples of that kind of political organization left in New York. This was called the Restoration Corporation, and its purpose was to interpret community needs, mobilize community support, develop operational programs, and then operate them.

The other—the Development and Services Corporation (D & S)—was all white and Manhattan-based. Presumably its purposes were to raise money, flex political muscle as needed, and recruit "the best" talent in all the categories relevant to the programs developed in, by and for the community. Its board included such luminaries as Andre Meyer, senior partner of Lazard Frères; Thomas Watson, chairman of the board of IBM; James Oates, chairman of the board of Equitable; William Paley, chairman of the board of CBS; and Douglas Dillon.

There were some serious problems built into this organizational scheme from the beginning. In practice the neat formal division of function and power between the two groups got confused, and because the two corporations were geographically separate and racially segregated, issues about who should call the shots were almost always colored black and white. The operational staffs of each corporation followed suit. Restoration came to be almost all black, and D & S had a roster of bright young white lawyers, accountants, architects and planners. (About a year ago, steps were taken to correct this situation.) On the militant side Jones and Thomas were outflanked on their own community board by young Turks like Robert (Sonny) Carson, the leader of CORE in the borough, and Albert Vann, who had achieved a certain notoriety in the city as the organizer of the Afro-American Teachers Association. Jones and Thomas walked a high-strung tightrope, balanced between aggressive, militant constituencies in their own community—eager to label them "Uncle Toms" —and the kind of do-business and "we know some things you may not" attitude of business, professional and political men of considerable substance in our society serving on D & S.

There was the additional problem—the backwash of the factional feuding in Bedford-Stuyvesant which had preceded the organization of Restoration. Unfortunately, the Kennedy formula did not completely heal those scars. Some groups and leaders in the community opposed the Kennedy approach. Pursuant to the LIU experience, I had friends in both camps.

I first met the senator in a VIP conference room at LaGuardia Airport. He had an hour or so between planes. I had been conditioned for the meeting, i.e., subjected to what I assumed was standard operating procedure in the Kennedy enterprise for sizing things up. As the plans had unfolded, the ideas I represented, and I, had been examined and cross-examined by many members of the senator's staffs in both the Washington and the New York offices. But in addition, some searching interviews had been arranged with Messrs. Paley, Meyer, Thomas, Jones, Adam Walinsky and others, and I even found myself at breakfast one morning talking about a new college for Bedford-Stuyvesant with Mrs. Jacqueline Kennedy and Richard Goodwin in her New York City apartment. And throughout all this, of course, I was keeping in touch with my friends back in the neighborhoods who had extended the original invitation. They too were looking at things as they developed.

The senator was cordial, but strictly down to business. He had read the documentation. He said he knew absolutely nothing about education, higher or lower, and then he proceeded to ask a series of incisive and most difficult questions about the proposal, indicating not only that he had read it carefully but that he knew quite a bit about education, higher and lower. He then asked me what precisely it would take to attempt the project, and whether I would do it.

I told the senator what I wanted: more than a quarter of a million dollars for the design effort over a twelve-to-eighteen-month period, a clear understanding that my own commitment to the project would extend only to that period, complete freedom regarding the choice and deployment of the design staff, help in major fund raising in behalf of the design once it was completed, and the understanding that we would be free agents in moving among the various factions in the community in order to do our work. I said that the staff I had in mind would be black and white, simply because as I saw it, the talent needed happened to be both black and white. On the other hand, I expressed the conviction that the new college, if it was ever to be born, should be led by a black man—a point about which the senator had some reservations, saying we should look for "the best," regardless of color. We agreed that the new college should essentially be governed by the people in its own community, though distinguished people from the rest of the world might be added to a governing board in time.

The senator was anxious that the project develop a close working relationship with the Restoration and D & S corporations, so that the educational operations could be related to whatever happened in other community fields such as housing, neighborhood planning, job training, etc. I suggested the creation of a semiautonomous corporation subsidiary to the other two, with a black and white board chosen from among the others. This was an idea we were to explore further. But about the rest, green lights were turned on with dispatch.

During the following month I assembled the core staff. Abe Habenstreit, Patricia Parsons and Mort Abromowitz all came with me from LIU. Abe had been my right arm in our initial probes into these communities from the LIU base. Pat Parsons, an attractive young black woman, had been my Girl Friday at the university. She knew a great deal about people and colleges. Mort Abromowitz was the dean of teacher education at LIU—about the only really intelligent renegade in that business I knew of in town. James Farmer, now formerly assistant secretary in HEW, had recently left active leadership of the national CORE organization, which he had helped create. Preston Wilcox was teaching at Columbia and was a central figure in the public school controversy in Harlem. A bit later, three others were added to this team: Al Vann, who was teaching in the public schools in Bedford-Stuyvesant and was also a member of Restoration's board; Ed Goodman, quite fresh out of Yale and the son of the man who ran Bergdorf-Goodman in New York; and Frank Lennon, a recent graduate of LIU, and after Bedford-Stuyvesant, enrolled as a student in urban planning at MIT. Each of these people was a fighter. Along with some distinguished victories, each had lost at least one major battle. Each dissented from some major aspect of prevailing educational policy. Each gave up something secure to join this team, and each knew that he was coming to a short-term drill. For whatever else they may have lacked, among them there was no shortage of courage, capacity to think and to act, and willingness to take risks.

On the Tuesday after Labor Day in 1967, in rented rooms on the sixteenth floor of the Granada Hotel on the Fort Greene–Bedford-Stuyvesant borderline, we assembled to begin our work.

The Paper People Principle

I was dean of the New School during the backwash of the Hungarian Revolt and the Cuban Revolution when the academic and intellectual refugees came around looking for new careers and new lives. They were a people carrying with them their own paper tents, nomads who always came lugging folders and briefcases full of papers, clutching yellowed scraps in their hands, anxious to talk first not about themselves, but about the pieces of paper they were always so eager to spread out on your desk. Visas and work permits, frayed clippings reporting great achievements in the past, official letters of recommendation stamped with seals, diplomas and certificates decorated with ribbons, notarized statements of health—a few material possessions rescued from disaster to prove conclusively that they were in fact still alive, individually unique, really standing before you, breathing and warm.

I think it must be one of the laws of nature that societies or classes that are very old or very sick or in deep trouble reduce almost all of the significant relationships among their citizens to paper transactions. It is as if the people, terribly unsure of themselves individually or together, seek solace in some nonhuman, external evidence of their humanity. Having lost confidence in their ability to judge each other face to face, they rely on the "objectivity" of the credential to prove that they still breathe, that they have distinct talents, and that their world, sick and disordered, still has some rationale, some absolute "standard" which cannot be jailed, exiled, fired or impoverished, proving magically their humanity.

Our colleges and universities, among the most powerful and important institutions middle America has produced to serve itself, have launched a new era of credentialism. Our academic institutions, in their maturity, live more and more in paper bags. Subtly over time, but almost irrevocably now, we have institutionalized the formulas and computations upon which most of our business is based. Earned high school averages are squared and multiplied by composite college entrance examination scores. Budget lines are divided by Ph.D.'s and the number of inches a man's publication list is. Human beings requiring offices or classroom seats are multiplied by a square-footage exponent according to rank and class and define what a campus is. Finally, union cards are issued out of all this, imbued with a value essential to obtaining employment, finding a wife, enjoying the theater, or even living with one's self.

Having institutionalized our way of life in this manner, we exalt institutionalization as a way of life. The educational institution, being a collection of things living through hardening academic circulatory and congested respiratory systems, naturally is larger and qualitatively superior to any person or group of persons it is meant to serve. The institutions *live,* having become personalities more real than the persons in them. The highest service a human can perform is to his institution. Ask not what your institution can do for you. Join the team.

Unfortunately, many of us who get these union cards

start believing the myths. We become, especially in our professional operations, paper people, forgetting some of the important aspects of our flesh-and-blood selves. We get accustomed to dealing with other paper people, and soon the things that come to concern us most are external to ourselves and remote from reality. Soon we are living in a paper world, insubstantial and inflammable, a dangerous place in which to play with matches.

Shortly after we moved into the Granada Hotel, a group of forty or fifty of the black community leaders who had been such stout allies in the battle of LIU invited me to a welcoming meeting in a storefront office deep in Bedford-Stuyvesant. The chairlady greeted me cordially, and introduced "Dr. Birenbaum" to the group for a progress report. There was a prolonged and optimistic discussion. Some courses of action were adopted. I was assured of further support. Lists of volunteers for various things were drawn up. Lunchtime was approaching, and the lady in the chair gave some concluding remarks, which went something like this:

"Dr. Birenbaum, we are pleased that you have undertaken this important responsibility in our community. We rallied to your support at LIU. But we don't want you to misunderstand what that support meant, or what our support here now may mean. You may think that what you did at LIU was courageous. You may think that Senator Kennedy is really important out here. You may think you really know something about Bed-Sty, about our children, about our educational problems and our schools. Things we have said about you may lead you to think that you really do know something about these things. Well, whatever you do know is nothing compared to what you don't know. The past is the past. We'll see how fast you learn now. You've got a lot to learn, and we'll try to be helpful. But you'd better not come around here 'courageous hero of LIU,' 'distinguished educational leader,' 'trusted friend of the black people in this community,' 'Mr. Know-It-All!' You've got a lot to learn, and there is nothing you can say to us—nothing—that we may not challenge or know something more about than you, Jim Farmer, Preston Wilcox and all the rest of your so-called experts! So, Dr. Birenbaum, we've just called you 'Doctor' for the last time. From now on you're 'Mister' out here—just like us. Mister Birenbaum, welcome!"

Many substantive issues get hung up on problems of style. Even the problem of style has become a substantive issue in our country. Either we want to do business or we don't. If we don't, there are a million ways to avoid doing business. But if we do, there is certainly some business to be done. Once a black leader, thirty-two years old, came to see me when I was provost at LIU. He told me he had just been elected chairman of one of the Office of Economic Opportunity community corporations. The election had been complicated. Thirty-two people had to be elected to the board by the community, and the board then had chosen its own chairman. There had been a bitter struggle to make the board "representative." X Puerto Ricans had been elected, Y blacks, and Z "others." After he had been elected chairman, and then revealed that he was also a practicing Catholic, his election had almost been undone, so sensitive were the problems of balancing races, religious and ethnic groups. But now, he said, he wanted to plan a mass rally to mobilize the thousands of people living in a nearby public-housing complex. Since LIU had the only auditorium big enough in the neighborhood to accommodate the crowd he expected, he wanted to use it. He gave me a date, and I called and arranged for the room to be available.

He said "Thank you," but there was another problem. His board had decided that the only way it could attract three or four thousand people to a rally was to attack the largest institution in the neighborhood. LIU, my institution, he informed me, obviously was the largest. The problem was: What was the best issue upon which his group could attack mine? He had a list of possibilities— segregated dormitories, inadequate black and Puerto Rican enrollments and employees, real estate wheeling and dealing in the community, etc.—but he really didn't know the facts. Having obtained my auditorium, he wanted to know the facts and get my best advice about my vulnerability!

Some may think this man was naïve. But after you live in the academic world awhile, wheeling and dealing with the people there according to their styles and expectations, I'm not so sure. Now may be the last time for all good paper people to come to the aid of themselves. We need help. And of course we, like our detractors, *are* vulnerable. It's like the closing scene in the movie *Cool Hand Luke,* where Paul Newman, with a hole shot through his head, sinks to his death muttering, "There's been a little misunderstanding here."

Number Two

On the first day at work, my black colleagues proposed that I resign as president of the organization we had created— the Education Affiliate in Bedford-Stuyvesant. Their position was perfectly simple: only a black man could effectively lead and lend credibility to what we proposed to do. They assured me that I was absolutely essential to the effort. I was to be Number Two, designated by whatever title pleased me. But Number One had to be black, and on the extremely vital community front, he would lead.

This issue consumed the first four weeks of our existence. I was shocked and deeply offended by this development, and the black staff members were very sensitive and concerned about my feelings, doing their best to help me understand. I did not view their conduct as a simple powerplay at all. But I had, after all, personally persuaded each member of this staff to join this cause. I had personally conducted the negotiations with Senator Kennedy, establishing the terms to which we had agreed. They had signed letters of contract I had issued. In many ways I had had more experience with educational matters in Bedford-Stuyvesant than most of them. The origin and nature of the invitation to design a new college in this community was a matter of public record. Finally, I had expressed very clearly my conviction that the first president of the new college should be a black man, limiting my own connection to the project to a twelve-to-eighteen-month term.

But as time dragged on and my own sense of frustration mounted, I was prepared to do almost anything in order to get down to work. The issue of my leadership was resolved abruptly when the senator intervened. He declared that we'd better get moving as originally intended or close up shop. We got moving.

This four week debate was by no means a waste of time. I have often regretted that it was not recorded, for in many ways it was a revealing journal of where intelligent and dedicated black and white Americans are in their relationships with one another. None of us had worked together before. We knew one another only by reputation. Wilcox and Farmer were the teachers throughout our discussion; but we all learned a great deal, not only about one another but about the issues we were to face together in the future. Everything was put on the table at the beginning, our prejudices—black and white. Throughout the rest of our association I do not remember one single case in which a racial problem arose among our staff—except in jest. We all learned some good off-color stories in the course of our collaboration.

Theirs, Not Ours

One day not too long after we had moved into the Granada Hotel, Senator Kennedy walked into my hotel-room office unannounced. It was a warm September day. I had my jacket off, my tie loosened, and my feet up on the desk. "What are you doing?" the senator asked. "I'm thinking," I replied. "Fine," the senator said, "but what are you going to do when you put your feet down?"

In my personal relationship with Senator Robert F. Kennedy I had my ups and downs. His expectations were high; his patience was limited. In this respect we were somewhat alike. (I guess I would find it difficult to work for me.) But he was personally interested in what we were doing. I appreciated this. For me it confirmed his sincerity. Unexpected visits or phone calls proved that he was neither too big nor too busy to care. He really cared, and even when you disagreed with him or felt that he expected too much too quickly, you had to take that into account.

Gingerly, we were putting our feet down—in the community, in relationships within our multicorporation complex, in our minds. We talked with everyone we could —with youth groups, welfare-recipient organizations, lawyers, doctors and clergymen, businessmen, from black right to black left, from the militant to those who had already clearly joined the great American middle class. One message came through, loud and clear, almost immediately. It was a message reassuring to those who would work for change. But it was also a message reassuring to those deeply worried about the potential for violence in our country, the abuse of due process, law and order.

A reporter for one of the national news magazines, after spending a few days on our streets, told us he was amazed by his conversations with people in Bedford-Stuyvesant.

"These people," he said, "really believe that the democratic process will work. They are like pioneers. They really think they can control their own affairs in this city." It was clear to us too. Those most abused and oppressed in American society miraculously retained a deep, almost blind faith in the traditions and ideals of the American Revolution. Not only that—they had a deep, and of course generally unrealized desire to possess, to own, to control their own physical environment. They were staunch advocates of the constitutional rights of property!

In these respects I consistently found these people more straightforward than most of the powerful men with whom I was accustomed to doing business in our society. The men of affairs, appearing to be more sophisticated, were generally far more cynical about how things got done or should get done in America. If there was an ideological problem here, it was on the part of those in charge. The dispossessed had actually believed what those with possessions were saying about the way America was, or at least should be. Those in possession, taken more literally than they expected, were stuck with their version of the *American* ideology. It was a curious situation, economic and political, but not ideological.

This point became very clear: the people would honor and respect what they really, not fictitiously, had a stake in. Clearly, our new college had to be organized so that the people it was meant to serve owned it. It had to be theirs, not somebody else's. Not the possession of some remote board, some external power structure. *Theirs.*

This led to some very fundamental propositions. The governing board had to emerge primarily from the immediate community. The college had to address itself first and foremost to the youth of that community—for the most part rejected by the institutions elsewhere. That youth, together with those who would teach them, had to possess the primary power to operate the college on a day-to-day basis. In other words, insofar as the administration and governance of a profession could be democratized, this college had to be democratized. Those to be most directly affected by the college had to have a stake in it.

There were refinements of these propositions. For example, all the service functions of the college—student and faculty housing, restaurants, health clinics, bookstores, barbershops, etc.—were to be organized so that those who were actually a part of the institution and the community itself *shared* possession, managerial responsibility and control, and the services provided. We concluded that the cooperative principle (under the laws of the state of New York) contained great potential in this situation.

Later, after funding negotiations with City University were opened, a member of the Board of Higher Education in New York expressed his fear that a college so organized in Bedford-Stuyvesant would turn out to be "segregated." As Bedford-Stuyvesant was more than 90 percent black, he argued, we might very well turn out with an essentially black board, a black student body, a black president and a black faculty. "A public university in New York cannot support the idea of a segregated college." But of course, as we pointed out, most of the units of City University *were* segregated. With one or two exceptions, all were more than 90 percent white. What's segregated?

Given the way that our cities and our institutions are, there is a dangerous gap between what we practice and what we preach, between what we expect those who want "in" to do, and what those of us who are "in" actually do. In fact, we have asked the dispossessed racial minorities to "integrate" before we ourselves have practiced or achieved "integration" even among ourselves.

I am convinced of the continuing viability of a very fundamental part of the American *business* ethnic. No bargain, no negotiation can succeed in the absence of some parity between those who bargain or negotiate. To compel a "deal" between unequals is to ensure that pigeons will someday come home to roost. There will be no instant integration. *The first step toward an integrated society is to empower its various segregated parts so that there can be no question about the integrity and the bargaining power of those who must eventually do business with each other.*

Red-White-and-Blue Expectations

A college addressed to the youth of Bedford-Stuyvesant obviously would be open to young people possessing high school diplomas of virtually no value. It would also be open to others, of whatever age, who had simply dropped out. They were the majority. We were greatly concerned about an adult clientele without many of the educational skills which it is assumed adults in America should have. This disparity between the reality of the humans and the operational expectations of the society in which they live is the most practical definition of our race problem. A country that creates such a disparity has committed a terrible, terrible crime. A country that tolerates it commits a worse one.

In the United States we have yet to invent an educational institution addressed to grown-up people who are "uneducated," or who are in need of further education. Our adult education programs are seldom seriously offered (especially as high schools and universities present them), or seriously received by those for whom they are intended. By and large they project the academic status quo, sometimes saving the grown-up people from the embarrassment of sitting in classrooms with children, even while they study subjects designed for children taught to them the way children are taught.

Some think the two-year colleges may provide a new option. They still may, but they've gotten themselves into some very difficult bags. By allowing themselves to become filters for the "regular" four-year colleges, they have tied their curricula to a national academic norm which is probably not appropriate for the new clientele and possibly not even for the traditional one. What they produce is popularly regarded as something less than the coin of the realm. The colossal inferiority complex of the two-year college movement reveals that those in charge—administrators and faculty—look "up" instead of out. It is, at best, second-best, often producing educational results far afield from the real educational needs.

In many of the older European countries, at least until very recently, a layer of technical institutes or vocationally oriented training centers provided a further educational outlet for young adults excluded from a university education. These schools are almost totally devoted to making the young people employable in the technological economy, creating a supply of workers to fulfill the manpower needs of national economies. Under Hitler only 5 or 6 percent of Germany's youth were admitted to the universities, and even under the German Reform Law, adopted a few years ago, only 12 to 14 percent will be admitted. Industrialists in West Germany argued against the Reform Law, claiming that an enlarged university admission would imperil the national supply of technicians and technologists.

In our own country, where about half of the youth of high school graduating age are now admitted to our colleges, and where a little more than half of these actually graduate, there is a growing feeling that too many of our young people are encouraged to choose the college option. Some fear the impact of the new student clientele upon the traditions, the "quality" and "standards," the established ways of operation in our universities. Others believe that our university system is overextended, trying to do too many things at once. Still others think that for a large number of our young people, withdrawal from the workaday world, extended isolation within formal educational institutions, works against their mental health, their intellectual and social development. On this last point, men of such divergent views as Bruno Bettelheim and Paul Goodman seem to agree.

But American society is, in its expectations and pretensions, strikingly different from European countries. And the plight of our racial minorities is unique in terms of both its scope and its history. The technology, its centrality to almost everything we do in this country, is most advanced. What job seekers and holders have to know to survive now in our economy is rapidly changing, requiring higher and higher levels of knowledge-acquisition and use. Perhaps industry itself, alone, could provide this input as well as or better than educational institutions organized separate and apart from industry. But unfortunately for those looking for simplistic answers, economic survival is not the only issue.

Of course young people in a community like Bedford-Stuyvesant want and expect to survive in this economy. "Jobs," "income," "decent and rewarding work" are high on the agenda. But no longer *any* job, *any* income, or without question, *any* definition of what is "decent and rewarding." There has been a tendency in our job-training programs and in the two-year-college technology options offered, especially to minority youth, to limit economic opportunity within a very definite range of the technological economy. In the normal progression of the entry of immigrant or underprivileged groups into the American middle class, stages of development have been the routine rule. First things first, and all that. Sons a rung or two higher on the ladder than fathers; second and third generations further along than the pioneering first one.

But ours is not a situation now where a "normal progression" is possible. "Black Is Beautiful" is a slogan which goes far beyond economics. So does the disaffection of many of our brightest middle-class white youth. What we expect from adults in American society now is different from what was expected from adults in Hitler's Germany. Our expectations are even different from current expectations in the German Federal Republic. In many ways our problems are simply symptoms of our differences. Perhaps we really are insane to persist in the operation of this economy within the terms of the humanistic Constitution adopted in 1787. Or perhaps the thrust toward human equality, dignity and integrity is built into our genes, just as the intellectual fruits of our science, technology and bureaucracy are genetic results, revealing the built-in genetic contradiction which seals the doom of our species.

Today's campus disruptions were born in the years 1776 to 1787. Although the mind of Thomas Jefferson was anchored in the traditions of Heidelberg, Oxford, Paris, Bologna, Rome, Greece, the religions of the early Christians and the ancient Hebrews, minds like his transformed the old into something quite new, as in the case of his proposal for a university in Virginia. What was created then was not, of course, the latest thing, nor was it necessarily the Truth. But it was an adventure, a genuine new departure, unlike most of the institutions of learning we have created in this country since the Morrill Act—that is, most of our higher-education establishment.

The traditions of the university in the West are anti- if not counter-revolutionary. Operating within these traditions, the university has produced revolutionary knowledge, but institutionally the uses of the knowledge have been directed mainly toward the confirmation of the status quo, particularly the political and cultural status quo. The themes of peace, integration, equality, freedom and the humane uses of knowledge are ones which traditionally fall beyond the purview of the university.

But in principle the main themes of our society run counter to this deployment of knowledge. In spite of Vietnam, poverty, racism and the overbearing logic of our technology—in spite of Bedford-Stuyvesant—the main themes of our country, in principle, were and still are revolutionary. They are reflected in such questions as these: Can the revolutionary knowledge developed in the universities be used humanely, to conform with what Jefferson and his colleagues apparently meant? What does equality mean, and whatever it meant or means, can we still achieve a version of it consistent with this adventure? Are reason and democracy really consistent? Is war in behalf of peace, given what we know now, realistic? Can Negroes who were once property suddenly become people? Are some genocides more decent than others, some cesspools more fragrant than others?

In any event, I *know* that Bedford-Stuyvesant is crammed full of red-white-and-blue Americans. They really believe that we ought to practice what we preach, and that's the problem. We've oversold America to ourselves, and so many of my very good friends—looking at the street violence and the circuses in the courts and on the campuses—who believe we confront a deeply un-American phenomenon, who think we face a serious threat to American values, completely misread what is going on there. We face a vibrant, far-reaching reassertion of what this country claims, what it has always claimed it is.

A Design for Learning

Tom was twenty-four, just back from Vietnam, a high school dropout, determined neither to make the army a career nor return to the way things were before he went in. He came to the Granada Hotel for advice. He wanted to be a lawyer because he was convinced that the "police court," the only place where he had ever seen a lawyer in action, was "corrupt." Tom was unusually articulate. He was mature. He had been around. But Tom at twenty-four didn't have the vaguest idea what a lawyer is. He didn't know what lawyers do. He didn't know how one becomes a lawyer. He had no idea what life as a lawyer might actually be like.

I do not fault Tom for what he didn't know. *I had grad-uated* from one of the country's best law schools before I began to understand what the practice of law is all about, what lawyers are really like, and what they have to do to survive. And I didn't grow up in Bedford-Stuyvesant, black.

I am astonished over and over again by how many collegians I meet do not understand the realities of decision-making in American society, how real influence and power are exercised, what is really involved in the professions and callings to which they officially aspire, how the real business of America is transacted, gets done. Most of them don't even understand how things get decided and done on the campus.

I have been reading a sampling of freshman themes written by black and Puerto Rican students admitted to Staten Island Community College through City University's College Discovery program. Incredibly insightful and sophisticated concepts and ideas are expressed in these papers—mature, adult thought, born of mature adult experience. But these thoughts are often written in an English language that would discredit an average sixth-grader. The contrast between the level of thought (pursuant to life experience) and the technical competence for expressing the thought (pursuant to prior formal education) is enough to make one cry. There are students, technically competent, whose life experience has been so limited and stunted that they have nothing to say. There are students who have so much to say, but who are hampered absurdly by the lack of the necessary technical equipment. All are young American adults. Each is a unique American educational challenge—at the adult level. And of them all we expect not only that they get jobs and support families, but that they also participate in the political process of the nation, the cultural and social life of the city, and the civic and familial responsibilities of the community. The American situation, in a manner distinct and different from almost any other, defines a distinct and different educational challenge.

The curriculum designed for the proposed Bedford-Stuyvesant college attempted to cope with some of these realities. Every student was to be exposed simultaneously to four levels of educational experience. Each, from the very first day on, was to engage in an internship position somewhere in the city. Each was not only to learn the nuts-and-bolts aspects of performance in some professional or business field, but to learn this in proximity to an important decision-maker in that field. We hoped that the students would begin to perceive the practical connections between work performance and the need to acquire specific bodies of knowledge, between knowing what you're doing and making decisions. Each student was to be paid for his work.

More than a hundred different retail corporations, manufacturing companies, banks, museums, hospitals, lower schools, brokerage firms, etc., were approached, and agreed to accept a cadre of students from the college. Each agreed that the students would be placed in a working situation proximate to a key decision-maker. Each agreed that the place of work would be staged as an auxiliary classroom of the college, and that the executive in charge would be given released time both for special instructional purposes and to participate in the life of the college as a member of the faculty.

In the overall design we figured, first, that throughout

his collegiate education, each student would spend one fifth to one fourth of his total time in the urban internship program. This approach meant that if a student was interested in becoming a teacher, he would find himself in working school classrooms from the word "go"—that if he proposed to be a lawyer, his apprenticeship to a practicing attorney or a civil or criminal court judge would begin when he began his collegiate education, and that if he didn't know what he wanted to be, he would nevertheless, after discussion of his interests, tentatively engage on some front, keeping open the option for a future shift.

Second, at the same time each student was to have access to a skills studio through which the mastery of basic language and numbers skills would be directly linked to the practical exigencies growing out of the internship environment and the parallel requirements of the academic curriculum. The skills studio was to rely heavily upon the tutorial way of teaching.

Third, the liberal arts portion of each student's program —the presentation of the formal academics in subjects such as psychology, economics, literature, philosophy, the basic sciences, etc.—was to be organized around key problems arising out of the internship situation and/or the life of the student's community, the college itself, or where he lived, or both. The main theme here was the connection between thought and action, between relevance and the motivation of the student.

Finally, there were to be master designs of core curricula in each of the college's professional areas of concentration —at the beginning in teacher education, administration and management in business, government, educational and cultural institutions, the creative arts, and pre-law; later, in the science professions—nursing, premed and medical technology. But the student's study in one of these areas was to be related to his response and progress in the internship and liberal-studies components.

This design assumed that the *motivation* of our prospective students was the primary *educational* problem we would initially face. The design attempted to link work and community experience with formal study, the *need* to learn with learning, the need to master thought systems with the need to decide, to commit specific acts. We hoped that the conquest of the weaponry systems essential to thinking—the skills required—would become a subsidiary part of understanding the need to master thought. We hoped that the ultimate decision about career or profession would be stimulated and informed by an interaction between the practical internship exposure and the more formal studies. Out of this we thought that primary teams of three—the internship teacher, the skills studio tutor and a member of the academic faculty—would emerge as a special counseling cadre for each of our students.

This approach led to other practical conclusions. About *time,* for example: it seemed absurd to assume that young people who had dropped out of or emerged from inadequate, even failing lower-school systems, could achieve in two years—in a community-college context—what far more successful high school graduates were taking four years to do. And it seemed wrong to prescribe, that because of past failures, they might only do less. We concluded that the new college had to be a four-year institution, at least. But we really meant *four* years—four *calendar,* not four *academic* years; years that had twelve months in them, which meant that the internship and study scheduling could conform to the realities of urban life patterns rather than to the agrarian calendar, to which most of our academic institutions still adhere.

When one tampers with time, one tampers seriously with the credit-hour method of pacing academic study. Credit hours seemed irrelevant in this case, except as an annual accounting to external agencies of what our students were doing. Fifty-minute class periods and four or five different subject courses each day also seemed inappropriate, given the educational targets involved. We planned for solid study days in disciplinary clusters, accommodated in special physical resource centers. There was to be a language arts day, starting at eight or nine in the morning and running through to four or five o'clock, during which the English language, the appreciation of literature, speech and the dramatic arts would form a composite whole. Not just a single teacher but a team of teachers would work with the students throughout an entire day. There would be a science day, a social studies day, etc. These days might include lectures, seminars, tutorials, library study, as well as field and project experience. It was assumed that students might move through the college at varying rates of achievement—that some might take four years, some more and others less.

These plans grew out of extensive consultations not only among the staff but also with young people, teachers, parents and others in the community we aimed to serve. We knew these proposals contained problems unique to themselves. Some young people, for example, raised the question: Wouldn't the internship experience brainwash or co-opt the participants? Wouldn't such an experience encourage them to feel that the way the Establishments in our society now do business is the *only* way business can be done? Wouldn't success in the context of Chase Manhattan, Macy's or the Museum of Modern Art dull the impulses for reform which the students might naturally bring to this stage of their learning lives? It is a possibility. But we thought that this fear underestimated the students with whom we intended to deal, underestimated the variety of counterexperiences this college would provide, and underestimated the importance of knowing what there is to reform as a precondition to the formulation of reform proposals or courses of action.

As things progressed we became less concerned about

the design of a new college than about the design of a new learning situation. We came to be more concerned about the standards and expectations of the *people* we planned to educate than about preconceived standards and expectations of an *institution* which would somehow accommodate the process.

The Politics of High Finance: Academic Style

Putting together a $20- to $30-million-dollar package to start a new college is not quite like putting together a package to start a new business enterprise or industry. The entrepreneural spirit in education is a bit different.

Very early in the game Senator Kennedy brought us together with the United States Commissioner of Education, Harold Howe II. "Doc" Howe was interested in what we were saying. He came to Bedford-Stuyvesant personally, spent considerable time there meeting people in the community and on the streets, talking with our staff and going over our plans. He was enthusiastic about what he saw, and arranged for members of our staff to meet with members of his in Washington over several days to assess funding possibilities under federal law. Together we made a rather astonishing discovery. Several million dollars were available through various statutory programs to support an operating, recognized, accredited college. But not one federal law as of 1967–1968 had anticipated the need for money to *start,* to *open* the doors of a new college. You actually had to be in business to obtain federal support.

To get into business required compliance with the laws of the state of New York for the chartering of new academic institutions. With Commissioner Howe's endorsement, we traveled to Albany to discuss our problems. In the office of the Commissioner of Education for the State of New York, our reception was plainly positive. There was a willingness to waive intricate regulations policing the credit-hour rigmarole and teacher training requirements in order to permit our deviant approach. We were told that the average lapse of time between the first submission of a plan for a new college and actual chartering was five to seven years. But in our case all stops would be pulled out, and if we did our homework it was conceivable that this period could be cut substantially.

But there were other statutory requirements that could not be waived. We would have to show evidence of a bank balance roughly equal to the cost of operating the college through its first year. We would have to produce a library, or evidence that we could quickly assemble one of a given size and quality. We had to show in advance that we had adequate facilities in which to start classes. And there were other requirements with dollar signs. We estimated that about $3 million would be needed to satisfy these requirements.

Needing a $3-million key to open the door to the federal treasury, we approached the Ford Foundation. Now our endorsements and support included not only Senator Kennedy's and Commissioner Howe's but also Albany's. Executives at Ford studied our plans with their usual meticulous care and expressed keen interest in what we proposed, but they were concerned about the future. Assuming that a package could be assembled to sustain the college over the first four years of its life, who would pick up the tab thereafter? Without commitment, it was suggested that some Ford support might be forthcoming, given a reasonable answer to that question.

Now, this was a proper question—but one to which we had no ready answer. We knew that the continuing needs of the college would probably exceed what private philanthropy alone could or would produce. We knew that federal policy was erratic and undependable. In New York there were two public higher-education systems—the state and city universities. But the former, by law, was precluded from operating four-year colleges in New York City—this was City University's private turf just as State monopolizes the public sector beyond the five boroughs of the city. Both, in our estimate at that time, were suspect, anyway. City University looked to us like a vast, encrusted, tradition-bound and segregated university, hopelessly ensnarled in its own bureaucratic red tape. In Harlem the black community was plainly hostile to City College, CUNY's nearest campus. And in our own territory, City University had declined, a few years before, to establish a new community college, preferring instead, after a heated public debate, to invest in a site at Manhattan Beach, on a remote white edge of Brooklyn. City University was not a beloved enterprise in Bedford-Stuyvesant. It was, we thought, a major part of the problem. If City had been doing what it should have done, there would have been no need for our collegiate effort in this community in the first place.

We hoped vaguely that the new college, proving itself during its first four years, firmly establishing its own terms of existence, could then, by negotiating with public funding sources, create a stable fiscal base, half public and half private—a unique funding situation through which one half could check and balance the other. But this was not the kind of assurance Ford or other foundations sought. Their risk-taking propensities, however honest, did not extend to *ultimate* risks. They too, finally, were academic.

Though the Education Affiliate had been in existence less than six months, these matters had already arisen—the development of the preliminary outline of the collegiate design and the initial probes on the dollar fronts. The deeper we got into the Bedford-Stuyvesant situation, the more desperate and urgent the community's educational needs and problems seemed. We confronted a crisis, and we were operating in a crisis-laden atmosphere. Conveying this sense of desperate urgency to others was often a frustrating and discouraging undertaking—but not with Senator Kennedy.

Early one morning in the fifth month, a call from the senator summoned me to breakfast in his United Nations Plaza apartment. It was a rainy and perilous day on the East River Drive, and I arrived on an hour's notice, breathless, a little late. The barefooted senator in a bathrobe, his wife and several staff members were roaming around making phone calls, caucusing in corners and bedrooms, munching Danish pastry and drinking coffee.

"Have you got your twenty million?" the senator asked. He knew very well I didn't, but I explained how we had been kicked in the front end by the federal problem and in the rear by the foundation. "Well, where are you going to get it?" he wanted to know.

I told him that we had informally opened discussions with the State University system in Albany about the possibility of a unique combined State University-City University approach, through which these two systems might join in a common collegiate effort in New York City. Knowing that the two systems were politically competitive, I foresaw an interesting and fruitful opportunity in behalf of our experiment if we could constructively capitalize upon the competitive impulses of these two bureaucracies. But the senator would have none of it. He was impatient. He wanted—as indeed we did—the college open and operating by the following fall, and he wanted to make the fact of that public as quickly as possible. He turned to an aide and asked that a call be placed to Al Bowker, the chancellor of the City University system. On the phone he told Dr. Bowker that City University ought to start a new college in Bedford-Stuyvesant—the college we had been working on—and arranged for a meeting within the week in the offices of William Paley, chairman of the board of CBS and a board member of the Bedford-Stuyvesant Development and Services Corporation.

I had of course been in touch with Dr. Bowker and members of his staff about what we were doing in Bedford-Stuyvesant. He had shown keen interest in the progress of the plans, but was cagey about his own intentions. I was convinced that it was not quite time to enter serious negotiations with City University. Two things looked definite to me. First, City University could not long avoid making some public commitment in Brooklyn, offering some solution to the growing higher-education problems confronting the minority communities. Second, from all I could gather then, City's answer would be another two-year college—vocationally oriented, concentrating on the technologies, essentially within the going terms of doing educational business, City University style. If correct, my estimate suggested profoundly important compromises of our proposal. It meant that City Universiy would mis-interpret the real needs and circumscribe the recruitment of relevant talents. It meant that CUNY would never establish effective community "ownership" of its own in-stitution, would never regard the community's youth in terms of a four-year educational opportunity, would never deviate from its conventional way of building campuses, hiring talent and establishing working conditions, what-ever made sense in our situation.

Politically, considering Senator Kennedy's stature, our bargaining position was not to be dismissed. But on educa-tional terms, unless we could get State University involved, and move toward commitments from HEW and the foundations, I didn't think we had a leg to stand on. My own staff and the community people to whom we were reporting were terribly upset by the prospect of what they all regarded as a premature negotiation with City University.

The discussions in Mr. Paley's office, and the two or three meetings that followed them, had very little to do with educational designs or programmatic plans. They focused strictly on the politics and economics of starting a new public college in a black urban community. Some research on these negotiations, done by Arthur Tobier, a member of the staff of the Center for Urban Education in New York, was reported in that organization's journal, the *Urban Review*:

Birenbaum still hoped to find a private "buyer," but the Kennedy organization and the businessmen of the D & S Corporation finally felt that too much persistence on the part of the Education Affiliate would interfere with their own ordering of the priorities. The school should be funded through City University and Birenbaum's unique plan for it would take form in the course of time. "What we're trying to do," explained one Kennedy aide, "is to get in a nick here and a nick there, and another nick over there, without the Man noticing, until before long the fat is flowing out into the gutter. The important thing is to get the institutions up, make them visible, and the community will identify with them." Thus the proper approach would be to take on the City University, particularly its Chancellor, Albert H. Bowker, directly, with Senator Kennedy himself providing the necessary political muscle. . . .

In the first meeting with Bowker, Kennedy tried to impress upon him how much importance the Kennedy organization attached to having the City University choose Bedford-Stuyvesant as the site for its next community college. In fact, there were plans to open a new college, but had been tentatively reserved for a distant and rival area in the Bronx. Bowker, too, praised the Education Affiliate's prospectus, but said that his institution could not possibly submit to having an autonomous community governing board and student administration; nor could he guarantee that if there were to be a college in Bedford-Stuyvesant, it would be, as required by Birenbaum's program, a four-year school. Birenbaum replied that these particular two points could not even be open to negotiation. For this remark, he was taken aside by Kennedy and told not to pursue his objections any further. The group agreed to meet again after the Chancellor had had an opportunity to reason among his peers.

Both Bowker and Edelstein left the meeting feeling extremely wary about getting involved in Bedford-Stuyvesant. [Julius Edelstein had served as administrative assistant to Senator Lehman, and then as education assistant to Mayor Wagner. He was during these negotiations, and still is, City University's vice-chancellor for urban affairs.] A first principle of the political mechanic, Edelstein said, is "never build on ground someone else has prepared." As for Bowker, he had no money in his current budget for seeding such a project. . . . Above all, the lack of a clearcut focus of power in Bedford-Stuyvesant—reapportionment had just given the area a seat in Congress for the first time and half a dozen people were jockeying to run for the seat and for the political leadership it would mean—put the instinctive politician in Bowker off. The lesson of instinct was to keep one's distance. [Among those jockeying for position regarding the new congressional seat was James Farmer, a member of the Affiliate's staff, and Judge Thomas Jones, chairman of the board of the Restoration Corporation. The seat was finally won by Congresswoman Shirley Chisholm.]

A call went through from Kennedy's office to Anthony Travia, speaker of the New York State Assembly in Albany, who owed his position of leadership to Kennedy's support in 1966. Travia was asked to support the Bedford-Stuyvesant site, and to impress Bowker with the urgency of the Senator's desires. The Chancellor, perhaps mindful that the solvency of his expanding university must ultimately depend on the good will of the state legislature, needed no promoting. A further meeting with the D & S Corporation—this time Kennedy was absent—found Bowker ready to agree that the university's seventh community college be committed to the Negro community. The educational questions would be left to be worked out in committee. In order to placate the old-line political organizations in Brooklyn, not particularly sympathetic to the Kennedy program, and in order not to appear to be reneging on his promise to the Bronx, Bowker's announcement on January 22 [1968] referred to the Board's having approved *three* new colleges for the coming three years.

The meaning and nature of the settlement with Bowker was not lost on Bedford-Stuyvesant. Some 30 community groups, represented by a panel of more than a hundred people, had for months been sought out by the Education Affiliate, and had offered their advice. Ordinarily competitive with one another—ranging ideologically from the most conservative to the most extreme, from the integrationist matriarchy to separatist youth—these various groups had spontaneously constituted themselves a coalition to represent the community in dealings with City University.... Moreover, in an action without precedent, the University system immediately granted the coalition legitimacy as spokesman for the community. (The *Urban Review,* Vol. iv, No. 1 (September 1969), "A Political Education," Arthur Tobier, p. 21)

Assuming the accuracy of Mr. Tobier's report, I was unaware of the details of the behind-the-scenes political maneuvering going on. Naturally I suspected more was going on than was available to my eye, but there was nothing I could do about that. My concerns were elsewhere, with the design we had produced. After the final session in Mr. Paley's office, when an understanding was reached, Senator Kennedy, pleased, pulled me aside to congratulate me, to tell me once again how great our design for the college was, and to reassure me that the things given away to obtain the result—the idea of an autonomous community board and a four-year institution —could readily be regained in more elaborate negotiations to follow. But I was not so sure. I was deeply depressed by the "victory." Surprised, and a little bit annoyed by my mood, the senator said; "All right. Are you so sure that you are right that you would stand up on a public platform

and tell the people of Bed-Sty that you rejected a twenty-
to thirty-million-dollar City University commitment just
because they might do their kind of college instead of
yours?" Put this way, there was but one answer. No one
embarking on a real experiment can predict the outcome,
be sure that he is "right." That fact is implicit in the
definition of "experiment."

After a flashy press conference in Brooklyn's Borough
Hall, at which almost every politician in town—the mayor,
the borough president, state assemblymen, local congress-
men, the senator, and various and sundry others—took
their proper credits for arranging a new college in Bedford-
Stuyvesant, the community coalition and City University
embarked upon months-long negotiations about the
details. And as Mr. Tobier describes it: "The Board of
Higher Education pretty much conceded to the coalition
the college laid out by the Education Affiliate. That is,
it accepted the demand for a four-year institution, community involvement in decision-making, an innovative
admissions policy; all in all a new form. But exterior events
intervened in the matter of the school's leadership."

It was a foregone conclusion that the president of the
new college would be a black man, but things fell apart
when a specific selection was faced. Eventually, the board
broke off negotiations with the coalition and moved along
another line. On March 3, 1970, City University issued a
press release announcing the appointment of the first
president for a new college in Bedford-Stuyvesant:

> A president for the City University of New York's long-
> planned experimental college in the Bedford-Stuyvesant
> section of Brooklyn was announced today. . . . The
> new presidential appointment came in a joint announce-
> ment by the six elected public officials of mid-Brooklyn
> and the Board of Higher Education. The six elected
> officials are: U.S. Representative Shirley Chisholm, State
> Senator Waldaba Stewart, Assemblyman Bertram L.

Baker, Assemblyman Thomas R. Fortune, Assemblyman Samuel D. Wright, and City Councilman William C. Thompson. They served as a consultative committee to the executive committee of the Board of Higher Education which served as a presidential search panel . . .

CUNY Chancellor Albert H. Bowker said: "Without the vigorous firm and unanimous support of the elected public officials who represent the people of mid-Brooklyn, plans for this new college could not have been realized . . ."

Chancellor Bowker, commenting on [the] appointment, said, "The University is redeeming a pledge made when Kingsborough Community College was permanently located in the Manhattan Beach area. We then promised that the next college for the Borough would be located in Central Brooklyn . . . we look for this college to be a pioneer on a vital urban educational frontier . . ."

There usually is a tremendous gap between the good intentions stated in press releases and the realities to which such statements refer. Between the press conference in Brooklyn's Borough Hall in January of 1968, when City University pledged itself to a new college in Bedford-Stuyvesant, and the university's press handout in March of 1970 announcing the appointment of a black president for this college, Senator Robert F. Kennedy had been lowered into his grave. Press releases may ignore history; but they do not, in and of themselves, make history either.

Shortly after the senator's murder, I left the Bedford-Stuyvesant project, and shortly after that, the Education Affiliate was officially dissolved, its meager possessions and dreams contractually handed over to City University. But the Restoration Corporation's effort to rebuild Bedford-Stuyvesant continues, and a new college will open its doors in the fall of 1971. What Senator Kennedy meant is not dead in Brooklyn.

To Albert Bowker's credit, to the credit of the colossal bureaucracy he led, where there was in fact to be no

college, now there was one. Richard Trent, the new
president for the college, is intelligent and eager. And
the college he is starting will not be just another two-
year technology training center. He and his colleagues
assembling there are shaping their own dreams, and this
is, after all, as it should be. Who is to issue a bulletin on the
state of their health? Being alive, well or seriously sick,
they represent the future's hope, and they have hope. And
so, in spite of it all, do I. Life and hope go together. Who
knows, finally, who or what is right?

But the ripened fruits of my own experience in Chicago
and Detroit and at Long Island University remain among
the most controversial and doubtful parts of the present
effort in Brooklyn. The architectural-planning design for
an urban campus built along the streets of the city, linear
and woven throughout its community, intimately connected to other existing resources and institutions and committed to a participatory role in the remodeling of neighborhoods economically and residentially—this part of our
proposal seems too complex to some, and to many too far
afield from what a campus in the city ought to be. Serious
consideration is being given to this approach to urban
campus development in other major cities in the country.
But in Brooklyn it is not likely that the innovation will
go this far.

The politics and the prejudices in this situation will
probably favor building new walls around Bedford-Stuyvesant's new campus. And in due course, inevitably, new
walls become old, serving all of the purposes that ancient
walls are meant to serve.

The Explosion of a Superblock

The more we came to understand the physical, economic,
and political characteristics of Bedford-Stuyvesant, the

more it became apparent that the medieval, Oxonian conception of a university campus corresponded, when transplanted onto the surface of the contemporary American city, to the ghetto. The wall, the enclave, the introversion, the apartheidness of the whole operation imbued the typical American urban campus with the same ghetto qualities and mentality that American society has imposed upon the territories where its black, Spanish-speaking and other urban minorities live.

It was a striking discovery: how the urban academic centers of intellectual liberalism—pro-integration, egalitarian, and all that—could be, by the way they built, internally organized and conducted themselves, elitist, segregated and essentially opposed to what they ideally stood for or meant to achieve. Moreover, we encountered very early in our work the colonial approach to the renovation of our inner-city slums. Urban renewal, perceived primarily as a technical and technological challenge, naturally leads to imperialistically imposed solutions. A slum, by definition, does not generate or contain the advanced, sophisticated technical or technological expertise American society has produced for the eradication of a slum. It follows that the slum does not produce a population capable of understanding who or how such resources are applied. Therefore the talent, the required thought and treasure, the "solutions," must be imported, and given the political realities of our cities, imposed. This is a traditional rationale for colonial exploitation.

For a while I. M. Pei, the distinguished Chinese-American architect whose career in its early stages was advanced by Bill Zeckendorf, was the house planner-designer for the Kennedy operations in Brooklyn. He came, he looked, and he recommended the superblock road to the resurrection of the deteriorating areas of the community. Streets were to be disrupted. Backyards were to be converted into inner parks. Two-, four-, or six-block squares were to be created, rearranging the horizontal, street-oriented flow of this community's life. Segments of the community were to be rebuilt so that they looked inward, away from the streets, away from the meaning of the whole, the sense of which was unfolding so slowly and tentatively. Suburban values infiltrated the plan. This approach seemed to ignore what we were learning about the people, what they thought they wanted, how they felt, their life habits. Renewal, clearly, was not simply a physical, technological puzzlement. Renewal also meant the proper accommodation of life styles and patterns unique to this population, imperfect not because they deviated from some external norm, but because they were improperly accommodated.

Typically, buildings and streets in the way of a new urban campus development are torn down or closed. The traditional prejudices about what a campus is or must be invariably take precedence over the ongoing life patterns and needs of the neighborhoods in which it is to be located. This approach was unacceptable in our case. To accommodate the educational programs we had designed, physical things had to be created in a pattern opposite from the superblock, the walled-in enclave, separate and apart from the community and the people we meant to serve. The new college, literally, had to be integrated into its community, even though the community was not "integrated" into its city.

We took these ideas to Harold Gores at the Educational Facilities Laboratories, a subsidiary of the Ford Foundation, and asked for money to hire an architect to help us spell them out. We found him in Atlanta, Georgia, of all places. Joe Amisano had grown up on the streets of Bedford-Stuyvesant. His firm contained a surprising number of young black architects, aggressively recruited from the five black colleges in the Atlanta metropolitan area.

In our situation Joe faced a formidable and unusual challenge. Architects on educational jobs must, first and foremost, contend with the educators. Of all the clients architects confront, educators are probably the most demanding and the least informed about what they want. Most academic administrators and professors cannot accurately generalize about their present activities, quite apart from predicting with any precision what they expect to be doing three to five years in the future. Consequently, a large part of new academic construction is imperfect before it is actually begun or outmoded long before it is completed or brought into use.

But in our case we insisted upon the community input in addition to our own. And not all elements in the community were completely sold on our conclusions. There was a faction, mainly professional and middle-class, which felt that a college in the black community should be designed just like one in a white community, only more so. While acknowledging the need for *programmatic* innovation, they felt that the physical presence of the college should show whitey, in his own terms, that Bedford-Stuyvesant could do as well or better. Exteriors should say to the world: This is what *you* mean by a college. Interiors should be just a shade plusher. But the majority of those with whom we worked understood. The problem was mainly one of detailing a reasonable translation of the new ideas into the physical result.

At the outset we recognized a few very basic nonacademic facts. We estimated that a four-year college, ultimately to serve eight to ten thousand students in addition to its adult and community programs, would require, minimally, a 25-to-40-million-dollar capital investment. This would represent the largest single capital investment in Bedford-Stuyvesant for any purpose—housing, industry, public construction—made since World War II. We knew that once the college was at full strength, its annual operating expenditures would range between 15 million and 20 million dollars. This would make our college one of the largest, if not the largest, single economic enterprise in the community. It was evident that what we intended to do carried implications far beyond issuing diplomas. Our operations and investments would have a tremendous impact upon patterns of doing business, housing renovation, jobs. The decisions about where to put the college and how to build it went far beyond what the academic entrepreneurs alone should or could properly decide. Obvious as this conclusion seems, it is not one commonly accepted by those with the responsibility to expand educational premises in the city.

Moreover, what we had planned educationally meant that we had to honor and respect the life style of the community, its rich existing architecture and the substantial resources already there, as a potential contribution to what the college would be. There were many public schools, fine parks, hospitals, centers of commerce and civic enterprise in Bedford-Stuyvesant. We saw direct relationships between these resources and our teacher training programs, what we planned in the field of recreation, the internship program and adult education. What we wanted was a "campus" which blended into the community, one woven throughout a substantial territory (finally about forty blocks), a decentralized, antisuperblock operation which intimately connected, at the street level, with the ongoing life of the neighborhood.

A building-by-building inventory of almost any substantial section of Bedford-Stuyvesant reveals a mosaic of contrasting conditions. There are some superb buildings, well preserved and maintained. There are large deteriorating sections, essentially solid stock, on the way downhill but worth rescuing and still rescuable. There are slums, beyond saving. And there is the ever-present pattern of decayed cavities—bombed-out lots, vacant holes full of refuse and the skeletons of dead automobiles. Nor are these various conditions always compacted—centralized contiguously. More often single blocks contain examples of each.

The art of weaving would be complex. A scalpel, not a meat axe would be required. What was needed was a precise and skillful deployment of our chips, putting them down where they could do the most good, given what we would confront on any block in the territory.

Together with Amisano and his team, we hit the streets of Bedford-Stuyvesant. We went everywhere and at all hours of the day and night, sometimes, we thought, literally taking our lives in our hands. The result was the design of an attitude as much as of an architectural scheme. (The plan has been published by the Educational Facilities Laboratories, *A College in the City: An Alternative*, New York, 1969.) Amisano says:

> It's not to be a school with a front gate which lets some people in and keeps others out, and which you lock up at night and which you impose on people who might be intimidated by it. It's a school that has doors everywhere which give you immediate access to where you want to go. We are interested in the walkup college. We want to attach it to the subway system, and put up glass walls around the sub stations where it passes through the college so it can be seen as an integral part of the college. The public buses that circulate in the area are our campus buses. The facilities will be where the community can get at them. The library will be a dispensary giving away paperbacks, instead of just maintaining an expensive collection of hardcover volumes. The school cafeterias will be as available to a plumber working on Fulton Street as to the students—maybe there will be a Chock full O'Nuts franchise run by students. On the level above the street is a place to bring your lunch if you want, a place to sit and relax. There'll be about 50 stores along Fulton, and another 50 store fronts for other functions. The businesses will all be cooperatives, some will be arrangements between the student government and private interests. Whatever

the case, it ought to be flexible. There's no reason why the students can't handle all of it.

"Everything we're going to try to illustrate in our plans is taken from the milieu and context of what is happening in Bedford-Stuyvesant today. This is a viable, living community. Some of the brownstones and limestones here were done by architects doing houses on Fifth Avenue at the same time. The densities are intolerable, but it's the density that gives the place its special character, and to assume otherwise is like defoliating the whole forest so you can see the trees. There's a tremendous need for open space in Bedford-Stuyvesant. But you don't have to tear the place down to establish it. Just find those places meaningful to the people. Look for the values that exist; incorporate what's to be seen. You can't ignore these people.

"Not ignoring the people" led to some other departures in academic planning. The library, for example. The central problem in most academic libraries is the security of the main floor. Books are imprisoned. The success of library administration is often measured by how efficiently what goes out is policed, how difficult access can be made, how little is "stolen." In this community there were very few decent bookstores. We knew that our library would have a major role to play throughout Bedford-Stuyvesant. Our first floor had to be a supermarket, not a prison. This conclusion went beyond architectural design.

It led into the problems of budgeting and financing an academic-community library, and this, in turn, led to intensive discussions with the publishing industry in New York where tentative agreements were reached for the inexpensive production, experimentally, of large new bodies of printed materials.

As for housing, we traveled to a large Midwestern state university where we were told the most up-to-date dormitory construction had been completed. On the edge of a prairie we saw sixteen-story towers, typical rabbit-hutch dormitories, room priced out at $8,000 each to accommodate two students per room, exclusive of land and common-area costs. Students ate in impersonal, noisy cafeterias. They shared bathrooms. Sexes were segregated. Generally it had been assumed that all decent recreation and relaxation should occur in public, in common areas where privacy was next to impossible. The typical walk-up or town-house-type construction in Bedford-Stuyvesant is three stories high, each floor containing a two- or three-bedroom apartment. In a two-bedroom apartment, with its own sitting room, kitchen, bathroom, dining and study room, four students could be housed. At the costs involved in the Midwest example, the construction cost of housing four students in such an apartment would be $16,000. Multiplying this by three, we asked: What kind of new three-story town house could we build in this part of Brooklyn for $48,000, exclusive of land cost? Obviously, we could house students, faculty and community people in common buildings this way, under conditions where normal, decent urban life styles could be respected, where people could live together in an atmosphere different from the army barracks so typical of what many of our colleges provide for their students. The Educational Facilities Laboratories Report of this plan concludes:

> The kind of challenge represented by housing is exactly what this new kind of college and this new kind of planning process is all about. It is one of the main reasons why this plan so far has stressed the necessity for flexibility in the distribution of college facilities, the maintenance of the urban mix and joint occupancies, and the establishment of close links with every segment of the community. An academic ghetto would obviously contribute nothing to the solution of these problems. But a college that works with the community, that occupies only one or two floors of a building, a college that can

move out of a building if it is suddenly needed for other purposes and move into a new combination with other functions, can solve problems and meet challenges that conventional college planning is incapable of dealing with.

But, of course, the fundamental questions remains: Is this what a college is all about, should be about? We remain at a very primitive point in the process of the reconstruction of our cities. We are primitives in the translation of the American ideals into the life patterns of the people in our great cities. And worst of all, our commitment, *our will to act* remains, in the estimate of those who must believe in us most of all, in doubt.

A Hole in the Head

Following the agreement with City University, the staff of the Education Affiliate continued to work on the details of its design, knowing that CUNY would probably follow its own course. About the college, we were in a depressed limbo. But we hoped.

We also turned our attention to a new and urgent problem. The battle for the decentralization of the governance and management of the giant public school system was at its height. It appeared that some decentralization plan would result. We began the design of a community resource center in anticipation of that result, a desperately needed agency to equip parents' groups, clusters of local school administrators, teachers and students, and leadership in the community with the technical resources, expert talents, and knowledge required at the neighborhood level in order to confront the complicated task ahead—popular participation in the development of educational policy.

Meanwhile, Senator Kennedy had finally thrown his

hat into the Democratic presidential nomination ring. A
new excitement and urgency touched all of us who worked
in any of his enterprises. Most of us, because of the Vietnam
war, rejected the Johnson-Humphrey option. And in Bedford-Stuyvesant we felt keenly Eugene McCarthy's utter
lack of understanding for what concerned us most. We had
eagerly awaited Kennedy's move, and during those busy
days when he occasionally was in our neighborhood, we
were inspired afresh both by his commitment and by the
fighting trim he displayed.

Late on the afternoon of the senator's great California
primary victory, I received a telegram from him reading:

> I WOULD GREATLY APPRECIATE YOUR
> SUPPORT IN THE DIFFICULT MONTHS
> AHEAD AND HOPE YOU WILL AGREE TO
> SERVE AS A VICE CHAIRMAN OF THE
> NEW YORK CITIZENS FOR KENNEDY
> COMMITTEE

The senator was due in New York the next day to begin
his primary campaign in our own state. After the telegram
arrived I received a call from the New York Kennedy
office arranging for a meeting with the senator and others
late the next afternoon. But, of course, events intervened,
and for some of us, the next afternoon never came. Within
a day or so another telegram arrived.

> YOU ARE INVITED TO ATTEND A RE-
> QUIEM MASS IN MEMORY OF ROBERT
> FRANCIS KENNEDY AT ST. PATRICKS
> CATHEDRAL IN NEW YORK CITY ON
> SATURDAY, JUNE 8, 1968 AT 10 A.M.
> INTERMENT WILL BE AT ARLINGTON
> CEMETERY, ARLINGTON, VIRGINIA AT
> 5:30 P.M. THE KENNEDY FAMILY

I was shaving on the morning of the day we were to meet in New York when I heard on the transistor what had happened a few hours before. Few events have ever struck simultaneously at so many of the foundation stones of my being—at the meaning of my work, at my personal conduct, at the very meaning of myself. The tragic, irrational, unbelievable hole in Robert Kennedy's head blew open a vast hole in my spirit. My emotional reaction to that time has grown into a deeper understanding of the great vacuum Robert Kennedy's death left. For me this is not an abstract feeling or a conclusion related to ideology. It is instead a sadness born of knowing him in a real place—Bedford-Stuyvesant—at a real time—in 1967 and 1968—in the midst of real combat. Not everyone in Brooklyn agreed with what he was trying to do. Not everyone liked him. He was controversial and complicated, responsible for a multitude of decisions, big and small, right and wrong. But he was seriously moving, deeply moved by what he saw and heard, politically muscular and hard, capable of the tough decision and the determination to make it. He gave a unique visibility to the problems. He inspired people—including me, sometimes in spite of myself, and in spite of him. For those of us who take our political responsibilities seriously, he was a viable American option at a time (and since) when there weren't too many.

Today, as then, Bedford-Stuyvesant is there—its rat-infested miseries; its annual winter celebrations—the deaths of its little children in the tenement fires; and its hopes, its strengths and the enduring genius of its humanity—not to be denied. Not to be denied by what we do to ourselves, to John and Robert Kennedy, to Martin Luther or Malcolm. Not to be denied. It all goes on. It, we —each in our own place, in our own way, in our own time.

And it *does* mean something, even if we are not yet sure what. For one thing, it means there will be a new college in Bedford-Stuyvesant—a college for the people there—named after Medgar Evers.

Chapter Ten

The Inauguration

Islands, Staten and Others

New York is a city of islands, inhabited, I have learned, by millions of insular people, resident mainly inside themselves, disconnected from each other by deep moats and turbulent rivers of misunderstanding, suspicion and distrust.

Except for the Bronx, which is on the mainland, everything depends on bridges and boats. For most continental Americans, accustomed to the landlocked solidity and immensity of the land, a nickel trip on the Staten Island ferry is a rare adventure, a trip which, by the very mechanics of it, anticipates the excitement of an arrival at an alien port. But when the ferry arrives, when it docks, America is there waiting, solid, determined, convinced of its own right meaning, usually silent, but potentially volatile and violent.

Just before Bunker Hill, the Continental Congress was about to send marshals to Staten Island to compel its

people to elect representatives to the confederated legislature of the several states. In Staten Island they wanted no
part of it. They could manage their own affairs without
outside help, thank you.

At the outset of the Revolution, General Howe established the main British headquarters on the island, commanding the port of New York. To service the twenty
thousand troops under his command there, he stripped the
territory—requisitioning the local livestock, chopping
down the forests. And yet, most of the local population
remained devoted to the Crown.

After the Civil War, before Newport was developed,
Staten Island was the summer spa for the rich, especially
from the South. There is a place, obscure, not honored,
near the ferryboat terminal where the proclamation was
read abolishing slavery in the last place where it persisted
north of the Mason-Dixon line. Then there was a larger
proportion of blacks on the island than now—roughly
one-third, compared with less than 10 percent now. The
island is rich with history. Garibaldi worked in a brewery
there for two years before he returned to Italy to do his
thing. Thoreau walked along its magnificent beaches now
marked by signs saying "SWIMMING UNSAFE. POLLUTED
WATERS." Emerson summered there.

Until its beautiful new bridge was opened a few years
ago, Staten Island's connection to New York City was as
brittle as the paper on which a treaty is written. Even now,
many of its people are not so sure they want to join. But
America is in Staten Island, holding in her hands the keys
to a part of what we want to know. And Staten Island is in
New York City, close, precariously close to the city's fate,
to the future of itself.

The Ball and the Little Red Book

I had been president of the Staten Island Community College for more than a year before the Board of Higher Education and the college itself ventured to confirm the fact officially through a formal inauguration. And even now, given the flow of events, there are probably some who feel the authorities acted precipitously.

Senator Kennedy's death had dramatically made me realize that the fruitful part of my own work in Brooklyn had come to an end. Within a week after that horrible event in June of 1968, I went to see the chancellor of City University, Albert H. Bowker, looking for my next job. During my Long Island University crisis, Dr. Bowker had been among the first to call offering a sympathetic hand. Though we sometimes represented divergent views during the subsequent Bedford-Stuyvesant negotiations, the debates were, I believe, honest, and did not diminish our respect for each other. At times, I'm sure, he thought my educational positions were a little way-out. But as he once commented to a newspaper reporter, City University was big and many-splendored, and it could, or ought to be able to, tolerate the likes of me, along with everything else it encompassed. Perhaps the concept "If you can't beat them, join them" was present to some extent in both our minds. In any event, the Long Island and Bedford-Stuyvesant adventures left me in no revolutionary frame of mind. More than ever I felt committed to an all-out effort to reform, a commitment which naturally led me back into the Establishment in the hope, perhaps misplaced, of disrupting from the inside.

In Bedford-Stuyvesant I argued vigorously against the junior or community college format in that new design. But in that situation I realized for the first time how many chips those in charge of higher education at every level were placing upon the two-year college as *the* response to the growing minority-group pressures for access to education beyond the twelfth grade. Though I had worked in almost every other kind of institution during my career, with the community colleges I had virtually no experience. They represented an important deficiency in my professional education.

At the time I saw Dr. Bowker, Staten Island was in search of a new president. As I spoke to the faculty representatives and the students, and for the first time began to explore the island itself, I knew that if they asked me to come there, I would go.

I had never been inaugurated before, and I was not quite sure what was expected of me. It was to be a large and complicated event, and I thought perhaps I would have some administrative responsibility for it. But I had underestimated Arleigh Williamson, founder of the college, prime mover in the creation of the city's two-year college system, now over eighty—a man to whom our college meant something deeply personal. Arleigh was chairman of the board's committee for the governance of our college, and he, together with a committee of deans, the faculty and student government, took charge of the show, relieving me of my worries. They asked me to do but two things: to give a proper speech (hopefully, brief), and to supply them with a list of special guests I might like to invite. My response on both points gave them cause to pause.

About guests, I wanted our students to be there—all four or five thousand of them. This seemed reasonable to me, even though I knew that students usually are not encouraged to attend inaugurations, other than through a few token representatives. Usually the president of the student government is programmed to extend greetings from the student body to the new president. Usually a corps of students is mobilized to act as ushers or to sing in a choir. But as for the rest, they are seldom encouraged to come, and from their point of view, given how most of these pomp-and-ceremony occasions are, they are not eager to get involved.

But in addition to my mother, my wife and children, and a few close friends, I wanted the students there. This presented complications. How would we get them there? A cocktail reception was planned for the faculty and the guests from the board and the community. Would the students be invited to drink? If they came, where would we put them? I was not interested in the details. I knew how to get them there. Equip them with the money to hire one of the leading groups to which they dance—the Beatles, or something like that. They'd come. About the rest, others could worry.

And so it came to pass. The students held an Inaugural Ball, engaging the Brooklyn Bridge to play. Thousands came—not only the students in the college but their friends from other colleges and high schools in the city. It was a wonderful, rollicking gala event. And when it came time for the president of the student government to greet me, he called several other students forward to share in the greeting—the leader of the black student organization, the editor of the paper, captains of the athletic teams, the chairman of the Maoist leftists. Together they presented me a bronze plaque inscribed with an informal motto I had adopted reflecting the spirit of community possessiveness I hoped we could develop inside the college. It read: "Its Ours, Not Theirs." (It meant: We are not the pawns of elusive external forces.) And in front of the assembled multitude, the chancellor, the board, and the people of Staten Island, one of the students presented me with a copy of Mao's Little Red Book, signed by all of the students who belong to the group who subscribe to that sort of thing on our campus. The audience roared, accepting this friendly gesture in the spirit in which it was made.

It was a rare moment of good will on our campus, of close feeling between the faculty, the students and the citizens who paid our way. My mother beamed. It was one of the few occasions on which she could actually see what I was supposed to be doing. It was, in her estimate, the kind of constructive activity about which she had always preached to her son.

To Honor and Respect the Young

My speech was another matter, calling as it did for the abolition of the very kind of college of which I was then being inaugurated president.

I came to Staten Island knowing virtually nothing about the two-year college. There was a growing mood in the public policy-making places to offer the junior college as *the* equal educational opportunity for minority-group youth. And most of the minority-group thought and experience to which I had been exposed took a very dim view of the two-year college as an answer to their higher-education problems. Clearly, one way or another, the two-year college was a central piece in the urban educational picture—a piece about which I had to learn.

After my first exploratory year, I had reached some preliminary conclusions:

> "I am convinced, after twelve months as president of this college, that the present two-year format of the community colleges is no longer viable in the city. Two years is just not long enough to accommodate the kind of education our students are demanding and ought to have. It is not long enough to convey all that we must convey, and to establish the sense of community which is so necessary in a teaching and learning situation."

I proposed some guidelines for a new college—a model college we might create.

"First, the new institution we invent to provide a universal educational opportunity beyond the twelfth grade must be solidly based upon a new amalgamation of the resources of the high schools and the colleges. It makes no sense for a secondary school system to educate more and more people who will require some formal educational experience beyond the twelfth grade, separate and apart from the activities of systems claiming jurisdiction beyond grade twelve. It makes no sense for the colleges to receive more and more students from the high schools into larger and larger remedial programs . . .

"Second, we must launch new colleges—which stand for real and total integration—the integration of races, and of cultures, of classes, and of life styles, and most important of all, of bodies of knowledge bearing upon vocation with bodies of knowledge bearing upon what Americans must know beyond making a living, in order to be free. . . . We must bring the technologies together again with the liberal arts, the younger with the older students, the students with the teachers, the two-year degree with the four-year degree . . .

"Third, our new college for the urban community must take a realistic and humane view of time. It must perform within the scope of twelve-month calendar years. . . . It must regard the infinite variety of human styles, commitments and talents, and deliver its rewards not in terms of credit hours, but in terms of the humans it serves. For some this may mean a year; for others, six or seven. The variable should be the person, not the scheme. . . .

"Fourth, the new college must be honest about the Establishment's prejudices regarding quality and credentials. . . . We possess no testing instrument which reveals the real potential of the high school dropout, the potential of the urban poor, the urban oppressed. . . . There is only one way—one expensive way—to test their

potential, and that is to offer them an honest chance . . .
We should concentrate on the quality of those who finally
get the degree, and relax a bit about the quality standards
at the beginning when we make the educational opportunity available. . . .

"Fifth, the new college must re-establish the connection between thinking and acting. . . . Decision-making
action is often the best context through which people
learn. . . . In a city like New York, in industry, government, the arts, and technical institutions of great variety,
there are exciting new possibilities for revitalizing the
apprenticeship or internship concept, for building our
educational programs around the relevant problems of
our time—Higher education should not be a pause in the
life of young adults—it must be a vibrant and exciting
part of adult life. . . .

"Finally, the new college should recognize that although older generations do have something they alone
can convey to the younger, what the young may teach
each other is at least as important. We must honor the
capacity of the young adult to run his own life, to share in
the direction of institutions specially created for him . . .
Institutions which are for the young must honor and respect the young.

Twelve, Eighty-one, Eighty-seven—HIKE!

Arleigh Williamson presided at my inauguration, and
Horace M. Kallen came. Leaning on his cane, Kallen
marched in my ceremonial parade wearing Santayana's
ermine-collared academic robes. At the end of my speech
I asked him and Arleigh Williamson to stand, and I said:

"Look at Arleigh Williamson, age eighty-one, distinguished member of the Board of Higher Education,
founder of this college and others, professor emeritus of
New York University and revered citizen of this borough

and this city . . . and Horace M. Kallen, age eighty-seven, honored student and partner of William James, professor emeritus of the New School for Social Research, author of more than a score of great books, philosopher honored in all lands . . .

"These men are great teachers of your new president and even now, in the agility of their minds and the youth of their spirits, they are as young as or younger than their student.

"To the younger people here I say: *Look at these men and wonder about the meaning of age, about being wise and about being young, about the bridge of wisdom which spans the gaps not of generations but of epochs. We may grow young by being wise, and grow wise through those simple and decent things which are age-less.*"

Finally I asked my son Charles to stand up.

"Charles is twelve years old. He plays soccer and the cello, and he writes poems. He wrote a poem for his dad to commemorate my inauguration. It reads:

"Everyman needs a heart
  To reach into,
  To pull out the very soul
  Which blooms in his mind.

"He needs a heart
  To light the fire,
  The fire of life which burns
  In the core of his knowledge.

"He needs a mind
  To know the meaning
  Of war and of hatred—
  And of love.

"He needs a mind
  To reach into,

To touch the core of his being—
His reason to live in a world made by man."

"Charles thinks thoughts which never occurred to your new president when he was twelve. He should give the students of this college pause. *To Charles your version of the future may seem as unacceptable as mine may to you.*

"It is a time to celebrate the meaning of ourselves. For from Charles at twelve to Professor Williamson at eighty-one and Dr. Kallen at eighty-seven there is a direct line into the meaning of this college. We need each other, all four. Through this simple truth we may yet—black and white, young and old, teacher and taught, town and gown—do something together of which we will be proud."

And so, with great luck and hard work, we may.

Bleeding Hearts and Hard-Hats

And now—in the seventh autumn after Berkeley, in the third fall after the fall of Morningside Heights, as the leaves are turning red again for the second time since Jackson State and Kent and the capture of City College's campus, twenty-six autumns after I arrived on Chicago's Midway eager to learn—here I am, on Staten Island, needing to learn, and eager.

My university has committed itself to let more in—anyone who has "earned" any high school diploma, even those whose high schools have somehow failed to teach them the nation's language, to master the mathematical systems to which economic success in America is so vitally linked. It is a magnificent commitment, a fresh and tender vote of confidence in the future of a springtime in this country, in a season of new life we hope will come after this winter.

Perhaps not all those undertaking this commitment were dreaming the American Dream. In New York City our campuses have been embattled, gates locked, police coming and going. Perhaps pragmatic political pressures more than humanitarian ideals or even educational convictions led some board members to cast their votes for open doors. It is not a particularly friendly time for pleaders of principle. I have heard them called "bleeding hearts" at recent meetings of our board. No matter. Hearts are bleeding on our campuses, in the city, all over America. It is a time for hearts to bleed a little.

On Staten Island, at this college where I am now the president, we have all these unfinished humans, these miraculous creations, each one flawed somewhat, some more, some less, a crack here, a chip there. Who are we to say they should not aspire to perfection? Are we to tell them not to argue for new definitions of beauty? I am impressed. They are here. To debate whether or not they should be here is not my bag now. Like them, I'm here.

And so, we must meet. We meet.

I have known, during this past year at the college, some finished humans too: the handsome blond boy, sitting hunched on the toilet stool in the third-floor men's john, dead; the syringe which injected the fatal dose of heroin lying on the floor at his feet. The black star of the basketball team in the pool of his own blood, lying on a curbstone in Queens, dead. The police bullet entered the back of his head after he, according to the press, opened fire on the two patrolmen "for reasons unknown." His mother and father showed me the three commendations he received in Vietnam, the gold seal on the statement describing the valor which earned him the Bronze Star. It cannot be true, they said. We do not understand, they said. He was my friend. But now our friendship is done. I do not understand.

This president's office is full of people all the time, and

it is so lonely. So little understanding passes over my
desk.

They've been turned off, off, off. Off by mothers and
fathers who have lost touch. Off by churches that preach
what they too seldom practice. Off by politicians who play
their professions like games. Off by the teachers and administrators who really don't seem to care. Off by slaugh-
tering wars, fought at the wrong time in the wrong places.
Off by the violence, by the corruption and the dirt, by the
apparent meaninglessness of so much of it. They come in
wearing their hard-hats of skepticism, cups of armor protecting the fragile skulls in which there is so much desire
to believe, to trust, to find what is honest and to know it
when it is found. They have made simple honesty, the
truth, trust, conditions of their education. They insist
upon the impossible. Never before has a college president
been so urgently called upon to live the ideals for which
his enterprise stands. Never before has he been called upon
to think so clearly—*to act in keeping with what he thinks.*

There is a huge difference between knowing what is
wrong and doing something about it; between designing
the ideal program and implementing it; between thinking
about what you'd do if you had the power and confronting
the responsibility of actually having it. It helps tremendously to have an idea, to experience the coming together
of intelligence and integrity. But now we are at a point
where delivery itself is crucial. People are really getting
hurt. Boredom and aimlessness, police and blood—these
are no laughing matters for a nation's young.

The subject matter of my work is really quite complicated. Harmonizing what I think with how I act is almost
hopelessly involved because there are so many people who
do not think what I think, who would not act as I wish to
act. Were I an "out" hoping to get "in," perhaps it would
matter less. But I am an "in," possessing a cutting responsibility for the welfare of so many of those who disagree

with me. The exercise of my presidential power is forever tempered by that. In other words, my professional life is one grand compromise.

Many of my young friends do not understand what it takes, what it means to compromise. Often quixotically critical of the fact of power, they are also critical, quixotically, I think, of temperance in its exercise. They see in the fact that I compromise a breach in my integrity, a flaw in my honesty, a reason for distrusting me. If a new building is to be built, build it. Forget the dozen university and city agencies, the legions of bureaucrats and piles of red tape which stand between the conception and the result. If a new curriculum seems to make sense, do it. Forget the faculty unions, the need for new dollars, the mountain of personal piques, the many mistakes that stand between the status quo and the new idea. If the war is stupid, stop it.

The trouble with this is that I have a deep feeling, even an understanding for their lack of understanding. Too often, it seems to me, intelligence, even justice, is on their side, not mine. But, unhappily, for most of these things, I am accountable, not they. I am accountable for my power. Worse, I am accountable for the use of a collectivity of power far beyond what I actually possess, for what happens in places when I am not even there—like the meetings of the faculty in the English department, like Vietnam, the john on the third floor, the curbstone in Queens.

There is no way to teach people accountability for possessing power other than, as a first step, to empower them. In America we have a generation of young adults, grown to be as old as eighteen or more, old enough to drive our cars, drink our booze, soon to vote, to fight our wars, whom we have kept relatively powerless, inexcusably ignorant about the connection between thinking and acting. How are they to understand my loneliness and our country's travail?

And as for the masses of Americans who are "out" but

who may still want "in," if their style is not ours, if their values are not ours, it is because we have not shared. We have not taught. We have selfishly hoarded what we know about the ends, and stupidly monopolized the means. Our stupidity leads us into our own paradox. Under the circumstances, the more we urge them to be like us and the more they respond to this invitation, the more we search for an escape and flee. Flee to suburbia, flee to segregation, flee to reaction, flee to the comfort of old habits and of being older, flee to the more arbitrary exercise of our superior powers.

At Staten Island we are on the threshold of another grand experiment. We will try to revise the freshman year precedent to setting the entire college in a new direction. We have admitted almost a thousand freshmen more this year than last. Admitted them into our departmentalized boxes, into the master plan that has worked so well for so long, until lately. Admitted them into our status quo, which is now the past. At this moment the design is pure. We are on the threshold of our compromises; on the brink, perhaps, of new disasters.

Our system's persistent durability is its foremost characteristic. Empires rise and fall, but the university goes on forever. Presidents and students get shot in the head, but it makes no difference. The system resists change, and so now we will try to change it.

We are supposed to double the size of our campus within the next few years. The townsfolk living in the $100,000 homes near our fences are outraged. More cars, more pot, more noise, more long hair, more disrespect for Flag and Motherhood! We have fought the new plan through the Park Commission, the Board of Estimate, the Site Selection Board, the Office of Education and University Headquarters in Manhattan, through the borough president's office, the neighborhood landowners association, and the Conservationist League. It will be a miracle, but finally we will do it. We will build a Learning Town here with its own pedestrian streets and its own town hall. We will bring this college into human scale, create our own walk-up learning places, our own moments of city beauty in the dimension of the people, who, to learn here, must also work here together, humanely. We will restore some measure of privacy and urban physical beauty to this campus. We will do it. We must.

Knowing that any urban design is only as good as the sense of community felt among the people for and by whom the design is made, we will try to restore a community among scholars, between teachers and the taught, the decent community of ideas and habits of life essential to any learning endeavor. We aim to return the curriculum, the learning plan and the facilities supporting it to the level of the blocks in the Learning Town, to empower the blocks to govern themselves, each regulating its own traffic in ideas, each planting and maintaining its own green garden of what we ought to know together. The thousands will be reorganized into groups of two hundred students each, with a score or more of teachers and counselors who will develop their own places in the Learning Town and be responsible for the design of their own part.

What is new often takes us back to ancient and eternal questions, to the significance of history. The future and the past are brothers. What should every man know now, and how may we best encourage the knowing? We are confident of a part of the answer to this question, but we are still groping. Every man must know the language of his country, how to read, write and speak it, the literature and drama of it, the power to get things done through the persuasive use of it. Every man must know the numbers systems upon which modern science depends, the methods of thought through which the science works, the science upon which the country's economy and health depend. There is no more impressive chapter in our history than the saga of how we have gotten, scientifically, technologically, to where we are. Every man must know the sources of his own community's politics, its culture, its dependence upon evolution, the reasons for its revolutionary birth and for its turbulent existence. To change anything one must know what there is to change. And every man must know not only how ugly he can be, but how beautiful, for only through sensing this in his architecture, in his music and art, can he sense the reasons for knowing all the rest. Every man must know these things, and if sixty credit hours or a hundred and twenty, two years or four are not right, if this library and these departments do not help him know these things, then we must change what we do and how we do it.

Finally, our Learning Town on Staten Island can never be more than a neighborhood of this great city. Each student citizen will be an intern in some aspect of the city's life. Each student, each week will move from his block in the Learning Town to the streets of his city, seeking new connections between what he is learning and the use of it, between the need to decide intelligently and acquiring the knowledge upon which intelligence depends, between the necessity to act and the desire to know in order to act wisely.

It will be a miracle, but finally we will do this too. We will carry our plans forward through the departments and the curriculum committees, through the personnel and budget committees, and the board of trustees, through the accrediting associations and the board of regents, through the grievance committees of the unions. And when we have done it, when it is done, it will be unfinished and imperfect, a model for no one and for nothing except ourselves as we try to be better and for those who will follow us in Staten Island, knowing more than we know and thus, knowing how to be better. When it is done, we will be history and they will be the future. We will be what they criticize, the reactionary status quo they will change.

In the passage of time between my writing these words and when they appear in print, all these miracles and dreams, these commitments and convictions, may convert into nightmares and dissolve into ashes. Perhaps we want too much. Perhaps I will not survive long as president of the college. Perhaps the faculty will rise in righteous indignation, or in its fearful recoil from the challenges succumb to intimidation. Perhaps the board will panic, or perhaps the students will burn it all down. Perhaps anarchy will overcome the campus and tyranny the tax-paying community which claims it. Perhaps . . .

But if there is anyone around then to study the history of this time and this place, they will know—they will know that there were many here who with youth in their souls and courage in their hearts tried to be themselves, who took their time and their place somewhat seriously. They will know that our bureaucratic bungling, that the petty political maneuverings of departmental chairmen, ambitious academics, deans and presidents, militant Maoists and crew-cut hard-hats meant, after all, something. They will know that some of us knew we had a chance, and that having the chance, we tried. They will know that we were part of the continuity and that we did not turn away from the opportunity to make a difference. Being on our own, finally, leaves us not lonely and in despair, but joined anew with our brothers, newly aware of our own possibilities, full of hope.

About The Author

WILLIAM M. BIRENBAUM, one of the most creative and articulate advocates of reform in American higher education, was born in Macomb, Illinois, in 1923 and grew up in Waterloo, Iowa. After service in Greenland in World War II he attended the University of Chicago, where he received a doctorate in law as his first and only earned degree, and where he later served as a faculty member and administrator. In 1957 Dr. Birenbaum moved to Wayne State University in Detroit, and four years later he became dean of the New School for Social Research in New York. From 1964 to 1967 he was vice-president and provost of Long Island University in Brooklyn, a position from which he was dismissed.

After his controversial dismissal from LIU, the author assisted the late Senator Robert F. Kennedy with the educational planning for a project the senator was starting in the Bedford-Stuyvesant area of Brooklyn. Shortly after Senator Kennedy's assassination, Dr. Birenbaum assumed his present position as president of Staten Island Community College of the City University of New York, where he has instituted more than a dozen experimental and innovative programs implementing many of the ideas discussed in this book and in his earlier work, *Overlive: Power, Poverty and the University*, published in 1969.

Dr. Birenbaum is married to Helen Bloch, who is a college professor. They have three teen-age children, two in high school and one in college.

"A college president is not supposed to write a book like this. Not while he's still in office. Not if he wants to stay there."

But President William Birenbaum has written such a book, a candid, moving and intimate personal account of what it's like to be a college president and what it takes to remain one.

Dr. Birenbaum has spent his professional career in the turbulent world of higher education as Dean of Students at the University of Chicago in the early fifties, Assistant Vice-President at Wayne State in Detroit, Dean of the New School in New York City in the early sixties, a cataclysmic term as Vice-President of Long Island University in Brooklyn until 1967, head of educational planning for a new college in the Bedford-Stuyvesant area of Brooklyn and now President of Staten Island Community College of the City of New York.

Something for Everybody Is Not Enough is not simply an abstract account of the career of a college President. It is a personal and deeply felt memoir of a sensitive and complex man faced with the enormous problems of university administration.

With respect to the great issues of our time—Vietnam, racism, the impact of technology, the role of the individual—the author has not been neutral. He argues that the universities, no matter how they may proclaim their neutrality, have not been neutral either. In expanding their campuses,